Human Capital Policy

KDI/EWC SERIES ON ECONOMIC POLICY

The Korea Development Institute (KDI) was established in March 1971 and it is Korea's oldest and best-known research institute in the fields of economic and social sciences. Its mission is to contribute to Korea's economic prosperity by drafting socioeconomic development plans and providing timely policy recommendations based on rigorous analysis. Over the decades KDI has effectively responded to rapidly changing economic conditions at home and abroad by conducting forward-looking research as well as putting forth significant efforts in formulating long-term national visions.

The East-West Center promotes better relations and understanding among the people and nations of the United States, Asia and the Pacific through cooperative study, research and dialogue. It serves as a resource for information and analysis on critical issues of common concern, bringing people together to exchange views, build expertise and develop policy options. The Center is an independent, public, nonprofit organization with funding from the U.S. government, and additional support provided by private agencies, individuals, foundations, corporations, and governments in the region.

The KDI/EWC series on Economic Policy aims to provide a forum for scholarly discussion, research and policy recommendations on all areas and aspects of contemporary economics and economics policy. Each constituent volume in this series will prove invaluable reading to a wide audience of academics, policy makers and interested parties such as NGOs and consultants.

Titles in the series include:

Social Policies in an Age of Austerity
A Comparative Analysis of the US and Korea
Edited by John Karl Scholz, Hyungpyo Moon and Sang-Hyop Lee

Macroprudential Regulation of International Finance
Managing Capital Flows and Exchange Rates
Edited by Dongsoo Kang and Andrew Mason

Economic Stagnation in Japan
Exploring the Causes and Remedies of Japanization
Edited by Dongchul Cho, Takatoshi Ito and Andrew Mason

Competition Law and Economics
Developments, Policies and Enforcement Trends in the US and Korea
Edited by Jay Pil Choi, Wonhyuk Lim and Sang-Hyop Lee

Human Capital Policy
Reducing Inequality, Boosting Mobility and Productivity
Edited by David Neumark, Yong-seong Kim and Sang-Hyop Lee

Human Capital Policy

Reducing Inequality, Boosting Mobility and Productivity

Edited by

David Neumark

Department of Economics, University of California, Irvine, USA

Yong-seong Kim

Professor, Korea University of Technology and Education, South Korea

Sang-Hyop Lee

Senior Fellow, East-West Center and Professor, Department of Economics, University of Hawaii at Manoa, USA

KDI/EWC SERIES ON ECONOMIC POLICY

A JOINT PUBLICATION OF THE KOREA DEVELOPMENT INSTITUTE, THE EAST-WEST CENTER, AND EDWARD ELGAR PUBLISHING LTD

Cheltenham, UK • Northampton, MA, USA

Published by
Edward Elgar Publishing Limited
The Lypiatts
15 Lansdown Road
Cheltenham
Glos GL50 2JA
UK

Edward Elgar Publishing, Inc.
William Pratt House
9 Dewey Court
Northampton
Massachusetts 01060
USA

A catalogue record for this book
is available from the British Library

Library of Congress Control Number: 2020952075

This book is available electronically in the **Elgar**online
Economics subject collection
http://dx.doi.org/10.4337/9781800377806

ISBN 978 1 80037 779 0 (cased)
ISBN 978 1 80037 780 6 (eBook)

Typeset by Servis Filmsetting Ltd, Stockport, Cheshire
Printed and bound in Great Britain by TJ Books Limited, Padstow, Cornwall

Contents

PART IV HUMAN CAPITAL AND THE LABOR MARKET

Contributors

Julian R. Betts is a Professor in the Department of Economics of the University of California at San Diego, USA, the Bren Fellow of the Public Policy Institute of California and the Executive Director of the San Diego Education Research Alliance.

Flávio Cunha is an Assistant Professor in the Department of Economics at the University of Pennsylvania, USA.

Susan M. Dynarski is a Professor of Economics, Education and Public Policy in the Gerald R. Ford School of Public Policy, the School of Education and the Department of Economics of the University of Michigan, USA.

Sungmin Han is an Associate Fellow in the Public Policy and Private Infrastructure Investment Management Center of the Korea Development Institute, South Korea.

Harry J. Holzer is a Professor in the Georgetown Public Policy Institute of Georgetown University, USA.

Hisam Kim is an Associate Professor of Humanities and Social Sciences at the Gwangju Institute of Science and Technology, South Korea.

Jaehoon Kim is a Fellow in the Department of Human Resource Development Policy of the Korea Development Institute, South Korea.

Yong-seong Kim is a Professor at the Korea University of Technology and Education, South Korea.

Sang-Hyop Lee is a Senior Fellow of the East-West Center and a Professor in the Department of Economics of the University of Hawaii at Manoa, USA.

David Neumark is the Director of the Center for Economics and Public Policy and the Chancellor's Professor of Economics at the University of California, Irvine, USA.

WooRam Park is an Associate Fellow in the Department of Human Resource Development Policy of the Korea Development Institute, South Korea.

Yoonsoo Park is a Professor of Economics at Sookmyung Women's University, South Korea.

Foreword

The high quality of human capital in Korea is one of many factors that explain remarkable economic growth and the success of the Korean economy in past decades. The literacy rate increased from about 20 percent in 1945 to almost 100 percent within two generations. The proportion of the population with tertiary education is among the highest of Organisation for Economic Co-operation and Development (OECD) countries. International achievement tests such as Program for International Student Assessment (PISA) testing have ranked Korea at the top in mathematics, reading and science.

Despite the positive outcomes, Korean education is now at a crossroads, with many questions coming into view. Can the current direction of education support sustainable economic growth in the future? Are students' skills and competencies adequately nurtured in schools and at home? Do schools acknowledge and react to the human capital required by labor markets in the twenty-first century? Is academic achievement currently affected by socioeconomic background? Is educational support fair in providing opportunities to those wishing to invest in their human capital? Korean education has long promoted social equity, mobility and cohesion, but can that role be ensured in the future?

The future path of human capital policy must be reconsidered, and upgrading the educational system will be a policy priority as Korea moves toward an inclusive society and a more innovative economy. A new direction of human capital policy requires improving the public school system, reinforcing the competitiveness of higher education, and strengthening cooperation between education and industry. It should also be designed to reduce inequality and promote socioeconomic mobility.

In the context of these issues and their policy implications, the Korea Development Institute and the East-West Center commissioned an international team of experts for a study on "A New Direction in Human Capital Policy: Trends in Advanced Countries and Implications for Korea." Their findings, presented in this book with reference to educational systems in Korea, the United States and other OECD countries, will be useful in understanding the problems and designing future policies.

On publishing this volume, I would like to thank Dr David Neumark, the Director of the Center for Economics and Public Policy and the

Chancellor's Professor of Economics at the University of California, Irvine; Dr Yong-seong Kim, Professor at the Korea University of Technology and Education; and Dr Sang-Hyop Lee, Senior Fellow of the East-West Center and Professor in the Department of Economics at the University of Hawaii at Manoa, for organizing and editing the chapters for publication. I also wish to thank the authors and reviewers who contributed to the volume.

Jeong Pyo Choi
President
Korea Development Institute

Abbreviations

2SLS	two-stage least squares
AA	Associate of Arts (degree)
AAS	Associate of Applied Science (degree)
AO	admissions officer
APH schools	autonomous private high schools (Korea)
BA	Bachelor of Arts (degree)
CMO	charter management organization
CNLSY/79	Children of the National Longitudinal Survey of Youth 1979 (US)
CREDO	Center for Research on Education Outcomes (US)
CTE	career and technical education
DART	deregulation, accountability, responsiveness and transparency
ESEA	Elementary and Secondary Education Act (US)
GCOE Program	Global Center of Excellence Program (Osaka University)
GDP	gross domestic product
GED	General Education Development (US program)
GPA	grade-point average
GSL	General Student Loan (Korea)
HAMP	Home Affordable Modification Program (US)
HEA	Higher Education Act (US)
HIES	Household Income and Expenditure Survey (Korea)
HOME-SF	Home Observation for the Measurement of the Environment, Short Form
I-BEST	Integrated Basic Education and Skills Training Program
ICL	Income Contingent Loan (Korea)
IMD	International Institute for Management Development
IQ	intelligence quotient
IRS	Internal Revenue Service (US)
ISCED	International Standard Classification of Education
ISIC	International Standard Industrial Classification
K–12	kindergarten to twelfth grade (US education levels)
KDI	Korea Development Institute

KHS 2013	KDI Happiness Study 2013 (Korea)
KIPP	Knowledge is Power Program (US)
KLIPS	Korean Labor and Income Panel Study
KSAT	Korean Scholastic Aptitude Test
NCES	National Center for Educational Statistics (US)
NEETs	young people who are not in employment, education or training
NSLDS	National Student Loan Data System (US)
OECD	Organisation for Economic Co-operation and Development
OLS	ordinary least squares
PAYE	Pay As You Earn (US program)
PISA	Program for International Student Assessment (coordinated by the OECD)
PSID	Panel Study for Income Dynamics
R&D	research and development
SELS 2010	Seoul Education Longitudinal Study 2010
SES	socioeconomic status
SGL	state-guaranteed loan
SIPP	Survey of Income and Program Participation (US)
SNU	Seoul National University
SSA	Social Security Administration (US)
STAN	Structural Analysis (OECD database)
STEM	science, technology, engineering and math
UNESCO	United Nations Educational, Scientific and Cultural Organization
US	United States
WHO	World Health Organization
WIA	Workforce Investment Act (US)
WIB	Workforce Investment Board
WIOA	Workforce Innovation and Opportunity Act

1. Introduction to *Human Capital Policy*

David Neumark, Yong-seong Kim and Sang-Hyop Lee

Education is a subject of never-ending public attention, and that attention has contributed to numerous reforms. One starting point in the search for better human capital policy is a careful review of past accomplishments and shortcomings of the education system, as well as future challenges facing it. Moreover, for most people the goals of human capital policy encompass the efficiency and effectiveness of policy, as well as its contribution to equity and social and economic mobility. The topics of this volume therefore delve into the quality of education, the effectiveness of public school systems and means of improving them, the competitiveness and accountability of higher education, and linkages between education and labor market outcomes.

The authors focus on Korea and the United States. The Korean education system can be credited for much of the remarkable economic growth achieved by the country in recent decades, during its transformation into an industrialized country. The economy during this period is regarded as a textbook case of taking a leap from being a marginal player in the global economy to being a leading one. Many factors must be taken into account to explain this transition. Among them, the country's education system, well designed and effective for its time, played an essential role in achieving both industrialization and social mobility. In terms of the quantity and quality of its human capital, Korea has made astonishing progress since regaining its independence in the late 1940s. With the rapid expansion of enrollment in both primary and secondary schools, the literacy rate increased from about 20 percent in 1945 to almost 100 percent today. The proportion of the population with tertiary education is the highest among the Organisation for Economic Co-operation and Development (OECD) countries. The expansion of education was accompanied by a soaring academic record. Recent international achievement tests, such as the OECD's Program for International Student Assessment

(PISA), have ranked Korea at the top in mathematics, reading and sciences.

As Korea moves to a knowledge-based society and a more creative economy, however, human capital policy must be reconsidered. Recent declines in the rate of economic growth, and deterioration in labor market conditions, suggest that upgrading the education system may be critical to sustaining strong performance of the Korean economy in the longer run. A number of features of the Korean education system create potential challenges.

Stressful competition to enter universities, and intensive focus on test scores, have resulted in doubts about the quality of education received in public schools, which in turn has caused the proliferation of private tutoring and consequently a heavy economic burden on the average family. Difficulties encountered in the transition from school to labor market, including the retraining programs for new recruits that businesses have to carry out, raise questions about the quality of human capital accumulated under the current education system. At the same time, there are signs of deterioration in students' motivation, creativity, interpersonal communicative and cooperative attitudes, and other character skills. More foreboding for the future economy, the research and development (R&D) capabilities of Korea's universities are generally rated well below those in advanced countries. There are also emerging challenges with regard to equity and mobility, as academic achievement appears to be increasingly affected by socioeconomic family background. Korean education, which used to promote mobility, is becoming a less effective means of doing so.

As this volume demonstrates, the issues surrounding education are wide-ranging in scope and highly complicated in nature. By comparing Korea's human capital policies with those in the United States, the authors examine issues relevant to understanding Korea's human capital policies in the past and draw out useful recommendations for new directions that may be needed. The chapters cover education reform in Korea, quality of education, the effectiveness of the public school system, competitiveness and accountability of higher education, the linkage between education and socioeconomic status, and labor market outcomes tied to human capital policies. This book also places Korea's experience in a broader international perspective by comparing Korea's case with Western countries. The comparative perspective broadens the evidence base on human capital policies, and may stimulate additional thinking and research by contrasting primarily Western experiences and perspectives on human capital policy with those of a newly industrialized economy in Asia.

EDUCATION REFORM ISSUES

In Chapter 2, Hisam Kim shows that Korean society, once characterized by a high level of social mobility, faces decreasing optimism over the significance of efforts in moving up the socioeconomic ladder. He begins with very detailed analyses based on surveys of attitudes toward social mobility in Korea. These surveys, conducted at different points in time, generally show that: (1) pessimism about upward mobility in society has been increasing; (2) the correlation in socioeconomic status across generations has been increasing; and (3) the younger generation is skeptical about the role of education as a ladder of intergenerational upward mobility. Kim's analysis reveals two trends that reduce equity and mobility: first, that income inequality has been increasing over time; and second, that educational paths have become increasingly correlated with parental socioeconomic status.

The author then turns to possible policy remedies that may increase mobility, which include early intervention to prevent loss of talent and public support for vulnerable students to help them improve job market skills and social networks. Finally, Kim also suggests that opening multiple routes to success, other than a narrowly defined route (such as from select universities to good jobs), should be encouraged and supported. The last point implies that the role of education in social mobility in the future may need to be redefined away from a single ladder of upward movement in one-directional zero-sum competition for highly concentrated desires and toward multiple bridges to help individual students realize their own dreams.

ISSUES IN HIGHER EDUCATION

In Chapter 3, Jaehoon Kim discusses measures to enhance the competence and responsiveness of Korean universities in relation to socioeconomic needs. He begins with the competence measure of university education achievement in Korea. Although Korea routinely scores high marks in the OECD's Program for International Student Assessment (PISA), the author attributes this outcome not to the quality of the public primary and secondary education system but to the value-added from investment in after-school tutoring.

Korea has the world's highest university enrollment rate. On the other hand, its responsiveness to socioeconomic needs has lagged behind, and Korean universities do not compare well with their peers worldwide. An important turning point to increase the number of universities and so put universities in a more competitive environment was the institution of the qualification rule, adopted in 1996 and first applied in 1997, which allowed the establishment of new universities, on condition of meeting certain requirements. The new rule appeared to be a policy supposed to promote competition among universities, and thus to enhance the competence of universities and to reduce the involvement of the government in university affairs.

Kim analyzes data on Korean universities in order to examine their impacts and the possibility of adopting quasi-market competition. The empirical results for universities in the Seoul metropolitan area, even after the adoption of the principle of the qualification rule in 1996, reveal that their enrollment is still highly regulated, that the difficulties of gaining admission have greatly increased, and that university competence (as measured, for example, by the employment rates of graduates) is lower than that of nonmetropolitan universities without enrollment regulations. This situation suggests that one possible way to enhance the competence of universities overall and to make the higher educational market more competitive may be to offer financial incentives to encourage some universities in the metropolitan area to move to nonmetropolitan areas.

The 2013 Master Plan for the Development of Higher Education introduced a new university rating system and tied acceptance limits to these ratings. Given that government subsidies remain in place, however, the author speculates that the changes will do little to improve or eliminate underperforming universities. Since the rankings must have provided prospective students with information about university quality that was not previously available, why did some students continue to matriculate in the ones that received poor ratings?

In Chapter 4, Susan M. Dynarski discusses recent trends in student debt and policy prescriptions to improve the ways that higher education is financed in the United States (US). The author begins with a picture of student loans in the United States; one that is not as dire as many commentators have suggested. Indeed, contrary to many media reports, she argues that student debt is not out of control, and that although borrowing has risen over time, the typical US student holds debt that is well below the lifetime benefits of a college education. The typical student borrower is not under water, as were many homeowners during the mortgage crisis in 2008. In addition, while it is true that college tuition has risen dramatically over the past 20 years, many people do not pay the full cost. This may be desirable, as universities are engaging in a form of price discrimination, where different students pay different prices depending on their willingness or ability to pay. This is most likely efficient, and it may also expand access to higher education if richer students are subsidizing poorer students who otherwise could not afford college.

The real issue is that there is a mismatch in the timing of the costs of college and the arrival of its benefits, with payments falling due when earnings are still low and at their most variable. Ironically, this mismatch is the very motivation for providing student loans in the first place. The author offers some possible solutions. One is an income-based repayment structure for student loans, with payments automatically flexing with earnings over a longer horizon than the ten years that are currently standard. While income-based repayment options do exist within the current system, few borrowers take them up; perhaps because of administrative barriers to accessing them. Furthermore, the existing options do not adjust loan payments quickly enough to respond to the high-frequency shocks that characterize young people's earnings, especially during a recession. The author concludes that a well-structured repayment program would help to cushion borrowers against both micro and macro shocks. With an interest rate that appropriately accounts for the government's borrowing and administrative costs, as well as the default risk, such a program could be self-sustaining. Designing it, however, requires detailed data on individual earnings and borrowing, which are currently unavailable to researchers; including those within the government itself. If loan policy is to be firmly grounded in research, this gap in the data needs to be closed.

In Chapter 5, Sungmin Han examines the relationships between student loans, academic performance and default risk. He also examines how academic performance and default risk differ for students who borrow through Korea's two largest sources of student loans: the General Student Loan (GSL) program and the Income Contingent Loan (ICL) program.

Student loans can have a positive impact on student performance. If no loans were available, college students would probably have to work to pay tuition fees, whereas with a loan, students can spend more time on their studies, thereby improving their academic achievement. Even so, there are differences between the two types of loan in Korea. The GSL program requires that students begin paying off the loan while they are still in school, though students can choose the level of payment and repayment period. Although the repayment amount and period are flexible, the recipients may still have to work if they have difficulty paying off their debts. In addition, since students receiving a loan start their careers with debts, there is a high probability of selecting any job regardless of job quality in order to pay off the debt early. The ICL program, in contrast, does not require payment until after students leave school. It can allow students to focus more on their studies. But this provision may have a different impact and a negative side to it, depending on the purpose of taking the loan. Moreover, if it serves as an incentive to delay repayment by deferring graduation, the repayment can become more problematic than in the case of GSL loans.

As the author notes, empirical studies suggest that ICL recipients perform better than GSL recipients. In terms of default, however, the probability of delinquency is higher when loans cover both living expenses and tuition than when they cover tuition alone. These findings suggest that although the ICL program is more effective in reducing students' financial burden, the repayment system should be improved to minimize the negative impact. Han accepts, nonetheless, that a rapid shift from GSLs to ICLs may impose a financial burden on the government budget. Thus, a gradual change of student loan policy is required.

HUMAN CAPITAL INPUTS AND OUTCOMES

In Chapter 6, Flávio Cunha provides a theoretical model for examining the linkage between parents' information sets and human capital formation of children. He begins with a survey of the existing literature on inequality in investments in human capital during the first few years of a child's life. While there are several nonmutually exclusive explanations for the pattern between investments and family socioeconomic status, the focus of this chapter is parental information. The author builds a model in which maternal subjective beliefs about the technology of skill formation may be correlated with socioeconomic status. These beliefs partially determine maternal expectations about returns on human capital investments, which, in turn, determine investment choices. If markets are complete, and if mothers have low expectations about returns to investments, then mothers with low socioeconomic status will invest too little in their children.

The author then shows that the evidence is consistent with a model in which parents are subjectively rational. Although parents act to maximize a well-defined objective function, they lack information about the constraints that link parenting style and investments to child development. He then shows that empirical implications of the model have been validated in recent experiments that provide parents with information that is important for fostering child development. These findings provide useful guidance for the design of new policies for narrowing the human capital gap that opens up long before children reach school.

In Chapter 7, Julian R. Betts examines the rationale of charter schools and reviews the literature concerning their impact on student performance. He begins by describing charter schools as a test of the theory of school choice. Charter schools are now one of the most important and fastest-growing forms of school choice in the United States. Charter schools provide a new form of competition by allowing private agents to organize and operate schools financed partly or fully with tax revenues. However, the author also takes note of some issues that apply to charter schools but not to competing public and private schools, such as restrictions imposed by school districts on their expansion, problems with funding and special regulations.

The literature suggests the following. First, charter schools often generate positive increases in completion rates for high school and subsequently college. Second, some national and regional organizations that manage charter schools are highly effective while others are not. Third, black students appear to gain more from attending charter schools than other students do. Fourth, charter schools in urban areas appear to outperform charter schools as a whole. Fifth, charters are more effective in improving test scores in math than in reading. Sixth, charter schools produce some positive behavioral outcomes such as fewer disciplinary episodes, reduced pregnancy rates and less likelihood of going to jail, but with mixed results on attendance. Seventh, there is little evidence that charter schools skim the best students from public schools and thus reduce student achievement in public schools.

All of these findings vary substantially across charter schools, though. Betts concludes that variation in measured charter school effectiveness likely represents variation in the quality of charter schools and alternative public schools. In doing so, he provides a sobering reminder of the difficulties facing researchers in clearly identifying the source of differences in student performance in different types of schools.

In Chapter 8, Yoonsoo Park examines the question of whether private schools provide better education than public schools do. The study makes use of a survey of autonomous private high schools in Korea. It begins with the long-standing academic debate among education policymakers and interest groups in Korea since the High School Equalization Act of 1974. Under that Act, private high schools were required to operate in a way very similar to public high schools. In 2010, the government partially deregulated the equalization policy by granting a certain level of autonomy to selected private high schools. These schools are called autonomous private high (APH) schools and are essentially the first truly private high schools in Korea since 1974.

The author contributes to both the economic literature and the education policy debate in Korea by examining the effectiveness of APH school attendance on educational outcomes of students. To isolate a causal effect of the APH schools, Park uses birth order of students as an instrumental variable for APH school attendance, under the assumptions that first-born students have a higher chance of attending those schools than do their later-born peers, and that birth order does not affect educational outcomes of students directly, other than through parental educational investment decisions. Applying this idea to data tracing students who entered high schools in 2010 over a three-year period, he finds that the APH school attendance substantially improves levels of student satisfaction, in comparison with regular high schools. However, Park does not find any clear evidence that attending APH schools improves achievement test scores, which suggests that the large academic performance gaps observed between the APH school students and regular high school students are largely driven by sample selectivity.

HUMAN CAPITAL AND THE LABOR MARKET

In Chapter 9, Harry J. Holzer reviews the recent empirical evidence on human capital formation among disadvantaged youth and adults in the United States. He focuses on the skills and credentials that are well rewarded in the labor market, and the different means of attaining them. He begins with a literature review and lists the main culprits identified by empirical research. Disadvantaged students tend to face important liquidity constraints that prevent them from enrolling in or completing a college education. Conditional on enrolling in a college, disadvantaged students are also more likely to choose fields or majors that offer low returns in the labor market. Holzer suggests a range of policies to improve these outcomes, such as recruitment and admission policies that open high-ranking colleges and universities to more disadvantaged students, better academic and career counseling, reforms in financial aid and remediation practices, and state subsidies based at least partly on the academic and employment outcomes of their students.

The author also reviews a range of alternatives to college programs, including high-quality career and technical education, and work-based learning programs and sectoral training, which have great promise but need to be carefully scaled up (and evaluated) before they will reach their potential. Holzer argues for policies to encourage better integration of education and labor market programs and institutions, while making both more responsive to the job market. The author concludes with cautions, as there are likely to be many pitfalls in implementing the policies and practices suggested.

In Chapter 10, WooRam Park examines the effects of human capital on industrial structure and productivity among OECD countries. He begins with a review of literature on the impact of human capital on various outcomes pertaining to industrial structure and growth. The micro studies tend to provide a uniform picture: the majority establish a strong positive relation between years of schooling and eventual income. However, the effect of educational attainment at the macro level often appears to be much weaker. The chapter advances the macro-level literature by examining the heterogeneity in the effect of human capital on the growth of industries through technology intensity. In particular, the author argues that if human capital facilitates technology adoption, then an increase in human capital will mostly affect the growth of technology-intensive industries. Park tests this hypothesis by examining whether human capital increases the share of high-tech industries and lowers the share of low-tech industries in terms of value-added and employment in the manufacturing sector. In essence, he tests whether human capital accumulation increases the technology intensity of the manufacturing sector.

Park uses a dataset at the industry level from OECD countries, based on technological characteristics. He tries to overcome the limitations of the previous literature by using technology characteristics of industries that could be applied to most countries in the sample. Using these data, the study finds that educational attainment – regardless of the levels of educational attainment – does not increase the shares in terms of value-added and employment in the technology-intensive industries. This might imply that the technologies adopted by high-tech industries among developed countries are likely to be labor-saving, which allows using less labor to produce equal amounts of output.

In Chapter 11, Yong-seong Kim examines the intragenerational income mobility of Korea since 2000 and links it with income inequality. He begins with a comprehensive literature review. While studies on income mobility are growing in number in the West, in Korea they are at an early stage, in part because a dataset is still being developed. The author emphasizes that the financial crisis in 1997–98 dramatically altered the course of the Korean economy: income inequality soared suddenly, and then continued to rise, and consequently the gap between the haves and the have-nots widened. These trends in inequality portend a serious potential problem in income mobility. This is a motivation for the study, which examines the trends in intragenerational income mobility.

The main findings of the chapter suggest that rising income inequality observed since 2000 seems to be driven by an increase in within-group inequality, particularly for the less educated. By contrast, within-group inequalities among the more educated remain relatively stable over time. In particular, examination of the transition process based on relative income positions over time reveals that the direction of income mobility is negative for those who changed income positions.

In addition, a decomposition approach shows that income inequality is due primarily to the permanent component of income. When total variance of income is decomposed into its components, the share of variance of the permanent component increases over time and becomes dominant. This observation implies that a substantial part of income inequality has a persistent element, making it harder for income to be mobile. Limited income mobility of the less educated, together with the widening income gap, Kim argues, may make income polarization more serious.

PART I

Education reform issues

2. Intergenerational mobility and the role of education in Korea

Hisam Kim

INTRODUCTION

Parents matter when it comes to their children's life trajectory. But the degree of parental influence differs across countries and over time. A good knowledge of both the intergenerational transmission of socioeconomic status and its strength in a particular society can throw light on the opportunities for upward mobility in the next generation, specifically for underprivileged children. In addition, investigations into the main paths through which both intergenerational transmission and intergenerational mobility occur will hint at policy measures that ensure equal opportunity and prevent talent loss.

This chapter examines social mobility focusing on intergenerational mobility and evaluates the role of education in the rise and fall of such mobility. The reasons for paying special attention to the role of education are as follows. First, education can be a ladder for upward mobility if the rate of return to schooling (particularly higher education) is sufficiently high, which is a necessary condition for children from humble families to rise. Second, however, education can be a conduit for passing down the parents' socioeconomic status only if the quantity and quality of the children's educational attainments are largely influenced by parental wealth. The high educational return is then appropriated by children from affluent families. Third, education policy is a qualified measure of enhancing social mobility. In Finland, for example, intergenerational mobility was increased by the 1950s baby-boomers' widening participation in secondary education (Pekkala and Lucas 2007) and the 1972–77 education reform that provided homogenous education until age 15, postponing the academic-vocational track from age 11 until 16 (Pekkarinen et al. 2003). Fourth, governmental intervention by means of education policy, specifically reducing the educational gap in early childhood to strengthen social cohesion, is politically easier as well as economically more efficient compared with income redistribution in adulthood.

Among various datasets used for this study, two merit special notice. I conducted an Internet-based survey of 3000 Koreans called the Korea Development Institute (KDI) Korea Happiness Study 2013 (or KHS 2013), stemming from the commitment of the KDI to improve happiness among Koreans.[1] A special set of questions about intergenerational mobility for this study was included in the questionnaire of KHS 2013. For international comparison, it also incorporates some questions contained in the Osaka University 21st Century Global Center of Excellence (GCOE) Program, which allow us to compare Korea with Japan, the United States, China and India on selected question items.

Data for estimating intergenerational mobility were also obtained from the Korean Labor and Income Panel Study (KLIPS). KLIPS is an annual survey of 5000 households and their members (ages 15 and above) from the seven metropolitan cities and urban areas in eight provinces (excluding Jeju Island). Since its second-year survey in 1999, KLIPS has surveyed split-off children's households that include ex-members of the original 5000 households. The most frequent reason for a split-off is the children's marriage and start-up of their own new families. By matching split-off children's economic standing with that of their parents, father–son and father–daughter pairs can be used in estimating intergenerational mobility. By 2014, KLIPS had 15-wave panel data, with nearly 700 father–son pairs and 700 father–daughter pairs, although the valid sample size is smaller depending on the variable of economic standing. Individual wages and earnings are observed, as well as household income and net worth (that is, total wealth minus total debt). Multiple wave observations of each economic variable enable us to reduce measurement errors and temporary shocks in the variables of interest to us, by averaging them using real terms.

The next section explores the growing pessimism among Koreans regarding their children's upward mobility. The third section empirically analyzes intergenerational mobility and the role of education, examines people's mobility expectations for the next generation, and shows evidence for a growing divide in education. The fourth section discusses policy directions for enhancing social mobility, which include preventing talent loss, strengthening social inclusion and helping in opening multiple routes to success; and it is followed by a concluding section.

BACKGROUND

In the past, many Korean parents have devoted themselves to improving their children's future by investing heavily in education. Even during times when poverty prevailed, they were optimistic about the future and believed

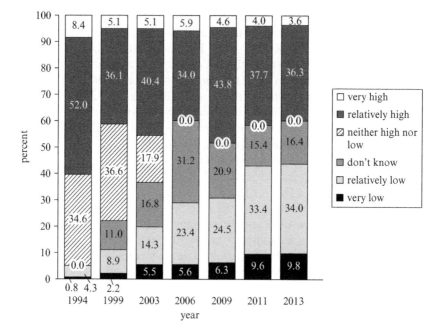

Question: What is your expectation on the chance that your children will fare better than you?

Note: The question was asked of the household head. Changes in the answer choice set before 2006 resulted in the nonexistence of a specific answer in a certain year.

Source: Statistics Korea, annual Social Survey data.

Figure 2.1   *Expectations about child's upward mobility in Korea, 1994–2013*

that their children would be better off, as illustrated in Figure 2.1. Does such optimism still exist among Koreans?

Figure 2.2 compares opinions about upward mobility in 2006 and 2013 by age cohorts. Expectations of whether the respondents' children will fare better than themselves turned pessimistic between these two years, as reflected in the change in the share of the reserved opinion (the "don't know" responses), which decreased, while the "relatively low" pessimistic responses increased. As a result, pessimism has surpassed optimism since 2011. Specifically, pessimism seems most prevalent among household heads in their thirties, who probably have young children and whose pessimistic expectations (51.5 percent in the two categories combined) outweighed their optimistic ones (35.9 percent) in 2013. I suspect that at

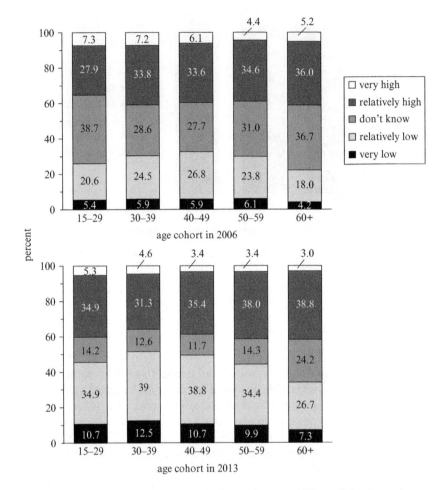

Question: What is your expectation on the chance that your children will fare better than you?

Source: Statistics Korea, annual Social Survey.

Figure 2.2   Reserved opinion about upward mobility turns to pessimism between 2006 and 2013

least part of their pessimism can be attributed to despair about catching up with affluent families in terms of their investment in their young children.[2]

Figure 2.3 reports a growing skepticism toward diligence and effort as the most important factor for success in Korea. In 2006, 41.3 percent of Koreans considered diligence and effort to be the most important factor,

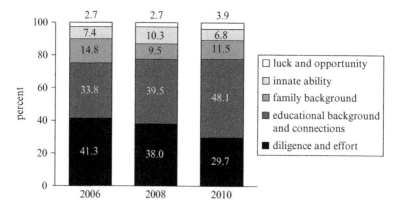

Question: What do you think is the most important factor for success in Korea?

Note: The responses were from 1200 adults in 2006 and 2008, and 1500 adults in 2010, ages 19 to 64, in nationwide household surveys.

Source: Korean Educational Development Institute, annual Public Opinion Survey on Education data.

Figure 2.3   Do diligence and effort still pay?

followed by educational background and connections (33.8 percent). Just four years later, however, diligence and effort (at 29.7 percent) yielded the top position to educational background and connections (48.1 percent), which are generally considered obstacles to meritocracy or fairness.

This weakening belief in recent years in the power of hard work as the key success factor is confirmed by age cohort comparison using survey data from KHS 2013. The corresponding statement in the survey is: "The most important factor for success in life is hard work rather than luck and personal connections." Since the same question was contained in Osaka University's GCOE 2012 survey, I can also compare across countries.

As Figure 2.4 shows, in contemporary Korea the fraction of people who think that hard work is the most important factor for success systematically diminishes the younger the respondents are. Optimism ("agree" plus "completely agree") dominates among people in their sixties (75.5 percent) but considerably shrinks among those in their twenties (51.2 percent). In other countries, however, such growing pessimism among the young is not observed. The figure does not show any evident pattern that the younger generation are less apt to believe that hard work pays in the United States (US), Japan, China and India. Instead, we can find a positive outlook among Americans in their twenties comparable to those in their fifties and

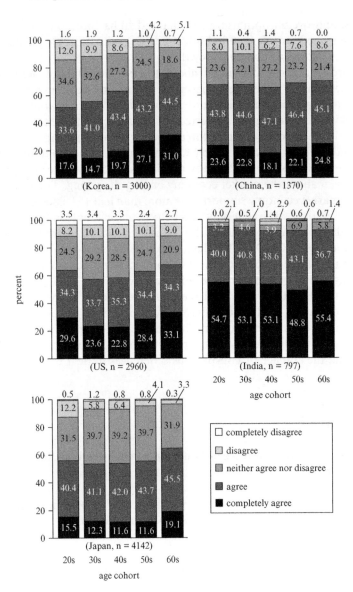

Proposition: The most important factor for success in life is hard work rather than luck and personal connections.

Sources: KHS 2013 for Korea; GCOE 2012 for other countries.

Figure 2.4   Opinions on the key factor for success factor in selected countries by age cohort

sixties, and overall optimism in China and India (people in urban areas were surveyed for this item in both countries), whose people are currently experiencing rapid economic growth.

A growing negative opinion about the pay-off of hard work seems to appear in the widening criticism of the market economy. Figure 2.5 shows age-specific opinions about the capability of the market economy in making the pie bigger, suggested by the survey statement: "Although an economy driven by market forces widens the income gap between the rich and the poor, it makes people wealthier in general; so in total, they are better off." The KHS 2013 survey provides striking evidence for growing skepticism about the market economy among the young. The proportion of pro-market economy supporters is more than half (53.3 percent) among Koreans in their sixties but only 29.4 percent among those in their twenties, and it decreases monotonically, the younger the age of the respondent.

According to GCOE 2012 data, other countries do not show such a systematic difference by age cohort in opinions about the market economy. Although people from stabilized advanced economies such as the United States and Japan seem to hold the market economy in low regard as a measurement of making themselves wealthier, their opinions are quite similar regardless of their age. In China and India, people have a very positive view of the market economy, reflected by the high economic growth rates and the absence of conspicuous differences in their opinions by age cohort.

ANALYSIS

Intergenerational Persistence of Economic Standing and the Role of Education

The degree of intergenerational persistence of economic standing is usually gauged by the intergenerational elasticity using the following regression model:

$$\ln Y_{k,i} = \alpha + \beta \ln Y_{p,i} + \gamma_1 Age_{p,i} + \gamma_2 Age_{p,i}^2 + \delta_1 Age_{k,i} + \delta_2 Age_{k,i}^2 + \varepsilon_i, \quad (2.1)$$

where $Y_{k,i}$ is child (usually son) i's economic variable (usually wage or income), $Y_{p,i}$ is the economic variable of the parent (usually father) of the child i, $Age_{k,i}$ and $Age_{p,i}$ are respectively child i's and his parent's ages, and ε_i is an error term. To reduce measurement errors and adjust temporary shocks of the economic variable, I use a multi-year average instead of an observation of a specific year. As the measure of economic standing, I use

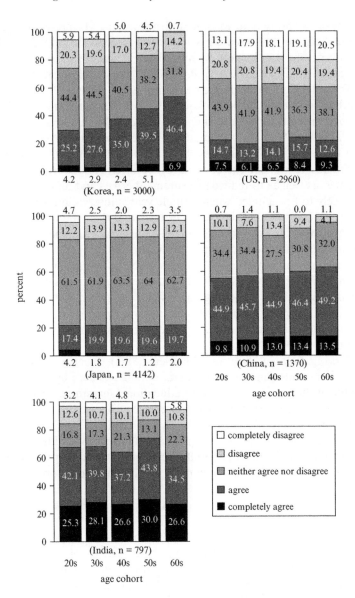

Proposition:　Although an economy driven by market forces widens the income gap between the rich and the poor, it makes people wealthier in general; so in total, they are better off.

Sources:　KHS 2013 for Korea; GCOE 2012 for other countries.

Figure 2.5　Opinion on the market economy by age cohort in Korea

wage, earning, household income and net worth. My preferred measure is wage, because this research is interested in how an individual's labor market outcome is influenced by his father via investment in education.

As mentioned earlier, the split-off children sample from the KLIPS data is used for empirical implementation. Since the KLIPS data provide the father's economic variables from 1998 to 2012 (not every year though, in case of retirement), I use the 1998–2012 real value average for valid observations as $Y_{p,i}$ to approximate the father's permanent income. As for the children's economic variables, $Y_{k,i}$, I use the 2008–12 real value average for valid observations to exclude split-off children's immature labor market outcomes, as well as to reduce measurement errors and temporary shocks more likely to be included when a single year's observation is used. I control for fathers' and children's average ages (and their squares) when their economic variables were observed in the data considering the age profile of economic standing (and potential no-linearity).[3]

The estimate of β in equation 2.1 represents the intergenerational elasticity, which answers the question: "By what percent will one's wage increase, compared with the average wage of his generation, when the wage of his father was 1 percent higher than the average wage of the father's generation?" Lower intergenerational elasticity means higher intergenerational mobility.

Following Solon (2004) and Blanden (2005), I consider the role of education in underpinning intergenerational persistence by extracting the component that can be explained by educational investment from the overall intergenerational elasticity. First, parental affluence can affect the educational attainment of children both through inherited ability ("nature"), which is associated with parental income and influences children's learning performance, and through parental investment in the quantity and quality of children's human capital ("nurture"), as shown in equation 2.2:

$$E_{k,i} = \alpha_0 + \psi \ln Y_{p,i} + \zeta_1 Age_{p,i} + \zeta_2 Age_{p,i}^2 + \upsilon_i \qquad (2.2)$$

where $E_{k,i}$ is the child i's educational attainment, $Y_{p,i}$ is parental income and υ_i is an error term. To consider the heterogeneity of the fathers' ages when their incomes were observed, I control for the average age when the father's income variables were observed in the data and its square. The degree of influence of the father's affluence on the child's education is measured by the magnitude of estimated ψ. Next, the benefit of the child's educational attainment on his economic standing can be estimated by the rate of return to schooling in a Mincerian wage equation:

$$\ln Y_{k,i} = \alpha_1 + \phi E_{k,i} + \eta_1 Age_{k,i} + \eta_2 Age_{k,i}^2 + u_i. \qquad (2.3)$$

Now, the overall intergenerational elasticity can be decomposed into the influence of parental income on the child's education (ψ) multiplied by the rate of return to education (ϕ), plus the remaining intergenerational persistence that is not transmitted through education and is represented by the influence of parental income on the residual u_i in equation 2.3. Therefore, β can be rewritten as the sum of two components as follows:

$$\beta = \frac{Cov(\ln Y_k, \ln Y_p)}{Var(\ln Y_p)} = \phi\psi + \frac{Cov(u, \ln Y_p)}{Var(\ln Y_p)}. \qquad (2.4)$$

It should be noted that $\phi\psi$ captures the component of intergenerational elasticity explained only by the quantity of education, because the data available allow education to be measured only by the years of completed final education. Thus, the quality of education such as the prestige of college education (that is, university ranking that affects labor market outcomes), as well as many other unobserved factors, will be included in the unexplained component. Consequently, the whole role of education in intergenerational persistence is bigger than the magnitude measured by $\phi\psi$.

Table 2.1 reports my estimates of intergenerational elasticity and its component explained by children's education level. According to the table, father–son elasticity varies in the range of 0.122 to 0.328 depending on the variable used to measure the father's and the son's economic standing. My preferred estimate of father–son wage elasticity is 0.225, which means when a father's wage was double (that is, 100 percent higher), his son will have a 22.5 percent higher wage.[4]

Here I reserve judgment of a large or small amount of mobility and will discuss it below in the next figure, through making comparisons of the extent of intergenerational mobility across countries. The rate of return to education ranges from 6.1 percent to 18.2 percent depending on the measure of economic standing. The influence of the father's affluence on the son's education has the largest estimate when I look at the association of the son's education level with the father's wage, which confirms my hypothesis that wage is an appropriate measure that reflects the labor market performance of both generations and will capture parental influence on the child's human capital via differing endowments and differing investments across families.

Now I can gauge the share of father–son elasticity explained by the father's influence on the son's education, and the son's return on education, by calculating the ratio of $\phi\psi$ to β. In the case of intergenerational wage persistence of father–son pairs, 40.9 percent of intergenerational elasticity can be attributed to the role of education (to be more specific, the quantity of education). Such an educational path explains 43.8 percent of their

Human capital policy

Table 2.1   *Intergenerational elasticity of economic standing and the*
               component explained by education level

Generations	Number of matched pairs n	Matched pairs elasticity β	Rate of return to education in child's generation φ	Influence of father's affluence on child's education ψ	Component explained by education $\psi\varphi$
Father and son					
Monthly average wage	356	0.225	0.063	1.463	0.092
		(0.034)	(0.007)	(0.195)	[40.9]
Monthly average earnings	606	0.130	0.061	0.930	0.057
		(0.025)	(0.007)	(0.132)	[43.8]
Yearly household income	693	0.122	0.078	0.702	0.055
		(0.028)	(0.008)	(0.129)	[45.1]
Net worth	603	0.328	0.182	0.454	0.083
		(0.039)	(0.021)	(0.069)	[25.3]
Father and daughter					
Monthly average wage	259	0.205	0.069	1.279	0.088
		(0.061)	(0.012)	(0.165)	[42.9]
Monthly average earnings	413	0.160	0.062	1.099	0.068
		(0.048)	(0.013)	(0.136)	[42.5]
Yearly household income	690	0.117	0.071	0.501	0.036
		(0.028)	(0.009)	(0.115)	[30.8]
Net worth	625	0.219	0.096	0.493	0.047
		(0.039)	(0.020)	(0.070)	[21.5]

Note: Standard errors are in parentheses. Percentage shares of explained components are in square brackets. Fathers' economic variables are the 1998–2012 average, and children's economic variables are the 2008–12 average. Considering age profile of economic standings, fathers' and children's average ages (and their squares) are controlled for, when their economic variables were observed.

Source: Estimated by the author using KLIPS data.

earning elasticity, 45.1 percent of their household income elasticity, and 25.3 percent of their net worth.

Similarly, I also estimated father–daughter elasticity as reported in Table 2.1. Their wage elasticity estimate is 0.205, of which 42.9 percent can be explained by the role of education. The number of father–daughter pairs is smaller than that of father–son pairs in the case of individual wage and earning, as the labor market participation rate is lower for daughters. Their intergenerational elasticity and the share of the explained component by education are, however, quite comparable to the son–father pairs. A noticeable difference in net worth elasticity by the child's gender

Table 2.2   Intergenerational transition matrix of wage, 1998–2012

Father's wage	Son's wage				Total
	1st quartile	2nd quartile	3rd quartile	4th quartile	
1st quartile	0.36	0.25	0.21	0.18	1.00
2nd quartile	0.30	0.27	0.20	0.23	1.00
3rd quartile	0.22	0.26	0.29	0.23	1.00
4th quartile	0.12	0.22	0.29	0.36	1.00

Note: The father's wage is the 1998–2012 average, and the son's is the 2008–12 average. The number of matched father–son pairs is 356.

Source: Calculated by the author using KLIPS data.

probably reflects the Korean custom of the groom preparing the house with financial support from his parents, which leads to higher net worth elasticity for son–father pairs than for daughter–father pairs.

Using the intergenerational transition matrix, I can figure out how parental income classes change into the next generation. Table 2.2 shows a transition matrix between the father's wage quintile and the son's. The intergenerational persistence rate defined by the share of the sum of diagonal elements (trace) is 32.3 percent. I note that 36 percent of sons whose fathers had the bottom (or top) quintile wages also had the bottom (or top) quintile wages, respectively, in their generation. There are success stories of rising from a humble family: 18 percent of sons who had fathers with the bottom quintile wages climbed up to the top quintile wages. I also note that men of the second quartile low-wage fathers seem vulnerable to downward risk in their generation.

International Comparison

The intergenerational economic mobility of Korea is relatively high. Even when using the highest intergenerational elasticity estimate of 0.225, which is found between a father's wage and a son's wage, Korea belongs to a low-elasticity group that includes Norway, Finland and Canada.

I add Korea into "the Great Gatsby Curve" that represents the relationship between income inequality and intergenerational economic persistence.[5] Figure 2.6 shows that Korea falls on a relatively good spot on which intergenerational mobility is fairly high and income inequality is not that high.

When observing the intergenerational transition matrix, I also find that the intergenerational transmission of economic standing in Korea is not

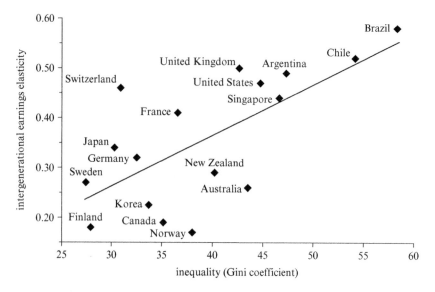

Sources: Intergenerational earnings elasticity (between father and son) for Korea are calculated by the author using KLIPS 1998–2012; for other countries, data estimates are in Corak (2013). Gini coefficients for market income are 1990–2000 averages calculated by the author using UNU-WIDER's World Income Inequality Database.

Figure 2.6   The "Great Gatsby Curve": intergenerational earnings elasticity versus inequality in selected countries

as severe as in the United States or the United Kingdom. Rather, Korea is more like Canada, where parental income distribution among the sons belonging to the top-income is quite similar to Korea. Comparing Korea with the United States, the intergenerational mobility difference appears to come from both differential upward mobility of the least advantaged and the differential probability that children of top-earning parents become top-earners in their turn (Table 2.3).

Intergenerational Correlation of Education

Education can be a "great equalizer" in society if parental influence on children's educational attainments is small. To examine whether education has indeed been an equalizer in Korea, I look into the intergenerational correlations of education of different generations using the KHS 2013 data. I asked 3000 respondents about the education levels of their grandparents and parents, of themselves and of their first children who completed school and are no longer students.

Table 2.3   International comparison of intergenerational transition matrix

Average monthly earnings of sons by country and quartile	Annual household income of parents by quartile				
	1st quartile	2nd quartile	3rd quartile	4th quartile	Total
Korea					
1st quartile	0.34	0.23	0.26	0.17	1.00
2nd quartile	0.30	0.27	0.19	0.24	1.00
3rd quartile	0.22	0.25	0.28	0.26	1.00
4th quartile	0.14	0.26	0.26	0.34	1.00
United States					
1st quartile	0.42	0.30	0.19	0.09	1.00
2nd quartile	0.27	0.28	0.29	0.16	1.00
3rd quartile	0.19	0.25	0.24	0.32	1.00
4th quartile	0.13	0.16	0.28	0.43	1.00
United Kingdom					
1st quartile	0.37	0.22	0.25	0.16	1.00
2nd quartile	0.29	0.31	0.24	0.16	1.00
3rd quartile	0.22	0.25	0.26	0.27	1.00
4th quartile	0.12	0.22	0.25	0.41	1.00
Canada					
1st quartile	0.33	0.29	0.22	0.16	1.00
2nd quartile	0.25	0.27	0.26	0.22	1.00
3rd quartile	0.21	0.24	0.27	0.28	1.00
4th quartile	0.21	0.20	0.25	0.34	1.00

Sources: The Korean matrix is adopted from Kim (2009) using 427 parent–son pairs from the Korean Labor and Income Study. Other countries' matrices are borrowed from Blanden (2005), and data sources are 526 pairs from the Panel Study of Income Dynamics in the United States, 1707 pairs from the British Cohort Study in the United Kingdom, and 428 022 pairs from the Canadian Longitudinal Tax Records.

Figure 2.7 shows the average years of schooling of these four generations. I divide the sample by gender and then observe male lineage (the grandfather, the father, the male respondent and his eldest son) and female lineage (the grandmother, the mother, the female respondent and her eldest daughter) separately. Owing to rapid educational expansion, the average number of years of men's formal education has increased remarkably, from 6.4 years in the grandfather's generation to 10.5 years in the father's generation, and to 15.2 in the male respondent's own generation. Their adult children's educational attainments, however, are quite similar to their own, because Korean education, including tertiary education, had already approached a saturation point in terms of quantity within their

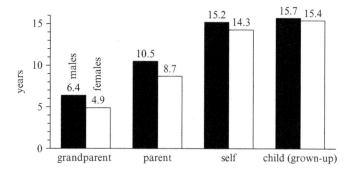

Note: The grown-up child is the first son or daughter who completed school and is no longer a student.

Source: Calculated by the author using KHS 2013 data.

Figure 2.7   Average years of schooling of four generations in Korea

own generation. Women's education has also increased significantly over the generations. The gender gap in educational attainment has narrowed in the respondents' generation and even more in their children's generation.

Before I observe the intergenerational correlation of educational attainment (years of schooling), I divide the KHS 2013 respondents into three age cohorts, which reflects potential differences between age groups. Young, middle-aged and old cohort respondents are divided into ages 20–35, 36–49 and 50–69, respectively, which produce similar numbers for the three age cohorts.

Figure 2.8 reports the intergenerational correlation of educational attainment by age cohort of men. The educational correlation between the grandfather and the father is 0.59–0.63. However, the educational correlation between the father and the male respondent is only 0.14–0.21, which shows the remarkable decrease of parental influence on children's education in the respondents' generation, specifically for the young.

Women's intergenerational correlation of educational attainment has also weakened substantially, as shown in Figure 2.9. In particular, the young female's educational correlation with her mother is fairly minimal, plausibly reflecting the recent change of social norms regarding the gender role in encouraging investment in daughters' human capital. Therefore, I can say that Korean parents had a strong enthusiasm for their children's education irrespective of their own education levels, which resulted in a weak correlation of educational attainments between adult Koreans and their parents.

In Figure 2.10, I also report the educational correlation between the

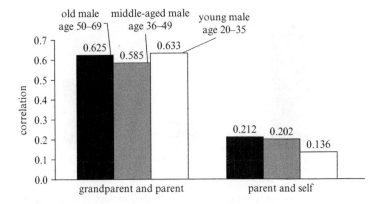

Note: Number of observations: 509 old males, 501 middle-aged males, and 515 young males.

Source: Calculated by the author using KHS 2013 data.

Figure 2.8   Intergenerational correlation of educational attainment by age cohort of male

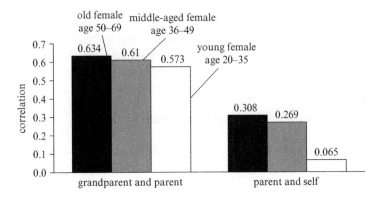

Note: Number of observations: 474 old females, 492 middle-aged females and 509 young females.

Source: Calculated by the author using KHS 2013 data.

Figure 2.9   Intergenerational correlation of educational attainment by age cohort of female

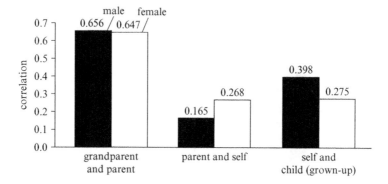

Note: Number of grown-up child observations: 229 first sons and 256 first daughters.

Source: Calculated by the author using KHS 2013 data.

Figure 2.10   Intergenerational correlation of educational attainment across four generations

male (or female) respondent and his (or her) eldest son (or daughter) who has completed formal education and is no longer a student. In the case of men, the intergenerational correlation of educational attainment takes a U-shape. Educational correlation between the male respondent and his father is far less than that between his father and his grandfather, but the intergenerational correlation seems to rise again between his eldest son and himself. On the other hand, women's intergenerational correlation does not take a distinct U-shape across the four generations.[6]

Mobility Expectation for the Next Generation

Educational attainment is a good predictor of socioeconomic status. In addition, I use a subjective measure of socioeconomic status (SES), which was included in the KHS 2013 survey. That was an imaginary ladder similar to the "Cantril ladder." The survey question is:

> How high or low do you think your family's social status is? Please circle the number that corresponds to the estimated status that each family member might be in their mid-ages (40s–50s) compared with all Koreans in the same age group. If your eldest child is very young or you do not have any children yet, please make a best guess of their future and circle the number that matches.

SES is based on comprehensive consideration of income, wealth, social status, living standard, and so on.

Respondents (both male and female) were asked to evaluate or project

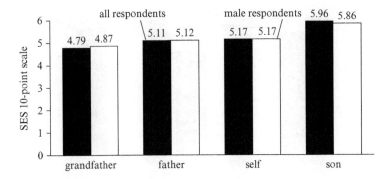

Note: SES is a ten-point scale subjective measure answered by respondents who were asked to place or expect each generation's status in their middle-age (forties and fifties) compared with other Koreans of their generation.

Source: Calculated by the author using KHS 2013 data.

Figure 2.11   *Average socioeconomic status of four generations*

the SES of their grandfathers (fathers' line), fathers, themselves and their eldest sons. The SES is a ten-point scale measure (with 1 the lowest and 10 the highest). Figure 2.11 shows the average SES of each family member, reported by the respondents. I report male respondents' subsample average as well as the whole sample average in the figure. The average SES reported by the respondents tends to be higher for the later generation, which may reflect their perception of socioeconomic improvement over a generation, although they were asked to report relative status in each generation.

Figure 2.12 shows the intergenerational correlation of subjective SES across the four generations. Again, I find a U-shape, a result of the rise in SES correlation between the respondents and their sons. As such, respondents tend to report that the socioeconomic similarity between parents and children will be higher for the next generation (0.6) than for their own generation (0.45–0.48).

In order to see the potential differences in respondents' evaluation of intergenerational SES correlation by their age, I split the sample into three age cohorts again. Indeed, Figure 2.13 shows that the young cohort (ages 20–35) report a relatively low SES correlation between their grandfathers and fathers but a higher SES correlation between themselves and their sons.

In order to observe men's intergenerational SES correlation only, I drop the female respondents' report in Figure 2.14. The improvement of intergenerational SES mobility in the previous generation and the growing pessimism (or fatalism) for the next generation's SES mobility can be clearly seen from the figure.

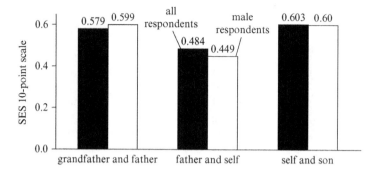

Source: Calculated by the author using KHS 2013 data.

Figure 2.12   *Intergenerational correlation of SES across four generations*
                 by sex

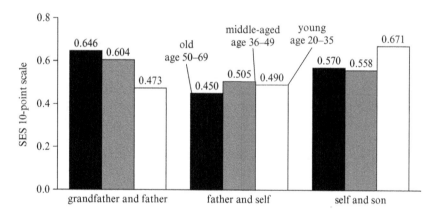

Note: Number of observations: 983 old, 993 middle-aged and 1024 young.

Source: Calculated by the author using KHS 2013 data.

Figure 2.13   *Intergenerational correlation of SES across four generations*
                 by age cohort

Education could play the role as a ladder for social mobility across generations or a conduit for passing down parents' social class position. In the
KHS 2013 survey, I asked respondents:

> How high do you estimate the probability of social mobility that generations
> of your grandparents, parents, your own and your child would have through

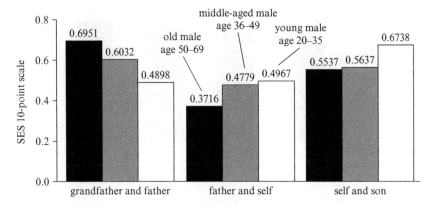

Note: Number of observations: 509 old males, 501 middle-aged males, and 515 young males.

Source: Calculated by the author using KHS 2013 data.

Figure 2.14   *Intergenerational correlation of SES across four generations by age cohort of male*

education? Please, circle the number that corresponds most closely to your level of agreement as to the role of education.

The answer format is given as an 11-point measure: a conduit for passing down parents' social class position equal to 0, and a ladder for social mobility across generations equal to 10. An average over 5 means that respondents are more likely to believe in the role of education as a ladder for intergenerational mobility. Figure 2.15 reports the sample mean of the responses for each generation. Respondents are more likely to consider education as a ladder for upward mobility for later generations. But I should take respondents' age variation into account.

In Figure 2.16, I compare respondents' opinion about the role of education regarding intergenerational mobility by their age cohort. The first panel is a sample mean comparison of the three age cohorts. The old (ages 50–69) respondents have the steepest gradient, representing the belief that Korea had become a land of opportunity for educated people thanks to rapid economic growth during the developing era. Thus they take a more positive view on the role of education for upward mobility for the later generation. The gradient, however, looks lower for younger cohorts.

In examining whether the differences between age cohorts are statistically significant, I regress the 11-point measure answers on the dummy variables of age cohorts with the middle-aged (ages 36–49) being the

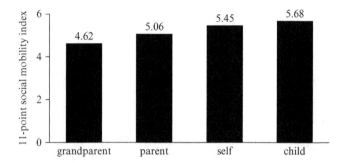

Note: A higher score means stronger belief in education as a ladder for upward mobility.

Source: Calculated by the author using KHS 2013 data.

Figure 2.15   Is education a ladder for upward mobility in each generation?

reference category. The second panel confirms the different views of the respondents by each age group on the role of education as a ladder for upward mobility. Compared with the middle-aged respondents, the old have lower evaluations for their grandparents and parents, but higher evaluations for themselves and their children. The young respondents, however, have consistently lower evaluations on the equalizing role of education for their parents, themselves and their children, although their evaluation for their grandparents is similar to that of their middle-aged counterparts. As such, the KHS 2013 survey also suggests that social belief in the role of education for intergenerational mobility has been weakening.

A Growing Divide in Education

Korea's tertiary educational institutions are ranked by the average Korean Scholastic Aptitude Test (KSAT) scores of the newly entering students. Most two-year colleges are ranked lower than four-year universities. The most prestigious of the four-year universities are located in Seoul or in metropolitan Seoul, with the exception of a few out-of-Seoul elite institutions in the fields of science or engineering, and local medical schools that admit high school graduates.

   Figure 2.17 shows that family backgrounds influence college entrance results. Parents' SES index (which incorporates household income and father's education level and occupation prestige reported in the ninth grade of children) is positively correlated with their subsequent outcomes in college entrance. For instance, three out of four students with the family background of the top quintile SES entered four-year universities;

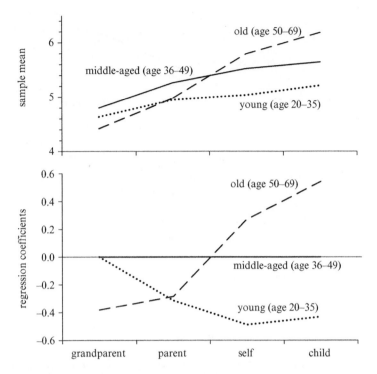

Note: Number of observations: 983 old, 993 middle-aged, and 1024 young.

Source: Calculated by the author using KHS 2013 data.

Figure 2.16   Different beliefs in the role of education as the ladder for upward mobility in each generation by age cohort

of these, 19 percent were admitted to the top 30 universities, and 10 percent to the top nine universities or medical schools. By contrast, among underprivileged students from the bottom quintile SES, two out of five entered four-year universities, but only 4.3 percent of them entered the top 30 universities and a mere 0.4 percent found themselves in the top nine universities or medical schools.

According to an online survey of 492 teachers or education professionals, conducted by the Korean Educational Development Institute in February 2011, the majority of respondents were skeptical about the possibility of being admitted to prestigious universities on the basis of individual ability and effort. In answering the question, "Do you think that one can enter prestigious schools by one's own ability and effort regardless of familial economic level?" 68 percent of education experts

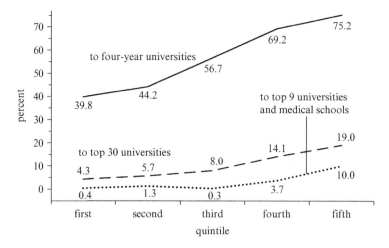

Note: SES index = (1/3)*(household income decile/10) + (1/3)*(father's education level category/6) + (1/3)*(father's occupation prestige category/5). These family background variables were measured in the ninth grade (third grade of middle school).

Source: Recalculated by the author using Table 2.4 in Kim (2011: 15), who examines the college entrance results of a sample of 1731 students (third grade of middle school in 2004) of Korean Education and Employment Panel (KEEP) data.

Figure 2.17   College entrance results by SES quintile in the ninth grade

including teachers answered "No." Moreover, younger respondents tended to be more pessimistic. The proportion of negative answers was 83 percent among those in their twenties and thirties, 71 percent among those in their forties, and 58 percent among those in their fifties.

Seoul National University (SNU) has a symbolic meaning for Koreans as the most prestigious university that guarantees a decent life. During the 1980s, a period when out-of-school private tutoring was banned by the authoritative government and nationwide equalization of high schools had already taken place, finding freshmen in the SNU campus who came from underdeveloped rural areas or islands was not difficult.[7] However, SNU became disproportionately represented by students from affluent families and from metropolitan cities such as Seoul. Kim et al. (2003) examined the family background of freshmen at the College of Social Sciences of SNU and found that the entrance ratio of students whose fathers belonged to the highest-paying occupations in comparison with other students had increased from 1.3 percent in 1985 to 16.6 percent in 2000.

Moreover, the regional distribution of the SNU entrance ratio has been concentrated in Seoul. Figure 2.18 shows that since 2010, when the

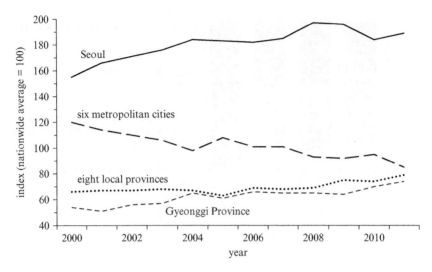

Note: The SNU entrance ratio is adjusted by the number of high school graduates in each region.

Source: The number of SNU entrants by high school, reported to the National Assembly by SNU.

Figure 2.18   Trends in the Seoul National University entrance ratio by region, 2000–2011

government ban on private tutoring was declared unconstitutional, Seoul and its surrounding Gyeonggi Province have outperformed other regions in terms of the SNU entrance ratio, adjusted by the number of high school graduates in each region. Meanwhile, the SNU entrance ratio of non-Seoul metropolitan cities has been decreasing. People suspect that the high performance of Seoul in entering this prestigious university is due at least partially to its booming market of high-quality private tutors.

Even within Seoul, the type of high school attended matters increasingly for being admitted into prestigious universities. Special-purpose high schools are regarded as better high schools that provide a competitive advantage in entering prestigious universities, owing to their privilege of selecting high-performing students, enhanced peer effects and better study environments than general high schools.[8] As Figure 2.19 shows, the proportion of special-purpose high school graduates among SNU entrants who graduated from high schools in Seoul increased from 22.8 percent in 2002 to 40.5 percent in 2011. In the meantime, general high schools, even including those in Gangnam district, were losing their shares in SNU entrance.

As a part of high school diversification policy, the government introduced

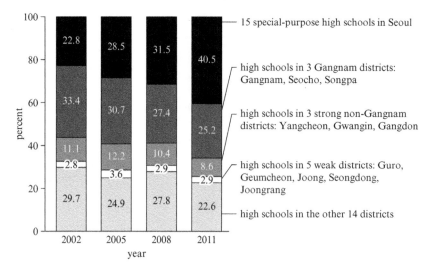

Source: The number of SNU entrants by high school, reported to the National Assembly by SNU.

Figure 2.19   Composition of Seoul National University entrants who graduated from high schools in Seoul, 2002–11

50 autonomous private high schools that have more autonomy in their curriculums, in return for financial independence, which means that each school does not receive any financial support from the government. These autonomous schools have attracted high-performing middle-schoolers from a broader region, because the top 50 percent of students in middle schools are entitled to apply for autonomous high schools. According to Table 2.4, autonomous high schools have revealed their competitive advantage in college entrance. Considering that the proportion of autonomous private high schools among all high schools nationwide is just 2.1 percent, their shares in four-year college entrants, four-year national/public college entrants and four-year Seoul metropolitan area college entrants were disproportionately high and even increasing between 2013 and 2014.[9] Their superior performance needs empirical investigation. It may result from the value-added instruction that autonomous schools provide, or from a mere selection effect that depends on students' higher abilities. The share of general high schools in four-year college entrants substantially decreased with the introduction of autonomous high schools. One might suspect, therefore, that the performance of autonomous schools can be largely attributed to "cream skimming" by monopolizing the high-performing middle-schoolers, who might have entered general high schools in the absence of autonomous high schools.

Table 2.4   Shares of four-year college entrants by type of high school in Korea (%)

Entrants to four-year institutions	2011	2012	2013	2014
All colleges				
General high school	83.4	85.7	79.4	78.0
Vocational high school	9.0	6.6	4.4	4.2
Special-purpose high school	4.0	4.0	4.6	4.5
Autonomous high school	–	–	7.5	9.2
National/public colleges				
General high school	87.0	89.4	81.9	79.9
Vocational high school	6.9	4.5	3.2	2.7
Special-purpose high school	3.6	3.6	3.7	3.8
Autonomous high school	–	–	8.0	11.0
Seoul metropolitan area colleges				
General high school	80.8	81.5	74.1	72.5
Vocational high school	5.7	4.7	3.3	3.3
Special-purpose high school	8.4	8.4	9.1	8.7
Autonomous high school	–	–	7.7	9.8

Note: The number of four-year colleges was 181 in 2011–12, and 174 in 2013–14. Among them, the number of national/public colleges was 26; and that of Seoul metropolitan area colleges was 67 in 2011–12, and 66 in 2013–14.

Source: Ministry of Education and Korean Council for University Education data.

The existence of outperforming high schools and their increasing superiority in college entrance results are closely related to the issue of intergenerational mobility, because high schools are differentiated by students' family backgrounds. Figure 2.20 examines the students in each of the four types of high school in Seoul and shows the systematic differences in the proportions of students based on the father's education level, occupational prestige and household income. In each case, vocational high school students have the poorest background (lower educational level of the father, lower occupational prestige and lower household income). General high school students are underprivileged compared with the autonomous private high school students. Special-purpose high schools appear to select the most privileged, richest students.

Korea's income inequality was not severe until the late 1990s. As Figure 2.21 shows, however, inequality has increased particularly since the economic crisis of 1997. I suspect that aggravated income distribution affected educational inequality because poor families could not afford

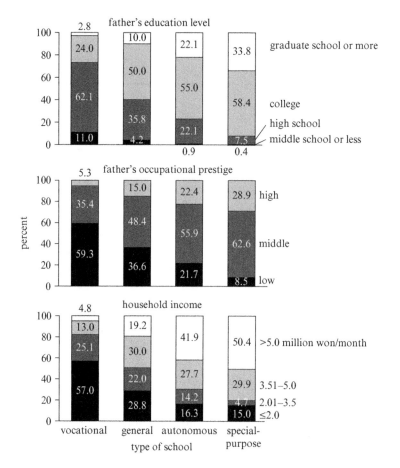

Source: Calculated by the author using Seoul Educational Longitudinal Study (SELS) 2010 data.

Figure 2.20   Family background of first-year high school students in Seoul by type of school, 2010

private tutoring or other investment to enrich their children's education, and the economic crisis was a shattering blow to many low-income families.

In this regard, Byun and Kim (2010) provide evidence for our suspicion. Using three cohorts (1999, 2003 and 2007) of eighth-grade Korean students from the Trends in International Mathematics and Science Study, they examine trends in the relationship between socioeconomic backgrounds and test score. The magnitude of the impact of socioeconomic

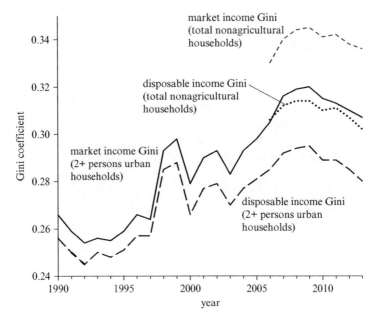

Source: Data are from the annual Household Survey of Statistics Korea. My thanks to Dr Gyeongjoon Yoo at the Korea Development Institute, who kindly shared data for this figure.

Figure 2.21 Measures of income inequality in Korea, 1990–2013

background on student achievement increased over time between 1999 and 2007. Meanwhile, American students' test scores improved regardless of socioeconomic background.

Educational achievement inequality results, at least in part, from the educational expenditure gap between income groups. Most Korean parents take part in the outrageous arms race of private tutoring, which is the main reason for the abysmally low birth rate. As Figure 2.22 shows, private tutoring cost continuously increased during the decade up to 2009, to the extent that it became almost double the public education cost for primary and secondary schooling. In particular, the current trend of sumptuous private tutoring, including English daycare services for very young children, is prevalent among rich families. As a result, private tutoring inequality, measured by the expenditure gap (ratio) between the top and the bottom income quintile households, also increased (the gap reached tenfold in 2009).

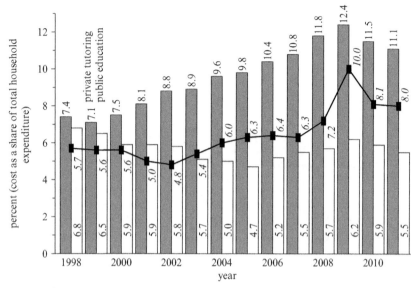

The solid line is the private tutoring inequality ratio.

Note: Cost (percentage) is the share in total household expenditure. Private tutoring excludes that for adults. Public education is for primary/secondary education. Private tutoring inequality = private tutoring expenditure of the fifth-quintile income household divided by that of the first-quintile income household. Data are for urban households with more than two unmarried children.

Source: Annual Household Survey of Statistics Korea.

Figure 2.22   Changes in child education expenditure share and private tutoring inequality, 1998–2011

POLICY DIRECTIONS

Preventing Talent Loss

When it comes to equal opportunity, as Corak (2013: 98) notes, "people tend to support policies that would assure a level playing field in access to jobs and education, and are less willing to take steps to offset genetic advantages." Therefore, I need to examine the potential ability gap at the beginning, from birth, between children from different income groups.

At the earliest ages, there is no significant difference in cognitive ability between high- and low-income individuals. Using data from the Early Childhood Longitudinal Survey, Fryer and Levitt (2013) find that the standardized mental function composite score of infants (8–12 months of age) has almost no correlation with the parental SES quintile (that is, a combination of income, education and occupation). Instead, other factors such as age, gender and birth order have a stronger correlation with the infant's cognitive ability.

Thus, the children of high- and low-income families are born with similar abilities on average, but rapidly diverge in outcomes by differential circumstances. The evidence suggests that even cognitive ability per se develops differently under the influence of parental SES. By examining the sample of British children born in 1970, Feinstein (2003) found that, in cognitive ability (Intelligence Quotient, IQ) distribution, the average position of low-income children who were near the top 90 percentile at 22 months of age continued to drop until age 10, when they were overtaken by high-income children whose IQ was near the bottom 10 percentile at 22 months.

The student achievement gap tended to widen in the higher grades of schooling, as insufficient development of literacy and numeracy skills hindered further studies in the next stage of education. Carneiro and Heckman (2002) find that long-term factors that promote cognitive and noncognitive ability are much more important determinants of the family income–college enrollment relationship in the United States than short-run liquidity constraints to pay college tuition and fees. Similarly, using data from the Korean Education and Employment Panel, Lee and Kim (2012) show that most of the higher education gap by family background can be attributed to the long-term accumulation of disadvantages from an underprivileged home environment, not the short-term constraint. In light of these findings, policies involving early intervention to prevent the widening developmental gap of children will be more effective in alleviating educational and subsequent income inequality than will providing college loans or reducing tuition costs.

However, the existing achievement gap often depicted in KSAT scores should also be addressed to prevent talent loss. In fact, standardized test scores show only partial information on students' ability and can be affected by private tutoring that is tailored specifically to solve the test problems. Therefore, an opportunity should be provided for underprivileged students, by taking affirmative action in the admission process, so that they can flourish in a better environment such as good colleges.

In an effort to enhance student diversity and regional representation, Seoul National University (SNU) introduced "regional balanced admission" in 2005 for high-performing students from rural high schools, which gave special consideration to the potentials not exhibited in the KSAT scores but recognized by teachers and principals. How were they doing

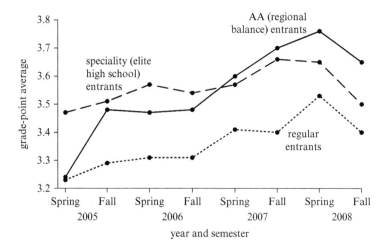

Note: SNU admitted 3224 students in total in March 2005, which consisted of 659 (20.4%) AA (affirmative-action) entrants based on rural area quota, 426 (13.2%) specialty entrants mostly from special-purpose high schools, and 2139 (66.3%) regular entrants. Among them, 702 students graduated in February 2009, composed of 84 AA entrants, 102 specialty entrants, and 516 regular entrants.

Source: Baek and Yang (2009).

Figure 2.23   *GPA of Seoul National University students until graduation by type of admission, 2005–08*

after being admitted to SNU? A four-year examination of those regional balance admission students shows that "a hidden gem will soon sparkle."

Figure 2.23 reports the changes in grade-point average (GPA) of the SNU students in the freshman class of 2005 until graduation by the type of admission. Three types of students were compared: (1) affirmative-action (regional balanced admission) entrants comprising mostly rural high schools; (2) specialty entrants comprising mostly special-purpose high schools; and (3) regular entrants. In their first semester as freshmen, the specialty entrants' GPA was higher than the other entrants, which may reflect their superior preparation and readiness for higher education. After four semesters of catch-up and adjustment process, however, affirmative-action entrants outperformed specialty entrants and finished their senior year with the highest GPA.

In 2008, with the encouragement and financial support of the government, Korean universities introduced the admissions officer (AO) system in their admission process. The main purpose is to find "a gem in the haystack" by the comprehensive consideration of a student's school record, letter of self-introduction, KSAT score, and so on. In spite of its potential to enhance social mobility, the AO system often faces suspicion or criticism that it only leads to a heavier burden for students (and parents) in preparing various specification packages to apply for college, and that it mainly serves the interests of students from rich families. Out-of-school curricular activities are believed to be necessary to prepare for an AO admission, which often require parental support and social networking. Therefore, the AO system needs to be developed more explicitly as an affirmative-action admission process, and more effort is required to reach out to underprivileged students with the potential to flourish, rather than to select the best students of the moment.

Strengthening Social Inclusion

Individuals from well-to-do backgrounds have various advantages in the labor market. The luckiest of them inherit firm ownership, as in the cases of family-owned Korean conglomerates or *chaebol*. Also, their backgrounds provide them with information about the labor market, or connections that help in the search for good jobs. For comparison, Loury (2006) suggests that, in the United States, up to half of jobs are found through family, friends or acquaintances.

In light of this, it is worth paying attention to the social network support perceived by Koreans and the difference by educational attainment. According to the Organisation for Economic Co-operation and Development (OECD) (2013), the percentage of people reporting relatives or friends they can count on is relatively low in Korea compared with other OECD countries. In particular, only 41.6 percent of the less educated Koreans without a college diploma reported that they have someone to count on. Although highly educated Koreans also feel weaker social network support than their foreign counterparts with a similar educational background, the feeling gap by education level is the greatest in Korea. This gap may reflect the relative deprivation of the less educated individuals, and explain people's obsession with specific college diplomas in recognition of the power of school connections in Korean society.

As Korean people, particularly the young, have become highly educated to the point where scholars are concerned about overeducation or an education bubble, the marginalization or social exclusion of less educated people may be more severe than ever before. In this vein, I need to take a closer look at the young people who are less educated.

Figure 2.24 shows the path of the high school graduates by type of school and its year-by-year changes from 2004 to 2013. The expansion of higher education also affected those in a vocational track, so that

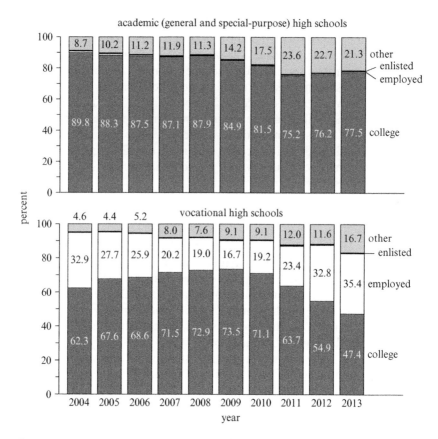

Source:　Calculated by the author using data from annual *Statistical Yearbook of Education* by Statistics Korea.

Figure 2.24　High school graduates' paths by type of school, 2004–13

the proportion of vocational high school graduates who went to college immediately after their graduation exceeded 70 percent from 2008 to 2010. However, their college enrollment rate began decreasing after 2010, as the government encouraged students to get jobs immediately after high school graduation and to apply to colleges later if needed. Also, it may be possible that the poor performance of many college graduates in the labor market might have influenced the high-schoolers' decision to directly enter labor markets. In this figure, 21 percent of academic high school graduates and 17 percent of vocational high school graduates are recorded as nonstudents, nonemployees or nonsoldiers.

As a matter of fact, the proportion of the young who are not in educa-

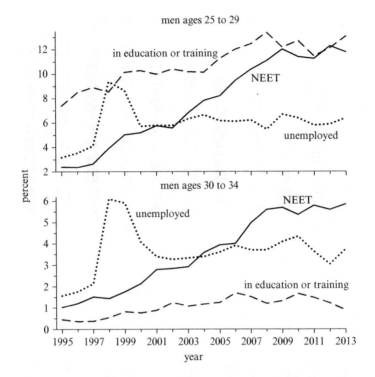

Note: "NEET" indicates unmarried young men who do not participate in education, employment or training. We exclude men who mainly participate in housekeeping from the NEETs.

Source: Calculated by the author using data from the Economically Active Population Survey of Statistics Korea.

Figure 2.25   Share of NEETs in the population of Korean young men, 1995–2013

tion, employment or training (NEETs) has been increasing. As Figure 2.25 shows, the proportion of NEETs among young men ages 25–29 increased from 2.4 percent in 1995 to 11.8 percent in 2013. Meanwhile, the proportion of NEETs also increased from 1.0 percent in 1995 to 5.9 percent in 2013 among men who are of the prime working ages from 30 to 34.

Moreover, as Figure 2.26 shows, the employment rate of the least educated (less than high school) men aged 30–34 dropped remarkably, from 84.9 percent in 2000 to 60.4 percent in 2013. They have become more and more marginalized as the average level of education has increased, which is reminiscent of Lester Thurow's "job competition" theory. In fact, as a result of overeducation, highly educated young people currently take

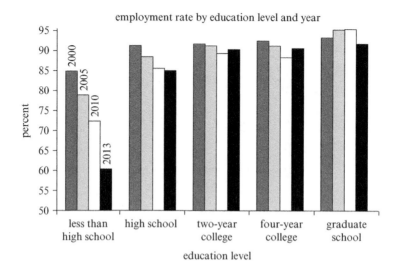

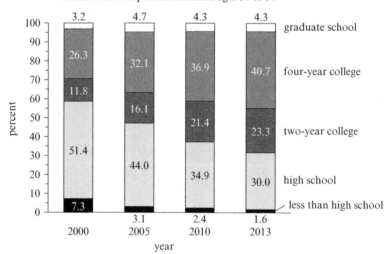

Source: Calculated by the author using data from the Economically Active Population Survey of Statistics Korea.

Figure 2.26   *Employment rate by education level and educational composition of Korean males, ages 30–34, 2000–13*

jobs that were conventionally taken by the less educated. For example, I can hardly find a young bank teller currently who graduated only from high school, despite the fact that the majority of employees in the banking industry were just high school graduates a few decades ago. In this fashion, the least educated young (specifically, high school dropouts) have lost employment opportunities.

Therefore, I need to pay special attention to the unemployed young people, specifically the least educated, because they are the weakest group in job competition and face the risk of falling into poverty or turning to crime. Preventing dropouts in secondary schooling and providing vocational education and training for these vulnerable young people should be listed in policy agendas for strengthening social cohesion.

Helping to Open Multiple Routes to Success

As Kim and Ohtake (2014) mention, most Koreans share a common definition of success, meaning working in the government and its allied enterprises, the banks or large enterprises that provide secure, well-paid and prestigious jobs. Thus they compete too narrowly for established routes of success, which becomes a zero-sum game that makes the vast majority of people feel like losers.

In the context of contemporary Korea where the education bubble has burst (which is implied by the recent drop in enrollment rates shown in Figure 2.24), a college degree is not always and not for everyone a gateway to a good job. Therefore, multiple routes to success should be opened for those who choose not to go to college. Korean vocational education, however, has failed to attract an adequate number of students needed in industry and has become degraded in the era of expansion of higher education. Despite the existence of the excessive supply of college graduates and increasing numbers of the highly educated jobless in the labor market, parents have continued to encourage their children to enter colleges because they have not been made aware of the existence of other paths to good-paying jobs.

To raise the attractiveness of vocational education and the employability skills of vocational high school graduates, there is a need to develop vocational education programs in collaboration with leading firms. In this vein, Korea introduced the German vocational education system to some pilot schools under the so-called Meister ("master" in English) high school program, which combines academic content with apprenticeships. It is a part of a new dual-track system for secondary education in Korea, which benefits firms by supplying relatively low-cost, entry-level workers with firm-specific skills, and at the same time, helps the graduates of the

Meister program pursue advanced degrees, if they later choose to do so, with the support of employers.

Of course the employability skills of high school graduates from common vocational high schools other than Meister high schools and general high schools should likewise be improved. Also, support must be given to young entrepreneurs for their business start-ups and to those searching for jobs abroad, especially if they have ideas and skills but do not have access to resources or networks.

CONCLUSION

Korea is often regarded as an exemplary model of achieving both remarkable economic growth and social equity, starting from the ashes of war in the 1950s, and today on par with the average of OECD countries. Furthermore, Korea's intergenerational economic mobility, measured by intergenerational elasticity and the intergenerational transition matrix, is also fairly high, and comparable to that of Canada or the Nordic countries.

The reasons why the intergenerational persistence of SES has been low in Korea are at least threefold. First, rapid economic growth has created many jobs in modern sectors that require skilled or semi-skilled labor. Second, after the abrupt abolition of the pre-modern social stratification in the Japanese colonial era, most Korean parents earnestly invested in their children's education, regardless of their SES, to help the next generation take advantage of new opportunities in the process of modernization and industrialization. The merit-based personnel practices such as hiring and promotion of government officials stimulated the demand for education.

Third, education policies also contributed to social mobility. In line with the pace of economic development, the Korean government developed educational capacity sequentially. Initial emphasis was placed on universal primary education, then on secondary education, and subsequently expanded to tertiary education. School finance was nationalized for private schools as well as public schools, up through secondary education, which equalized educational resources for each school. Also, the government introduced an equalization policy for secondary education (for middle schools in 1969 and for high schools in 1974) by using a lottery-based assignment of students in place of school exams, which indeed reduced achievement gaps between schools and enhanced student diversity in select universities. Moreover, the government banned out-of-school private tutoring in 1980 and curbed the expansion of the private tutoring market to some degree, until the ban was declared unconstitutional in

2000. All those policies countervailed the influence of family background on student achievement and, therefore, contributed to social equity including intergenerational mobility. In this vein, Jang and Han (2011) find that banning private tutoring and equalizing middle schools actually enhanced intergenerational mobility of the treated cohort compared with the previous age cohort.

Now, however, Korea faces a different situation. Economic growth slowed down after the Asian crisis of 1997, and the pressure of international competition became stronger with the rise of the Chinese economy. Jobs for both low-skilled and high-skilled labor have been lost due to the increasing imports of cheap goods and labor and the offshoring of large enterprises, as well as labor-saving technology. Income inequality has increased since the 1997 crisis and, in the meantime, the labor income share has decreased because wages have not caught up with labor productivity.

The educational environment has also changed, in ways that impede rather than facilitate social mobility. A heated pace of private tutoring begins at a very early stage of life, even while a child is still a toddler. High schools are no longer equalized but vertically differentiated, due to the introduction and expansion of prestigious high schools that absorb high-performing middle-schoolers. A college degree is less promising than before, and the college premium is concentrated among a few select universities. The NEETs are increasing and the least educated young (high school dropouts) are being marginalized in society.

Considering these circumstances, young adults today may well have a much more pessimistic expectation of their children's upward mobility compared with the older generation who experienced high growth and mobility. Growing pessimism among the young exacerbates the abysmal birth rate of Korea, which increasingly is becoming a serious problem. Rising income inequality coupled with falling social mobility is bound to undermine social cohesion and sustainable economic growth.[10]

Focusing on the role of education in the rise and fall of social mobility, this chapter suggests three policy directions. First, loss of talent should be prevented by early intervention as well as school loans or scholarships. Pro-mobility education policies in place of private tutoring have proved effective (Kim 2011), including enhancement of the quality of school lessons specifically in underprivileged regions and provision of low-price, high-quality enrichment classes such as after-school programs.

Second, it is necessary to take care of the less educated young to prevent them from becoming NEETs. Their deficiency in employable skills and social networks needs to be addressed by giving them public support. And to prevent dropouts before high school graduation, schools should bear more responsibility in guaranteeing the minimum level of achievement for every student, and provide special care to vulnerable students in cooperation with local governments and regional communities.

   Third, opening multiple routes to success other than a narrowly defined route (such as from select universities to good jobs) should be encouraged and supported. Limited public resources must be given to people who will deploy their talents and energy in pursuit of innovation, production and job creation.

NOTES

1. The KDI researchers selected Macromill-Embrain, Inc., the top web survey agency in Korea, which boasted a database of 980 380 Korean panel respondents nationwide at the end of July 2013. Data were obtained on 3000 Korean respondents aged 20 through 69 using stratified random sampling from the panel. The company executed the survey under the direction of the authors and the survey experts of the KDI Economic Information and Education Center from October 17 to November 13, 2013. We used payment incentives and email or a support notification service to encourage participation, and made additional efforts (telephone calls and follow-up surveys) to ensure that previous web responses were accurate. Researchers often have concerns about the potential selection bias of a web survey because of the possibility of excluding those who have only limited access to the Internet, such as elderly people or those living in rural areas. However, Korea has a world-class Internet penetration rate. In December 2011, Korea's high-speed wireless Internet penetration rate reached 100.6 percent, becoming first in the world, owing to the well-established information technology infrastructure and rapid increase of smartphone users nationwide, whereas the OECD average was 54.3 percent. This penetration rate partially relieves our concerns about selection bias.
2. For example, the so-called "English divide" appears among kindergarten children. Koreans tend to value English proficiency because they believe it helps them to get better jobs. According to data from the Ministry of Education reported to the National Assembly, the number of private English daycare centers where children are given English-only lessons increased from 181 in 2009 to 235 in 2014. Among them, the number of expensive ones (those receiving more than 1 million won per month for each child) also increased, from 20 in 2009, to 133 in 2014. As English is a foreign language that requires deliberately huge investment to acquire proficiency in Korea, more salient income-based differences were observed in English scores on the KSAT than in math or Korean (Kim 2012).
3. In the sample of son–father pairs, and in the case of the subsample for analyzing intergenerational wage elasticity, the average birth years of father and son are 1946 and 1976, respectively, and their average ages (standard errors) when wages were observed are 57 (6 years) and 34 (4 years), respectively. In the corresponding subsample, the average birth years of father and daughter are 1947 and 1977, respectively, and their average ages (standard errors) when wages were observed are 56 (6 years) and 33 (4 years), respectively.
4. Other studies that used data from KLIPS also produced similar estimates of intergenerational income elasticity (Kim et al. 2009; Choi and Hong 2011). The magnitudes of the elasticity estimates are higher when instrumental variables (for example, education level) are used for father's income (Kim et al. 2009; Choi and Hong 2011; Yang 2012) or when children who live with their parents are included in the sample (Yang 2012). For international comparison, however, I do not use instrumental variables but use averaged real earnings observed in the data and confine the children sample to adults who do not live with their parents, as most studies do for other countries.

5. Considering that the sample average of Korean sons' birth year is 1976 and that parental investment in enriching the human capital of their children used to be concentrated in their secondary and postsecondary education via providing private tutoring or tuitions in those days, I use the average of Gini coefficients during 1990–2000 while they were 14–24 years old. The intergenerational earnings elasticity estimates of other countries use data on a cohort of children born during the early to mid-1960s whose adult outcomes were measured in the mid- to late 1990s (Corak 2013: 81).
6. When the sample is confined to those who have adult children who completed all education, the educational correlation between the grandfather and the father is 0.589, and between the father and the male respondent is 0.256, which still show a U-shape intergenerational correlation across four generations of men. In the case of women, the subsample of those who have grown-up daughters produces the educational correlation of 0.582 between the grandmother and the mother, and 0.411 between the mother and the female respondent. Therefore, the U-shape is found only in men's intergenerational correlation, which may hint at the possibility that "like father, like son" is coming again.
7. In 1974, Korea adopted a "high school equalization" policy that abolished entrance tests and introduced a lottery system to assign middle school students to high school. The purpose of the equalization policy was to ease overheated competition for admission to the better high schools.
8. Special-purpose high schools have been introduced as a modification to the equalization policy, beginning with science high schools (1983) and continuing with foreign-language high schools (1992) and international high schools (1998). These schools have their own objectives for educating students with special aptitude. They have, however, become objects of parents' envy as well as public criticism, because the reason for establishing them became diluted by their focus on getting their students into prestigious universities. For example, only a very small fraction of foreign-language high school graduates actually choose corresponding majors in college, and some students even enter medical schools.
9. Autonomous high schools in Table 2.4 include 58 autonomous public high schools designated and supported by the government to improve their disadvantageous educational environments. Therefore, most of the superior performance of autonomous high schools in college entrance probably comes from autonomous private high schools.
10. According to Chetty et al. (2014), intergenerational mobility has not changed appreciably in the last 20 years in the United States, although income inequality has increased. They suspect that improved civil rights for minorities or greater access to higher education played a huge role in why no plunge in mobility has occurred. In Korea, however, the situation is different. Nowadays, college admission does not guarantee upward mobility for the underprivileged young. And ordinary Korean parents are now more discouraged about the chance of upward mobility for their children, because the odds of moving up the income ladder were fairly high in their own generation (or the previous one, depending on the parents' age). This anchoring effect, which gave them high expectations for their children's future, may exacerbate pessimism in the current circumstances.

REFERENCES

Baek, Soonkeun and Jungho Yang (2009), "The achievements and challenges of regional balanced admission," in *Proceedings of the 27th Higher Education Policy Forum*, Seoul: Korean Council for University Education (in Korean).

Blanden, Jo (2005), "International evidence on intergenerational mobility," Centre for Economic Performance Working Paper, London: London School of Economics.

Byun, Soo-yong and Kyung-keun Kim (2010), "Educational inequality in South Korea: the widening socioeconomic gap in student achievement," *Research in the Sociology of Education*, **17**, 155–82.

Carneiro, Pedro and James J. Heckman (2002), "The evidence on credit constraints in post-secondary schooling," *Economic Journal*, **112**, 989–1018.

Chetty, Raj, Nathaniel Hendren, Patrick Kline, Emmanuel Saez and Nicholas Turner (2014), "Is the United States still a land of opportunity? Recent trends in intergenerational mobility," *American Economic Review: Papers and Proceedings*, **104**(5), 141–47.

Choi, Jieun and Kiseok Hong (2011), "An analysis of intergenerational earnings mobility in Korea: father–son correlation in labor earnings," *Korean Social Security Studies*, **27**(3), 143–63 (in Korean).

Corak, Miles (2013), "Income inequality, equality of opportunity, and intergenerational mobility," *Journal of Economic Perspectives*, **27**(3), 79–102.

Feinstein, Leon (2003), "Inequality in the early cognitive development of British children in the 1970 cohort," *Economica*, **70**(277), 73–97.

Fryer, Roland and Steven Levitt (2013), "Testing for racial differences in the mental ability of young children," *American Economic Review*, **103**(2), 981–1005.

Jang, Soomyung and Chirok Han (2011), "Education policy and social mobility," in *Changing Society and Social Mobility, Research Monograph 2011–20*, Seoul: Korea Institute for Health and Social Affairs, pp. 103–169 (in Korean).

Kim, Hisam (2009), "Analysis on intergenerational economic mobility in Korea," KDI Policy Study 2009-03, Seoul: Korea Development Institute (in Korean).

Kim, Hisam (2012), "Equity and efficiency of Koreans' English education investments," *KDI Policy Forum*, Vol. 245, August 22, Seoul: Korea Development Institute.

Kim, Hisam and Fumio Ohtake (2014), "Status race and happiness: what experimental surveys tell us," Policy Study 2014-01, Seoul: Korea Development Institute.

Kim, Kwang Ok, Dae-il Kim, Yi Jong Suh and Chang Yong Rhee (2003), "Who enters Seoul National University?" *Korean Social Science*, **25**(1–2), 3–187 (in Korean).

Kim, Minseong, Bonggeun Kim and Tae-wook Ha (2009), "Intergenerational income elasticity in Korea," *Kukje Kyungje Yongu*, **15**(2), 87–102 (in Korean).

Kim, Youngchul (2011), "Improving equal opportunity in admission to higher education," KDI Policy Study 2011-06, Seoul: Korea Development Institute (in Korean).

Lee, Seungeun and Taejong Kim (2012), "What causes the college entrance gap in Korea?" *Korean Journal of Labor Economics*, **35**(3), 51–81.

Loury, Linda Datcher (2006), "Some contacts are more equal than others: informal networks, job tenure, and wages," *Journal of Labor Economics*, **24**(2), 299–318.

Organisation for Economic Co-operation and Development (OECD) (2013), *Education at a Glance*, Paris: Organisation for Economic Co-operation and Development.

Pekkala, Sari and Robert E.B. Lucas (2007), "Differences across cohorts in Finnish intergenerational income mobility," *Industrial Relations*, **46**(1), 81–111.

Pekkarinen, Tuomas, Roope Uusitalo and Sari Kerr (2003), "School tracking and intergenerational income mobility: evidence from the Finnish comprehensive school reform," *Journal of Public Economics*, **93**, 965–73.

Solon, Gary R. (2004), "A model of intergenerational mobility variation over time and place," in Miles Corak (ed.), *Generational Income Mobility in North America and Europe*, Cambridge: Cambridge University Press, pp. 38–47.

Statistics Korea (annual), *Statistical Yearbook of Education*, Seoul: Statistics Korea.

Yang, Jung-Seung (2012), "Estimating the intergenerational income mobility in Korea," *Korean Journal of Labor Economics*, **35**(2), 25–41 (in Korean).

PART II

Issues in higher education

3.   Restructuring universities in Korea

Jaehoon Kim

INTRODUCTION

The principle of the "qualification rule" was adopted in 1996, and first applied in 1997. In contrast to the permission system in which the government decided on the establishment of universities in Korea, under the qualification rule, once certain establishment requirements are satisfied, universities can operate without any further administrative permission. As result, the number of universities in Korea soared. Despite such growth, however, the lack of quality improvement in university education has been criticized. The quantitative expansion of higher education has surely brought some positive outcomes, such as mass accessibility, but these benefits are overwhelmed by negative consequences, which mainly lie in the production of underperforming universities that fail to recruit either adequate numbers of students to fill their admission targets or faculty members to teach them. The social cost caused by these institutions staying in the market is believed to be huge. Adding to that, looming changes in Korea's demographic structure would accelerate the decline in its school-age population, leaving almost all universities with difficulties to face when filling their student admission targets until the year 2030.

In its master plan for the development of higher education released in August 2014, the Ministry of Education announced the abolition of the principle of the standing rule, starting from 2014. However, making it difficult to establish new universities will not help to solve pending problems of the existing, underperforming universities. As the school-age population decreases, the number of prospective university students is likewise on the decline, triggering a projection of excess supply of higher education. Given that the majority (80 percent) of private universities rely mainly on student tuition for their operation, there will be more underperforming universities as a result of the decline in the number of students, if current conditions persist.

By and large, the Korean government now faces two challenges: raising efforts to enhance the competitiveness of universities, and consequently coping with the decline in the school-age population. It would be reasonable to regard these two challenges as a single coin with two opposing sides. The government policy on higher education has so far focused on control through fiscal support based on multifaceted regulations. This has partly contributed to the complacency that Korean universities now espouse, pursuing the status quo instead of moving forward through competition. Within this context, this chapter intends to seek out measures to enhance the competitiveness of Korean universities and to respond to the decline in the school-age population. To that end, this chapter first outlines academic achievements made by Korean universities and reviews two fundamental regulations on Korean universities: university establishment regulations in the capital region and the principle of the qualification rule. Then, data on Korean universities are analyzed in order to examine their impacts and to ponder the possibility of adopting quasi-market competition.

CURRENT CONDITIONS OF KOREAN UNIVERSITIES

Achievements

If Korea is to serve as an economic and cultural epicenter of Asia, it requires a creative, innovative and talented workforce capable of generating added value to the knowledge-intensive sectors. The number of Korean universities has expanded rapidly over the past 50 years, but their global competitiveness has not lived up to such expansion. According to the International Institute for Management Development (IMD) World Competitiveness database for 2013, Korea ranks twenty-fifth among 60 nations, following Sweden (first), Denmark (second), Israel (eleventh) and Taiwan (twenty-first), in terms of university competitiveness.

A simple phrase can be used to describe the problem facing Korean university-level education: Korea is doubly regarded as having the world's highest university enrollment rate while, at the same time, being notorious for its low academic achievements. It is therefore imperative to seek out the underlying causes of the problem and to develop institutional measures to improve current conditions. In the IMD World Competitiveness database for 2013, among 60 subject nations, Korea ranked eleventh in the category of the number of students studying in higher education abroad (with 2.6 students per 1000 population) and forty-first in university education.

As shown in Table 3.1, Korea in 2013 ranked near fiftieth in the number of students (20 and 18, respectively) per teacher in elementary and secondary schools. On the other hand, Korea's secondary school

Table 3.1   *Korea's international rankings in education competitiveness by indicator, 2009–13*

Indicator	2009	2010	2011	2012	2013
Korea's international ranking	36	35	29	31	25
(number of participating nations)	(57)	(58)	(59)	(59)	(60)
Quantitative indicators					
Educated-related public spending					
as a share of GDP	36	36	33	31	32
(% of GDP)	(4.2)	(4.2)	(4.6)	(4.6)	(4.63)
per person	27	29	32	31	33
(US$ per person)[a]	(831)	(916)	(793)	(785)	(785)
Number of students per teacher					
in elementary schools	51	51	51	50	51
(number)	(26.7)	(25.6)	(24.1)	(22.4)	(20.9)
in secondary schools	50	51	53	53	52
(number)	(18.0)	(18.1)	(18.2)	(18.0)	(17.6)
Secondary school enrollment rate	6	8	6	8	10
(%)	(96.1)	(96.5)	(98.0)	(95.7)	(96.0)
Higher education completion rate	4	2	2	2	2
of population ages 25–34					
(%)	(53.0)	(56.0)	(58.0)	(63.0)	(65.0)
Foreign students studying in Korea[b]	37	34	33	34	32
(number per 1000 population)	(0.46)	(0.66)	(0.83)	(1.02)	(1.20)
Korean students studying abroad[c]	10	11	11	11	11
(number per 1000 population)	(2.11)	(2.17)	(2.32)	(2.54)	(2.56)
Scholastic achievement					
overall ranking	4	4	5	5	5
math	4	4	4	4	4
(PISA score)[d]	(547)	(547)	(546)	(546)	(546)
science	10	10	6	6	6
(PISA score)[d]	(522)	(522)	(538)	(538)	(538)
English proficiency[e]	48	48	46	46	46
(TOEFL score)[f]	(77)	(78)	(81)	(81)	(82)
Illiteracy rate ages 15 and above	32	32	33	34	34
(%)	(2.0)	(1.7)	(1.7)	(1.7)	(1.7)
Qualitative indicators					
educational system	32	31	20	27	27
standard deviation	(4.38)	(5.03)	(6.00)	(5.58)	(5.71)
science education[g]	–	32	20	37	23
standard deviation	–	(4.96)	(5.37)	(4.57)	(5.32)
university education	51	46	39	42	41
standard deviation	(3.95)	(4.28)	(5.00)	(4.57)	(4.93)
management education	42	43	35	43	41
standard deviation	(4.52)	(4.70)	(5.41)	(4.95)	(5.19)
linguistic ability	34	39	31	32	28
standard deviation	(4.88)	(4.98)	(5.60)	(5.59)	(5.88)

Table 3.1   (continued)

Notes: Numbers in parentheses are values as specified in row headings below each
indicator.
a.   Not used for calculating the ranking; included for reference to check the background of
     subject nations.
b.   Number of foreign students studying in higher education in Korea per 1000 population
     of Korea.
c.   Number of Korean students studying in higher education abroad per 1000 population
     of Korea.
d.   Scores from 2009 to 2010 are from PISA 2006, and those from 2011 to 2013 are from
     PISA 2009.
e.   Used as background information until 2008, but included in quantitative indicators
     from 2009 to 2012, and then again categorized as background information from 2013.
     The rankings and scores are based on *IMD World Competitiveness Yearbook* data and
     are therefore partly inconsistent with those published by PISA 2009.
f.   The Test of English as a Foreign Language (TOEFL) test was changed from the
     computer-based test (CBT) (0–300 scores) to the Internet-based test (iBT) (0–120
     scores), so the rankings from 2009 are calculated based on the iBT; the 218 score in the
     CBT is equivalent to an 81–82 score in the iBT.
g.   One of the detailed indicators for science infrastructure before 2010, when included in
     detailed indicators for education competitiveness. Rankings and scores for 2009 were
     not released.

Sources: *IMD World Competitiveness Yearbook* data cited in Korean Educational
Development Institute (2013).

enrollment rate recorded 96 percent and ranked around eighth to tenth
place. Its Program for International Student Assessment (PISA) scores
for math and science were ranked fourth and fifth, respectively. Such outstanding achievement can be understood as the result of parents making
large investments in private education, compared with the public sector,
which was making less investment in elementary and secondary education. Also, Korea ranked second, with 65 percent, in the category of the
higher education completion rate of population ages 25–34. By contrast,
Korea ranked among the lowest (at twenty-seventh, forty-first and forty-
first, respectively) in the educational system, university education and
management of education in 2013. Among 59 subject nations, Korea
ranked relatively high at tenth with 2.6 students per 1000 population
studying abroad, and relatively low at near fortieth in university education: the large number of students studying abroad and the low level of
university education can be interpreted to mean that many students opt
to study abroad to get a better education because of low-quality domestic
university education.
    As shown in Table 3.2, Korea is at the top of advancement into higher
education, though it remained during 2009 to 2013 among the lowest at
forty-fourth to sixty-fourth in the quality of the educational system, and

Table 3.2 Korea's ranking in WEF education competitiveness, 2009–13

Area	2009	2010	2011	2012	2013
Higher education and vocational training					
Total higher education enrollment rate	1	1	1	1	1
Quality of educational system	47	57	55	44	64
Quality of university/graduate school of business	44	47	50	42	56
Corporate innovation in university–industry research collaboration	24	23	25	25	26

Note: The number of nations varies: 133 in 2009, 139 in 2010, 142 in 2011, 144 in 2012, and 148 in 2013.

Source: World Economic Forum, *The Global Competitiveness Report* data.

forty-second to fifty-sixth in the quality of university/graduate school of business. In the university–industry research collaboration category, an indicator that measures the level of university–industry collaboration, Korea ranked twenty-third to twenty-sixth, a relatively low level considering the global status of Korea's economic power.

There was a popular belief that putting the supply of higher education in the hands of the private sector would result in an undersupply of higher education, because of the external effect of higher education. Confounding this belief, within the first 15 years students at private universities had become more than three times as numerous as those at national and public universities in Korea, according to 2011 data (Table 3.3). By contrast, in most nations that year, public universities accounted for 70–90 percent of all students. However, Korea and Japan remained exceptions, with only 23 percent and 25 percent, respectively, of all undergraduate students at institutions established as public universities.

As shown in Table 3.4, the employment rate of university graduates was 56.2 percent in 2012. It should be noted that these figures are possibly overestimated, as they contain the number of graduates employed on campus. Universities sometimes do this in order to raise the employment rate of their graduates.

The employment rate of graduates in the capital region was 56.7 percent in 2012, not very different from 55.8 percent in the noncapital region (Table 3.4). However, the gap between the two widens sharply when it comes to the employment rate by field of study. Even when considering that the market demand for a specific field of study varies, it is still reasonable to think that universities have not put in enough effort, such

Table 3.3   Proportions of undergraduates by establishment type in selected countries, 2011 (%)

Country	Public	Government-dependent private	Independent private
Australia	96	–	4
Austria	84	13	3
Finland	74	26	–
France	86	5	9
Germany	96	4	–
Italy	90	–	10
Japan	25	–	75
South Korea	23	–	77
Mexico	67	–	33
Norway	85	5	10
Poland	90	–	10
Spain	88	–	12
Switzerland	93	7	–
Turkey	94	–	6
United Kingdom	–	100	–
United States	70	–	30

Source: OECD (2013).

as adjusting student quotas (that is, numbers of places available) in each study field or creating market demand for particular study fields. In other words, a university might intend to raise its total employment rate by expanding quotas for medical sciences and pharmacy, while decreasing quotas for other unpopular fields of study. Interestingly, despite the fact that the market demand for education is almost fixed, the employment rate was only 45.9 percent in the capital region in 2012, and this implies that universities have knowingly refused to adjust the quotas.

The discussion so far might raise the question of whether low achievements in higher education in Korea can be the result of insufficient fiscal support in higher education, given that the proportion of private universities is high in Korea. But the objection to this question can be found in Table 3.5. Korea's expenditure on public education in 2010 was 2.59 percent of gross domestic product (GDP), higher by 1.61 percent than the Organisation for Economic Co-operation and Development (OECD) average, following Canada (2.71 percent) and the United States (2.8 percent) and leaving most countries behind. As seen in Table 3.3, it should be noted that despite the high proportion of students at private universities in Korea (77 percent), the level of govern-

Table 3.4   *Employment rates in Korea by region, field of study,*
              establishment type and gender, 2012 (%)

Region and field	Total			National/public college			Private college		
	Total	Male	Female	Total	Male	Female	Total	Male	Female
Capital region									
Subtotal	56.7	62.8	50.9	59.7	64.5	51.9	56.5	62.6	50.8
Humanities	50.0	55.2	47.9	51.0	52.9	49.6	50.0	56.3	47.8
Social sciences	56.4	59.0	53.8	62.7	66.6	56.0	56.0	58.4	53.7
Education	45.9	44.1	46.7	47.3	47.3	47.3	45.8	43.7	46.7
Engineering	71.0	73.4	62.8	70.2	72.6	61.0	71.0	73.5	62.9
Natural sciences	51.1	55.7	48.2	51.7	54.5	48.4	51.0	56.8	48.2
Medical sciences and pharmacy	75.8	81.3	73.1	84.2	88.7	79.8	75.4	80.7	72.9
Arts and physical education	39.1	43.2	37.2	42.3	49.2	35.4	38.9	42.5	37.3
Noncapital region									
Subtotal	55.8	58.5	52.9	52.7	58.4	44.8	57.2	58.5	55.9
Humanities	47.1	48.0	46.6	39.8	43.9	37.8	49.7	49.5	49.8
Social sciences	53.2	52.8	53.5	48.3	50.4	45.8	54.5	53.6	55.6
Education	50.2	47.4	51.5	32.7	37.3	29.6	60.4	56.8	62.4
Engineering	65.4	66.2	61.3	66.9	67.2	59.2	64.9	66.3	63.0
Natural sciences	52.8	54.9	51.1	50.2	53.8	46.9	55.4	56.1	54.9
Medical sciences and pharmacy	73.9	79.2	71.1	66.7	77.8	64.4	74.7	79.5	72.2
Arts and physical education	47.7	53.0	44.3	38.3	48.8	33.2	49.3	53.6	46.4
Total	56.2	60.1	52.1	53.4	59.1	45.5	56.9	60.4	53.5

Notes: The employment rate in 2012 is defined as (workplace health insurance
subscribers + graduates employed on campus + overseas employees + the employed in
farming business/persons eligible for employment) × 100. The employed (as of 2012)
include workplace health insurance subscribers, graduates employed on campus, overseas
employees and the employed in farming businesses. Graduates employed on campus (as
of 2012) refer to those with workplace health insurance, as of the date of survey, who
signed a contract for longer than one year with the university foundation or relevant
institutions (industry–academic cooperation foundation, university or corporate) and
are paid more than the minimum wage; the salary of a person employed at the per-hour
minimum wage of 4580 won (as of 2012) was 957220 won. Overseas employees are those
who work for more than 15 hours a week and maintain an employment contract for
longer than 91 days. The employed in farming businesses are those without workplace
health insurance working in farming business as of the date of survey. Persons eligible
for employment (according to 2012 guidelines): graduates (persons who are advancing
into higher education, undertaking their mandatory military service, unable to work,
officially excluded and foreign students). Persons who are unable to work are those
who are incarcerated, dead, emigrants overseas and hospital patients for more than
six months. Persons who are deemed officially excluded are those who are medical
aid recipients, graduates with a degree from a religious-leader training course, female

Table 3.4   (continued)

military officers attending a training course before being officially commissioned, and persons eligible for education courses provided by professional education institutes for aviation workers.

Source: Korean Educational Development Institute data.

ment spending is similar to that in the United States, where the private university proportion is only 30 percent but university achievements are much higher.

Regulations on Establishing Universities in the Capital Region

Pursuant to the policy to control the increasing population in the capital region, the government enacted the Seoul Metropolitan Area Readjustment Planning Act in 1984 and strengthened regulatory policies on the establishment and expansion of large-scale enterprises, universities (four-year, in particular) and public institutions (Table 3.6). The central government's policy to discourage concentration in the capital region is largely categorized into discouraging specific types of behavior themselves through the 1984 Act and restructuring zones and spaces through the readjustment plan. Total quantity control of university student quotas was adopted in 1994, in order to regulate the total number of prospective students for universities in the capital region.

The number of universities was growing steadily until 1979 and continued to grow in the noncapital region from 1980 (Figure 3.1). After the application of the principle of the qualification rule in 1997, the overall number of universities increased sharply. Since 1997, the number in the capital region and Seoul has been flat, whereas that in the noncapital region has been constantly rising. Similar changes took place in the number of students (Figure 3.2).

The ratio of universities in the capital and noncapital regions was mostly 6:4 until 1979, but it reversed to 4:6 from 2003, as the proportion of universities in the capital region had decreased continuously since 1979 (Figure 3.3).

The ratio of enrolled students in the capital and noncapital regions was mostly 7:3 until 1972, but the proportion in the capital region has decreased gradually from that time. The ratio has been about 4:6 since 1990 (Figure 3.4). Enrollment rates are reported in Table 3.7.

Table 3.5 Public education expenditure for higher education in Korea, 2010

	Public education expenditure on education institutes (% of GDP)				Annual expenditure on education per person (PPP-converted US dollar against GDP)			
	Education-focused services	Additional services	R&D	Total	Education-focused services	Additional services	R&D	Total
Australia	0.95	0.06	0.62	1.63	8831	548	5763	15 142
Austria	1.05	0.01	0.46	1.52	10380	108	4519	15 007
Canada	1.92	0.13	0.68	2.72	15120	1180	6176	22 475
Denmark	0.99	0.01	0.22	1.23	–	–	–	18 977
Finland	1.13	–	0.80	1.93	9802	–	6912	16 714
France	0.95	0.08	0.48	1.51	9473	836	4758	15 067
Ireland	1.14	–	0.43	1.57	11512	–	4496	16 008
Italy	0.61	0.04	0.34	0.99	5892	374	3314	9580
South Korea	2.12	0.02	0.45	2.59	8159	66	1746	9972
Mexico	1.16	–	0.22	1.38	6611	–	1262	7872
Netherlands	1.09	–	0.64	1.74	10818	–	6343	17 161
Norway	0.99	0.02	0.70	1.70	10741	191	7579	18 512
Poland	1.23	–	0.24	1.46	7281	–	1585	8866
Sweden	0.82	–	0.94	1.76	9143	–	10419	19 562
UK	0.80	0.11	0.46	1.37	9256	1290	5316	15 862
US	2.15	0.34	0.31	2.80	19672	3072	2832	25 576
OECD average	1.13	0.06	0.45	1.61	8889	564	4241	13 528

Note: Additional services include commuting, meals and dormitory costs.

Source: OECD (2013).

Table 3.6 Changes in school regulations in the Seoul capital region, 1983–94

Revision date	Scope of schools	Regulations on the relocation promotion zone (Seoul) and exceptions
October 20, 1983	High school and higher education	Ban on establishing or expanding new or more schools and academic courses The construction of a new facility requested by a junior college or more advanced educational institution is allowed within the minimum scope stipulated in the Decree on Standards for School Facilities.
October 10, 1985	University, teachers' college, colleges of education at universities, air and correspondence colleges, open university and junior college (or various kinds of schools)	Ban on establishing a new school and on expanding an existing one or increasing its student quota (except for night courses) The construction of a new facility requested by a junior college or more advanced educational institution is allowed within the minimum scope stipulated in the Decree on Standards for School Facilities. New facility construction for the Korea Aerospace University is allowed.
December 24, 1988	Same as above	Ban on establishing a new school and on expanding an existing one or increasing its student quota (except for night courses) The construction of a new facility requested by a junior college or more advanced educational institution is allowed within the minimum scope stipulated in the Decree on Standards for School Facilities.
December 23, 1989	Same as above (except for air and correspondence colleges)	Ban on establishing a new school and on expanding an existing one or increasing its student quota (except for night courses) The construction of a new facility requested by a junior college or more advanced educational institution is allowed within the minimum scope stipulated in the Decree on Standards for School Facilities. Establishing a new religious school is allowed when the head of the Ministry of Education, in consultation with the head of the Ministry of Construction, deems it necessary to foster educators. Establishing a junior college in the non-Seoul area is allowed.

December 31, 1992	Same as above	Same as above The expansion of the student quota for the fields of advanced science and engineering is allowed by 1995 (under review). Establishment of a small-scale college is allowed (in zones designated for reserved development and environment preservation). The establishment of the Korea National University of Arts is allowed.
February 20, 1993	Same as above	Ban on establishing a new school and on expanding an existing one. Establishing junior and open colleges in the non-Seoul area is allowed (under review).
April 30, 1994	Same as above	A total quantity control of student quotas is adopted. Establishment of a small-scale college is allowed (in zones designated for growth management and environment preservation).

Source: Cho (2008).

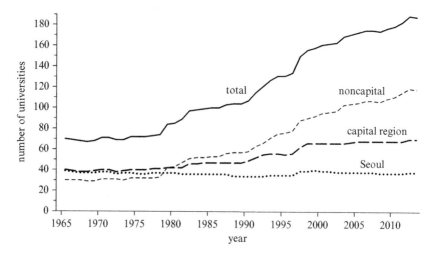

Source: Ministry of Education (1965–2013), *Statistical Yearbook of Education* data.

Figure 3.1   Number of universities in Korea, 1965–2013

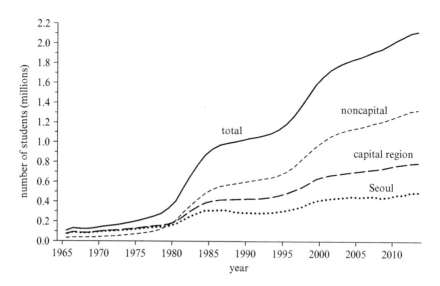

Source: Ministry of Education (1965–2013), *Statistical Yearbook of Education* data.

*Figure 3.2   Number of students enrolled in universities in Korea,
                1965–2013*

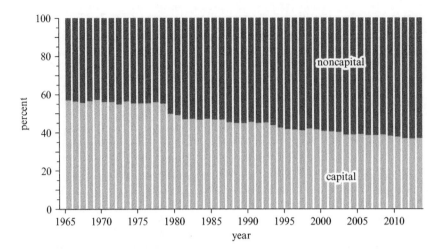

Source: Ministry of Education (1965–2013), *Statistical Yearbook of Education* data.

Figure 3.3 **Shares of number of universities in the capital and noncapital regions in Korea, 1965–2013**

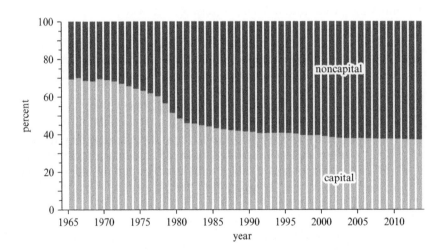

Source: Ministry of Education (1965–2013), *Statistical Yearbook of Education* data.

Figure 3.4 **Shares of number of students enrolled in universities in the capital and noncapital regions in Korea, 1965–2013**

Table 3.7   Enrollment rates, noncapital versus capital, 2011–13

Year and category	Observed value	Average (%)	Standard deviation
2011			
Noncapital	90	94.33	18.04
Capital	62	111.25	17.93
2012			
Noncapital	91	91.38	25.69
Capital	62	110.95	23.16
2013			
Noncapital	91	95.36	20.80
Capital	62	112.83	18.74
Three-year total			
Noncapital	272	93.69	21.74
Capital	186	111.67	21.74

Source: KCUE, "Higher Education in Korea" (www.academyinfo.go.kr) data.

Principle of the Qualification Rule in Establishing Universities

By initiating the educational reform (released on May 31, 1995), the government attempted to change the paradigm of Korea's higher education policy. The main goals of the reform are the principle of the qualification rule: deregulation in university establishment, and the liberalization of university student quotas. Some critics have blamed these two policies for Korea's overly enlarged higher education system.

To recap, the university reform policy can be outlined as follows:

- More diversity and specialty: to develop diverse university models and to adopt an (independent) specialized graduate school system.
- More liberalization of establishment, student quotas and academic program operation: the principle of the qualification rule (liberalization of student quotas).
- Pursuing first-class academic research: to upgrade its research level to world-class standards and to tie university evaluation with financial support.
- Globalization of education: to foster professionals in international relations, to attract more foreign students and to promote the establishment of overseas campuses.

Deregulation of universities was carried out by the adoption of the principle of the qualification rule and an (independent) specialized graduate school system – which runs no bachelor's degree program – while deregulation of student quotas was carried out by the acceptance of a phased "liberalization of quotas."

ISSUES

Regulations on Establishing Universities and Student Quotas in the Capital Region

Regulations on private universities in the capital region – mainly concerned with establishing them and setting quotas for numbers of students – have made universities depend more on tuition. Indeed, this is one condition that discourages investment aimed at offering better educational services. On the other hand, however, it means that existing universities in the capital region do not need to make extra effort to recruit students, since there is no new university to compete with them for prospective students.

Easy student recruitment and little new investment result in the fixation of university ranks. To put it another way, there are no incentives for universities to put in new effort or investment. Meanwhile, professors spend more time in commissioned projects, to be able to afford the high cost of living in the capital region, and have few incentives to invest in developing and upgrading their curricula for students.

Universities in the capital region are given government support that is two to three times greater than support to universities outside (Table 3.8). Support per student is on average 1.2 times greater in the capital region than outside (Table 3.9).

Without active investment from a robust corporation or foundation, it is actually impossible for private universities in the provincial region to compete with those in Korea's capital. Besides, their dependence on tuition is no less than that of their counterparts in the capital region. A high dependence on tuition leaves private universities in the noncapital region no choice but to be more dependent on government support (Table 3.10). The government's control of financial support is like actually controlling student quotas. Not only that, being away from the capital region works as a disadvantage for private universities in the provincial areas; less access to benefits and amenities in the capital city places them at a low ranking, which results in low student enrollment rates and causes difficulty in recruiting quality faculty members. As a result, the quality of their educational services cannot but be poor.

Table 3.8   *Government support (central government + local authority) per*
university, noncapital versus capital, 2011–13

Year and category	Observed value	Average (1 million won)	Standard deviation
2011			
Noncapital	75	7617	11671
Capital	47	16954	27963
2012			
Noncapital	82	10834	23771
Capital	56	18381	31564
2013			
Noncapital	80	9240	13627
Capital	52	24120	51161
Three-year total			
Noncapital	237	9278	17336
Capital	155	19873	38284

Source: KCUE, "Higher Education in Korea" (www.academyinfo.go.kr) data.

Table 3.9   *Government support (central government + local authority) per*
enrolled student (below or above the quota), 2011–13

Year and category	Observed value	Average (1000 won)	Standard deviation
2011			
Noncapital	75	1348	3901
Capital	47	1455	1791
2012			
Noncapital	82	2863	15352
Capital	56	1626	1982
2013			
Noncapital	80	1794	6361
Capital	52	2113	3348
Three-year total			
Noncapital	237	2023	9981
Capital	155	1737	2480

Source: KCUE, "Higher Education in Korea" (www.academyinfo.go.kr) data.

University Restructuring Policy

The October 2013 master plan for the development of higher education
contains the basic directions for the university structural reform and

Table 3.10   *Share of government grants in total educational revenue,*
          2011–13

Year and category	Observed value	Average (%)	Standard deviation
2011			
Noncapital	91	5.06	3.53
Capital	62	2.59	1.80
2012			
Noncapital	91	5.22	3.86
Capital	62	2.74	1.80
2013			
Noncapital	90	9.95	4.40
Capital	62	6.99	2.91
Three-year total			
Noncapital	272	6.73	4.54
Capital	186	4.11	3.02

Source: KCUE, "Higher Education in Korea" (www.academyinfo.go.kr) data.

evaluation system and suggests policy agendas for building the basis for sharpening competitiveness, strengthening industry–academy collaboration and lifelong education, reinforcing research capacity and promoting innovations in university education. Following the announcement, the Ministry of Education released the Action Plan for University Structural Reform in January 2014, with an aim to upgrade the quality of university education and to prepare for a rapid decline in the numbers in the school-age population. The Action Plan is mainly designed to carry out performance evaluations of all universities and to determine the reduction in student quotas according to the results of the evaluations.

Its main objective is to develop a pre-emptive and aggressive reform measure for restructuring so as to enhance the competitiveness of universities by significantly reducing their number and by upgrading their educational quality. All universities, except for those rated "excellent," are subject to a quota reduction. New systems for specialized university evaluations are to be adopted, and legal and institutional foundations for consistent and systemic structural reform are to be established. With this as a first step forward, the Action Plan includes detailed tasks as follows.

First, based on the results of performance evaluation, a quota reduction was to be implemented with targets of 40 000 by 2017 and a total of 16 000 by 2023, reflecting the numbers of prospective students after 2014 and the expected increase in the school-age population after 2025. The provisional

*Table 3.11   Student reduction targets per cycle: provisional projections
              from 2014 to 2022*

Evaluation cycle	1st cycle (2014–16)	2nd cycle (2017–19)	3rd cycle (2020–22)
Number of students	40 000	50 000	70 000
Period (academic year basis)	2015–17	2018–20	2021–23

Source: Ministry of Education (2014), plan dated January 28, 2014.

targets of reduction per cycle are shown in Table 3.11, and all universities were to be evaluated at every cycle. Based on the evaluation results, all universities except for those rated excellent were to be subject to a differentiated quota reduction, and those rated excellent were also to be encouraged to voluntarily reduce their quotas in connection with government-funded projects. The performance outcomes of the structural reforms are to be reflected in the evaluation of all government-funded projects, and detailed methods to be connected with structural reforms are to be suggested in respective project action plans.

Second, the Action Plan provides for the adoption of a new system for university evaluation to improve the quality of education. This is mainly about expanding qualitative evaluation instead of the existing quantitative evaluation, in order to formulate an evaluation system for university structural reform. In other words, strict evaluations will be conducted on all universities, and they are classified into five grades according to the result. The evaluations, using both qualitative and quantitative methods, cover all areas ranging from overall management and operation to curriculum, with both common and specialized indicators. Evaluation indicators applied to four-year universities and two-year colleges are set differently, while those applied to national, public and private universities are identical. Measures for structural reform according to the grade are shown in Table 3.12.

Third, to build legal and institutional foundations for consistent structural reform, the Action Plan aims to formulate an enforcement system and relevant laws. The process of formulating an enforcement system includes the establishment of a committee for university structural reform and the operation of a nonstanding evaluation task force and university council, attended by approximately 400–500 personnel, including incumbent and former professors and industry leaders. Relevant laws are mainly about the legislation of the provisional Act on University Structural Reform and Evaluation, as a way to implement structural reforms, such as a quota

Table 3.12   Measures for structural reform by grade

Grade	Structural reform measures
Excellent	Voluntary quota reduction, participation in government-funded projects
Good	Partial quota reduction, participation in government-funded projects
Average	Average quota reduction, participation in government-funded projects
Poor	A higher-than-average quota reduction, unqualified for participation in government-funded projects, unqualified for the National Scholarship II, partial restrictions on student loans
Very poor	A sharp quota reduction, unqualified for participation in government-funded projects, unqualified for the National Scholarship I–II, full restriction on student loans, induction of voluntary closure

Notes: A university rated "very poor" twice in a row will be forced to close. National Scholarship I: differentiated support in connection with income. National Scholarship II: support in connection with university's own efforts (reducing tuition, expanding scholarships).

Source: Ministry of Education (2014), plan dated January 28, 2014.

reduction, and to prepare a channel for voluntary closure of private universities according to the results of university evaluations.

To recap, the government's university restructuring policy intends to reduce student numbers at all universities according to evaluation results. When it comes to the goal of strengthening university competitiveness, it would be more appropriate for those deemed more efficient to continue to be the providers of educational services, and for those deemed not efficient to be out of the league. The current university restructuring policy, however, is to reduce student numbers in all universities, meaning that universities deemed inefficient are here to stay and will continue to provide educational services; a policy that could pose significant problems in the future.

Region-based establishment regulations and quota control have already been blamed for overall low-quality educational service in universities in Korea, and they even lack a timely response to social needs. In this situation, the planned restructuring policy – differentiated government support on quota reduction – could only lead to more inefficiency and even a paradoxical situation of a delay in university restructuring.

Inefficient universities which have low student recruitment rates, and hence enough capacity for quota reduction, will be the recipients of fiscal support through the reduction; whereas efficient universities with high student recruitment rates, and hence no capacity for reduction, will have fewer students to benefit from their better educational service after the reduction. In other words, the policy will make inefficient universities, which should be out of the market for university education, more dependent on fiscal support, leading to much greater inefficiency in university education. This restructuring policy therefore must be reconsidered, since it is highly likely to generate more universities dependent on government subsidies.

ANALYSIS

Data and Descriptive Statistics

This study is limited to four-year private universities that are subject to the evaluation for limited government support. Therefore, teachers' colleges, Korea National University of Education, cyber colleges, air colleges, technical colleges, cyber universities and graduate schools are excluded. Also, universities whose purpose is solely specialized in training religious leaders, and in arts and physical education, and hence are not subject to government support, are likewise excluded.

University data used in this study are drawn from the database of Higher Education in Korea, published by the Korean Council for University Education for the government (www.academyinfo.go.kr), and the articles of association of respective universities. Given that the analysis data of this study are based on three-year panel data from 2011 to 2013, a fixed-effects model might best fit a statistical analysis model. But this cannot be an appropriate analysis model, since variables used in the analysis cannot show drastic changes in such a short term. This is why a pooled ordinary least squares method was used in this study.

The number of observed values in this analysis is 390 in total, meaning that from 2011 to 2013, data from 130 universities were used. The following describes basic statistics on two dependent variables and 12 explanatory variables used in this analysis.

Among independent variables, admission competition is 9.19 applicants per place available on average, with minimum and maximum values of 0.6 and 35.2. The universities' operating margin in 2013 was 6.969 billion won on average, with minimum and maximum values of –35.529 and 273.938 billion won. Explanatory variables in the study are the capital region dummy as an institutional variable, the dummy for universities that were established after the adoption of the principle of the standing rule, and the interaction terms of these two variables. The average of the capital dummy is 0.4, an accurate reflection of 40 percent, the proportion of universities in the capital region in Korea. Meanwhile, the average of the dummy for universities that were established after the adoption of the principle of standing rule is 0.2, meaning that 20 percent of the universities were established after the adoption. As indicated in Table 3.13, the average of the interaction terms between these two dummy variables is 0.05, meaning that the proportion of universities established in the capital region after the adoption accounts for 5 percent of the total.

To control for the size of universities, the log value for the number of enrolled students was used. To control for differences in the quality of education between universities, the rate of full-time faculty member recruitment and the employment rate were used. The average of the full-time faculty member recruitment rate is 75.84 percent, with minimum and maximum values of 22.1 and 359.5 percent, while the average employment rate is 57.7 percent, with minimum and maximum values of 0 percent and 100 percent. This analysis uses the log value for tuition, the number of foreign students and the number of for-profit projects stipulated in the articles of association as explanatory variables for universities' current year operating margin and proportions of tuition, government grant and donation in the revenue as controlled variables. The average of the number of foreign students is 380.71, with minimum and maximum values of 0 and 3583. The average of the number of for-profit projects stipulated in the articles of association is 2.43, with minimum and maximum values of 0 and 13. The average proportions of tuition, government grants and donations in the revenue are 65.93 percent, 6.08 percent and 1.88 percent, respectively.

Regression Results

As mentioned earlier, a pooled ordinary least squares method was used to analyze the effect of explanatory variables on the admission competition rate and universities' current year operating margin. According to Table 3.14, universities established in the capital region after the adoption of the principle of the standing rule show a statistically significant increase in admission competition in all three models. Also, along with increases in the number of enrolled students, there are increases in the rate of full-time faculty member recruitment and the employment rate, the admission competition rate also increases, and those variables are all found to be statistically significant in the three models.

Specifically speaking, according to model 3 and when other conditions remain the same, the admission competition rate in the capital region was

Table 3.13 Descriptive statistics

Variables	Observed value	Average	Standard deviation	Minimum value	Maximum value
Admission competition (times)	390	9.19	6.17	0.6	35.2
Current year operating margin (1 million won)	369	6969	18272	−35529	273938
Log value for enrolled students (below or above the quota)	390	8.57	1.10	5.12	10.14
Capital region = 1 (Seoul, Gyeonggi-do, Incheon) (A)	390	0.4	0.49	0	1
Established after the adoption of principle of standing rule = 1 (B)	390	0.20	0.40	0	1
(A) * (B) interaction term	390	0.05	0.21	0	1
Employment rate (%)	390	57.71	10.18	0	100
Rate of full-time faculty member recruitment (%)	390	75.84	35.86	22.1	359.5
Log value for tuition	369	8.90	0.10	8.44	9.17
Number of foreign students	369	380.71	559.94	0	3585
Number of for-profit projects stipulated in the articles of association	369	2.43	2.79	0	13
Proportion of tuition in the revenue (%)	369	65.93	13.42	12.70	89.77
Proportion of government grants in the revenue (%)	369	6.08	4.16	0.15	24.47
Proportion of donations in the revenue (%)	369	1.88	2.51	0.05	30.99

Source: KCUE, "Higher Education in Korea" (www.academyinfo.go.kr) data.

Table 3.14   Regression results on admission competition rates

Variable	(1) Admission competition rate (times)	(2) Admission competition rate (times)	(3) Admission competition rate (times)
Capital region = 1 (Seoul, Gyeonggi-do, Incheon) (A)	8.319*** (0.431)	8.298*** (0.426)	8.431*** (0.423)
Established after the adoption of principle of standing rule = 1 (B)	2.354*** (0.619)	2.165*** (0.614)	1.942*** (0.642)
(A) * (B) interaction term	−3.490*** (1.095)	−3.793*** (1.084)	−3.728*** (1.083)
Log value for enrolled students (below or above the quota)	2.615*** (0.201)	2.663*** (0.199)	2.658*** (0.203)
Rate of full-time faculty member recruitment (%)	– –	0.018*** (0.005)	0.015*** (0.005)
Employment rate (%)	– –	– –	0.066*** (0.019)
Year 2011	2.006*** (0.466)	2.139*** (0.461)	2.209*** (0.462)
Year 2012	1.842*** (0.466)	1.917*** (0.460)	1.872*** (0.459)
Constant	−18.132*** (1.826)	−19.947*** (1.880)	−23.519*** (2.092)
Observations	369	369	369
Prob > F	0.0000	0.0000	0.0000
R-squared	0.6281	0.6387	0.6482

Note: Numbers in parentheses are standard deviations. * $p < 0.1$; ** $p < 0.05$; *** $p < 0.01$.

Source: KCUE, "Higher Education in Korea" (www.academyinfo.go.kr) data.

8.431 times higher (statistically significant) than in the noncapital region. After the adoption of the qualification rule, the admission competition rate of in the capital region was 6.645 times higher (statistically significant) than in the noncapital region. The admission competition rate of those established after the adoption of the qualification rule was 1.942 times higher (statistically significant) than those established before the adoption. The analysis also found that the admission competition rate in the capital region was higher than in the noncapital region and that, among those in the capital region before the adoption, this rate was higher than that of those established before it.

A 1 percent increase in the number of enrolled students (an indicator of school size), in the rate of full-time faculty member recruitment (an indicator of education quality) or in the employment rate leads to increases in the admission competition rate by 2.615 times, 0.018 times and 0.066 times, respectively.

Table 3.15 provides the results of the analysis on universities' current year operating margins. The log values for tuition, the number of foreign students, the number of for-profit projects stipulated in the articles of association and the proportion of tuition in the revenue are all statistically significant.

Model 1 considers only institutional variables, tuition and the number of foreign students as explanatory variables, while model 2, intended only to control for the size of university, considers the log value for enrolled students and the number of for-profit projects stipulated in the articles of association as explanatory variables. Model 3 is model 2 plus the variables of proportions of revenue by revenue type.

Analysis based on model 3 finds that a 1 percent increase in university tuition or a one-person increase in the number of foreign students result in increases, respectively, of 44.318 billion won and 5.46 million won in the current year operating margin and that both are statistically meaningful. Also, a one-project increase in the number of for-profit projects stipulated in the articles of association results in an increase of 1.353 billion won in the current year operating margin. The result in the case of foreign students reflects the fact that the admission of foreign students leads to extra revenue, since they are above the quota. The number of for-profit projects appears to bring positive effects on current year operating margins, as it is directly related to extra-education revenue.

A 1 percent increase in the proportion of tuition in revenue leads to a decrease of 253 million won in the university's current year operating margin. In short, normally, the higher the tuition rises, the greater the operating margin becomes, but when the proportion of tuition in revenue grows higher, the current year operating margin decreases. This observation can be interpreted to mean that a reduction in operating deficits in universities demands both higher tuition and less dependence on tuition.

Figure 3.5 confirms the positive correlation between tuition and admission competition rate. It is hard to say which causes the other, but the trend can be interpreted to mean that a university with a higher admission competition rate tends to have both higher tuition and a bigger operating margin.

Table 3.15 *Regression results on university's current year operating margin*

Variable	(1) Current year operating margin (1 million won)	(2) Current year operating margin (1 million won)	(3) Current year operating margin (1 million won)
Log value for tuition	42468***	38869***	44318***
	(10605)	(10962)	(10970)
Number of foreign students	9.748***	6.813***	5.458***
	(1.840)	(1.982)	(2.016)
Number of for-profit projects stipulated in the articles of association	–	1460***	1353***
	–	(336)	(334)
Proportion of tuition in revenue (%)	–	–	−253***
	–	–	(70.13)
Proportion of government grant in revenue (%)	–	–	−353
	–	–	(279)
Proportion of donations in revenue (%)	–	–	21.06
	–	–	(338)
Log value for enrolled students (below or above the quota)	–	184	1045
	–	(1219)	(1357)
Capital region = 1 (Seoul, Gyeonggi-do, Incheon) (A)	−1494	−572	−460
	(2254)	(2388)	(2493)
Established after the adoption of principle of standing rule = 1 (B)	−55.540	−60.90	−100
	(56.958)	(64.96)	(67.41)
Year 2011	537	914	544
	(2211)	(2166)	(2579)
Year 2012	798	947	510
	(2150)	(2102)	(2506)
Constant	−372408***	−344758***	−379490***
	(93592)	(94156)	(94219)
Observations	369	369	369
Prob > F	0.0000	0.0000	0.0000
R-squared	0.1605	0.2024	0.2358

Note: Numbers in parentheses are standard deviations. $* p < 0.1$; $** p < 0.05$; $*** p < 0.01$.

Source: KCUE, "Higher Education in Korea" (www.academyinfo.go.kr) data.

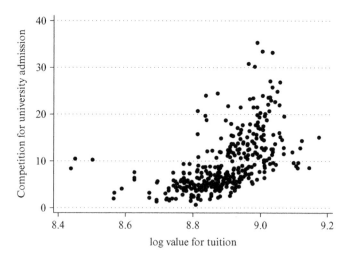

Source: Data from Higher Education in Korea (www.academyinfo.go.kr) reprocessed by author.

Figure 3.5   Positive correlation between tuition and admission competition rate in Korea

CONCLUDING REMARKS AND POLICY RECOMMENDATIONS

Experience with university reforms by the United States (US) and European countries could offer many insights for Korea, which is currently under pressure to restructure and raise the competitiveness of its universities, due to the decline in the school-age population. In the mid-1980s, universities in Europe were subject to both academic self-governance and strict government regulation and control. They were governed by many government regulations. Afterwards, new public management initiatives were introduced with emphasis on less government control and more quasi-market elements, based on the expectation that a university with more autonomy in its internal resource allocation and management system is likely to have high management efficiency through competition with others.

Schimank (2007) describes the new form of university governance structure with characteristics such as high competition, low academic self-governance, high stakeholder guidance, low state regulation and high managerial self-governance. Aghion et al. (2009) analyze the impacts of university governance structure on research outputs that are measured according to the number of patents and the global university research rank. The analysis shows a positive correlation between institutional autonomy and competition in public universities in the US and Europe, and their research outputs. When given additional financial support, public universities are the ones that produce more patents in a fierce competition with private research universities that enjoy comparatively more autonomy. This trend, according to the Aghion et al. (2009) interpretation, shows that quasi-market competition for research funding and students has been a foundation for the success of US university departments.

Schneider and Sadowski (2010) analyze the data concerning the employment of doctoral graduates in economics for 2001 and 2002 in Germany and elsewhere in Europe. According to their analysis, major characteristics in successful departments are transparency in academic achievement, no governmental or university regulations, and research funds that are allocated according to the degree of output performance. On the other hand, they find that governance characteristics in unsuccessful departments include a lack of transparency in academic achievement, the imposition of university regulations on the departments, and research fund allocation without consideration of relative outputs.

The Korean government has so far put in efforts for university restructuring through a series of projects, including the National University Restructuring Plan (1998), Structural Reform of Universities (2004), University Specialization Measures (2005) and the University Information Disclosure System (2008), but to no avail, according to evaluations. Subsequently, the Ministry of Education demonstrated its commitment to the closure of underperforming universities due to the declining school-age population. Current policy for university restructuring is likely to end up with a reduction of student quotas in all universities. In other words, considering that the current university evaluation is constructed to put a strong emphasis on qualitative elements, the policy appears to target university restructuring through reductions in student quotas and fiscal support based on evaluation results. This policy, however, could be problematic: not only in that the discretionary power of the Ministry of Education could become excessively broad, but also in that incentive structures in the universities could become distorted.

Region-based establishment regulations and quota control have already been blamed for overall low-quality education in Korean universities that are heavily dependent on tuition revenue. They even lack a timely response to social needs. Therefore, the government's planned restructuring policy and differentiated fiscal support on quota reduction can only lead to more inefficiency and an even more paradoxical situation of a delay in university restructuring.

Inefficient universities, which have low student recruitment rates, and hence enough capacity for quota reduction, will experience little impact and even become the recipient of fiscal support through the reduction. In other words, fiscal support will end up extending the survival of inefficient universities that should be eliminated.

On the other hand, efficient universities that have high student recruitment rates and no capacity for reduction will experience a decline in their revenue as a result of a quota reduction. The quota reduction in efficient universities would generate inefficiency through two channels: one is less opportunity for better educational services, and the other is a degraded quality of education services that follows decreased investment in education caused by the decline in university revenue resulting from the quota reduction.

The inefficiencies in university restructuring described so far are inevitable in any type of combination of quota reduction and fiscal support, because efficient universities that are capable of offering better educational services and deserve higher quotas are involuntarily forced to reduce their quotas. The inefficiency and weakening competitiveness resulting from such university restructuring policy could lead to undermining Korea's global competitiveness in the looming knowledge-based economy. This policy, therefore, should be amended.

Now, the question remains: "What would be the most desirable policy for restructuring universities in Korea?" The most likely solution could be a quasi-market competition in which universities have autonomy on quota adjustments and tuition decisions, provided that they transparently disclose academic achievements and operating results under the constraint that the university is a nonprofit corporation. Adding to that, it could also be necessary to develop a specific and clear manual on the process of university liquidation.

In sum, the restructuring policy for Korean universities should be revised in line with promoting DART: an acronym for deregulation, accountability, responsiveness and transparency. Various government regulations on universities should be eased so that they have autonomy on quota and tuition decisions. The structure of university governance should be improved so that universities demonstrate more accountability in society. All information on a university's operating results and academic achievements should be disclosed in a transparent manner, to make it easier to compare different universities, thereby minimizing information asymmetry and helping prospective students to make informed choices based on objective and accurate information. Universities should be keenly responsive to the choices of students and their parents, and to the needs of the society, so that they will be able to provide students, parents and society with needed educational services in a more efficient manner.

REFERENCES

Aghion, P., M. Dewatripont, C. Hoxby, A. Mas-Colell and A. Sapir (2009), "The governance and performance of research universities: evidence from Europe and the U.S.," NBER Working Paper 14851, Cambridge, MA: National Bureau of Economic Research.

Cho, Sung-ho (2008), "A study of policy evaluation on university location regulation in Capital Region," Gyeonggi Research Institute.

Korean Council for University Education (KCUE), website of "Higher Education in Korea," available at www.academyinfo.go.kr.

Korean Educational Development Institute (KEDI) (2013), *Analysis Report on the 2013 IMD Education Competitiveness*, Seoul: Korean Educational Development Institute (in Korean).

Korean Educational Development Institute (KEDI), *KEDI Employment Statistics Database*, available at http://swiss.kedi.re.kr (in Korean).

Ministry of Education (annual, 1965–2013), *Statistical Yearbook of Education*, Seoul: Ministry of Education.

Ministry of Education (2014), *Action Plan for University Structural Reform*, Seoul: Ministry of Education.

Organisation for Economic Co-operation and Development (OECD) (2013), *Education at a Glance*, Paris: Organisation for Economic Co-operation and Development.

Schimank, Uwe (2007), "Die Governance-Perspektive: Analytisches potenzial und anstehende konzeptionelle Fragen," in Herbert Altrichter, Thomas Brüsemeister and Jochen Wissinger (eds), *Educational Governance: Handlungkoordination und steuerung in Bildungssystem*, Wiesbaden: VS Verlag für Sozialwissenschaften, pp. 231–60.

Schneider, M. and D. Sadowski, D. (2010), "The impact of new public management instruments on PhD education," *Higher Education*, **59**, 543–65.

World Economic Forum (annual), *The Global Competitiveness Report*, Geneva: World Economic Forum.

4. An economist's perspective on student loans in the United States

Susan M. Dynarski

INTRODUCTION

Forty million people in the United States (US) were holding student debt totaling $1 trillion by 2013. While other forms of consumer credit declined during the Great Recession (Figure 4.1), student debt continued to rise. As a result, student loans are now, after mortgages, the largest source of household debt, outstripping credit cards and auto loans.

Defaults on student debt also rose during the Great Recession after 2007.[1] Nearly 7 million student borrowers were in default by 2013, with

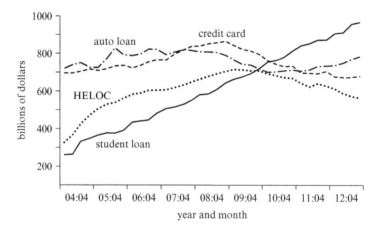

Note: Data are for the fourth quarter of each year. "HELOC" indicates home-equity lines of credit.

Source: Adapted from Lee (2013) based on data from the Federal Reserve Bank of New York.

Figure 4.1 Trends in US nonmortgage consumer debt, fourth quarter 2004 – fourth quarter 2012

more behind on their payments.[2] Proposed policy responses have included reductions in interest rates, forgiveness of student debt, more flexible repayment plans and increased regulation of college prices. In one effort to respond to widespread policy concern that there was a student debt crisis, President Obama in June 2014 signed an executive order expanding eligibility for the Pay As You Earn program, which offers reduced payments to borrowers in financial distress.

In this chapter, I provide an economic perspective on policy issues related to student debt in the United States. I begin by laying out the economic rationale for government provision of student loans. I show time trends in student borrowing and describe the structure of the US loan market, which is a joint venture of the public and private sectors. I then turn to three topics that are central to the policy discussion of student loans: whether there is a student debt crisis, the costs and benefits of interest subsidies, and the suitability of an income-based repayment system for the United States. I close with a discussion of the gaps in the data required to fully analyze and steer student loan policy.

To preview, I argue that there is no debt crisis: student debt levels are not large relative to the estimated pay-off to a college education in the United States. Rather, there is a repayment crisis, with student loans paid when borrowers' earnings are lowest and most variable (Dynarski and Kreisman 2013). As a result, there is a mismatch in the timing of the arrival of the benefits of college and its costs. Ironically, this mismatch is the very motivation for providing student loans in the first place.

One solution is an income-based repayment structure for student loans, with a longer window for repayment than the ten years that is currently the standard. While there exist income-based repayment options within the current system, few borrowers take them up. The administrative barriers to accessing these options are considerable, which may explain the low take-up rate. Further, the existing options do not adjust loan payments quickly enough to respond to the high-frequency shocks that characterize young people's earnings, especially during a recession.

A well-structured repayment program would insure borrowers against both micro and macro shocks. With an interest rate that appropriately accounts for the government's borrowing and administrative costs, as well as default risk, this program could be self-sustaining. Designing such a program requires detailed data on individual earnings and borrowing, which are currently unavailable to researchers within and outside the government. If loan policy is to be firmly grounded in research, this gap in the data needs to be closed.

THE ECONOMIC RATIONALE FOR GOVERNMENT LOANS TO STUDENTS

Education is an investment. Like all investments, education creates costs in the present but delivers benefits in the future. While students are in school, expenses include both direct costs (tuition, books) and opportunity costs. Future benefits include increased earnings, improved health and longer life. To pay the current costs of their education, students need liquidity. In a business deal, a borrower would put up collateral in order to fund a potentially profitable investment. The collateral would typically include any capital goods used in the fledgling enterprise, such as a building or machinery. Similarly, homeowners put up their home as collateral when they take out a mortgage.

Students cannot put themselves up for collateral: they cannot contractually commit to hand over their future labor to a lender in exchange for upfront cash, because indentured servitude is illegal. This is a market failure: there are good investments to be made, but private lenders cannot, or are reluctant to, make these loans, just as they are reluctant to make (and therefore demand higher interest rates for) other unsecured loans, such as credit cards. This market failure explains why governments play an important role in lending for education. While there have been occasional efforts to offer loans securitized by human capital (for example, My Rich Uncle), none has moved beyond a small niche market. Indeed, the public sector of most developed countries and many developing countries provides loans to students.[3]

Given their prevalence, there is remarkably little compelling evidence of the effect of student loans on educational investments.[4] Students choose to borrow, so estimating the effect of loans on outcomes is challenging: those who borrow likely differ from nonborrowers in ways that will bias naive comparisons of their educational attainment. A randomized trial would solve the selection problem, but there has been no experiment in which access to student loans is randomly manipulated.[5]

The best observational evidence comes from South Africa and Chile (Solis 2012; Gurgand et al. 2011). In these countries, students are offered loans only if they have a minimum credit score (South Africa) or test score (Chile). The papers that analyze these loan programs compare the college attendance of students right above and below these cut-offs, capturing the causal impact of loan availability. This research approach is referred to as "regression-discontinuity" design. In a well-designed regression-discontinuity study that is essentially random, someone ends up right above or right below the eligibility cut-off. A comparison of these two groups therefore yields a causal estimate of the effect of program eligibility.

In Chile, right below the eligibility cut-off, 20 percent of students go to college. Right above, the figure is 40 percent. The difference – 20 percentage points – is the estimated causal effect of loan availability on college attendance for these students. The South African study reaches a similar conclusion. Right below the credit score cut-off, 50 percent of students go to college, compared with 70 percent right above. Again, the estimated effect is a 20 percentage point increase in college attendance. These are large effects, indicating that student loans make college possible for many students, at least in these two countries. While we would prefer to have evidence from the United States, these studies currently constitute the best available evidence on the causal impact of student loans on educational attainment.

TRENDS IN STUDENT BORROWING

As noted earlier, the stock of outstanding student debt by 2013 exceeded $1 trillion. The flow of debt also increased, with annual borrowing doubling between 2001 and 2011 (from $56 billion to $113 billion, in constant 2011 dollars).[6] Borrowing has increased, in part, because there are more students: college enrollment rose 32 percent in the decade between 2001 and 2011.

But as the number of students increased, so too did annual borrowing per student, rising from $3500 to $5400, an increase of 54 percent.[7] This per-student increase in borrowing can be explained by one or both of two factors: an increase in the share of students taking out loans, and/or an increase in the size of the loans borrowers take out. Both of these factors appear to be at work over the past decade. As discussed later in the chapter, federal Stafford loans are the largest loan program, accounting for 75 percent of student loan volume (labeled as unsubsidized and subsidized federal loans in Figure 4.2). In 2001, 34 percent of undergraduates took out a Stafford loan; by 2011 that number had risen to 50 percent.[8] The average loan taken out by each borrower went up by only 8 percent, by contrast: from $7600 to $8200, in constant 2011 dollars. The increases in the Stafford program, at least, are therefore on the extensive rather than the intensive margin.

While we know that students now borrow more, the reasons are not well understood. Rising college costs are a natural suspect. The sticker price of college has risen for years, but so too has aid for college (Figure 4.2). At public colleges, where 80 percent of students are enrolled, the sticker price of college increased by $3450 in real terms from 2001 to 2011. But after netting out increases in grants and tax credits, the net price of college rose by just $1160. At private schools, which frequently offer grants to students,

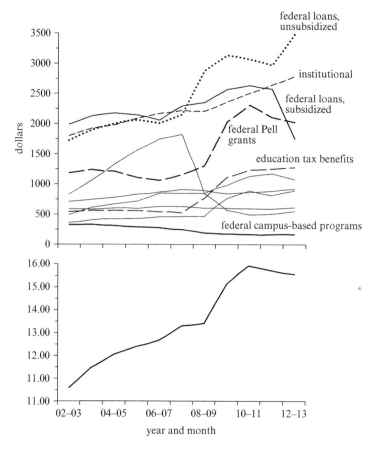

Source: College Board data.

Figure 4.2   Aid per full-time equivalent student in the United States,
2002–12

net prices rose even less, by $320. These increases in net price cannot fully
explain the $1900 increase in average borrowing.

    The family income distribution has become much more unequal over
the past several decades, with incomes dropping among the lowest-earning
households, stagnating in the middle, and rising only at the very top
(Piketty and Saez 2003). For the majority of families, flat college costs
represent a mounting share of family income. These shifts in the income
distribution may explain at least part of the increasing reliance on loans to
cover college costs.

Despite these increases in borrowing, the vast majority of students still borrow moderate amounts. As discussed below, in 2009, 69 percent of undergraduates had borrowed $10000 or less. Only 2 percent borrowed more than $50000.

STUDENTS' LOANS IN THE UNITED STATES ARE A PUBLIC–PRIVATE VENTURE

The modern student loan program dates to 1965, when the Guaranteed Student Loan, now known as the Stafford loan, was initiated. From the start, federal student loans were a joint venture of the public and private sectors. Private lenders provided capital, took applications, disbursed loans and collected payments. The federal government defined eligibility for loans, paid interest on some loans while students were enrolled in school, and guaranteed lenders against default. Congress defined interest rates, loan maxima and other loan terms.

During the 1990s, the federal government began offering Stafford loans without a private intermediary through the Direct Loans program. Private lenders continued to offer Stafford loans, side-by-side with the new Direct Loan program. Which program a student borrowed from depended on the college they attended, since colleges opted into Direct Loans.

The participation of the private sector in the federal loan programs was substantially scaled back in 2010. With the passage of the Health Care and Education Reconciliation Act, the Federal Direct Loan Program became the sole source of federal student loans in the United States. The private sector now participates in the Stafford program only as "servicers" for the Department of Education: collecting payments, keeping records and communicating with borrowers.

The shrunken private role in Stafford loans can be traced to two events. First, the financial crisis paralyzed the secondary markets that provided liquidity for private lenders. Short of capital, private lenders turned away applicants and delayed loan disbursements, throwing the Stafford program into disarray. The Direct Loan program, whose liquidity relies on the borrowing power of the federal government, was unaffected.

Second, scandals undermined the political capital of the private lenders, who had long campaigned against the expansion of the Direct Loan program. Media coverage depicted private lenders as bribing school officials in order to gain preferential access to their loan-seeking students.

While private lenders no longer offer loans through the federal loan programs, they market a product labeled "student loans." These private loans comprised as much as 10 percent of annual borrowing in the early 2000s.

The private loans differ from the Stafford loans in this crucial dimension: they require a creditworthy borrower or co-signer. As discussed earlier, Stafford loans are provided to students regardless of their creditworthiness and with no security: Stafford loans are "secured" only by the future earnings of the student borrower. By contrast, private student loans are extended only to borrowers who have a good credit record, or a creditworthy co-signer. Private student loans are essentially unsecured consumer credit, much like credit cards or personal loans.[9] Unlike these types of credit, however, private student loans cannot be discharged in bankruptcy.

The terms of private loans are typically worse than on federal loans. For example, these loans do not allow access to the Pay As You Earn program or other initiatives intended to ease repayment, nor do they allow for forbearance. Private loans are particularly prevalent at for-profit colleges, whose students are three times as likely as other undergraduates to hold private loans.[10]

The public–private partnership in the provision of student loans is sometimes strained. During the Great Recession, defaults on student loans spiked. The federal government introduced a variety of repayment plans intended to reduce defaults, but relied on the private servicers to move borrowers into these more forgiving payment plans. Borrowers trickled slowly into the new plans, frustrating policymakers eager to reduce defaults. The Consumer Finance Protection Bureau has documented that in many cases loan servicers are unresponsive to borrowers who want to restructure their payments.[11] This dynamic echoes that of the mortgage crisis, when the Home Affordable Modification Program (HAMP) was launched to help borrowers who were struggling with their mortgages. HAMP relied on mortgage servicers to move borrowers into the new plans, but progress was slow. While the goal was for 4 million borrowers to enroll in HAMP, 1.3 million did so.[12]

Here we have a classic "principal–agent" problem, with the agent (the student loan servicers) having little incentive to act in the best interests of the principal (the federal government). Student loan servicers do not have much incentive to prevent borrowers from defaulting, because the servicers either do not own the underlying loans or, if they do, face few costs if a borrower defaults. Restructuring a borrower's payments and preventing default require effort, and the beneficiaries of this effort are the government and the student, not the servicer. Carefully written contracts are required to make such relationships work well; an entire field of economics – mechanism design – is devoted to studying these contracts. In some cases, if the principal cannot get the incentives right, they should just do the job themself. In the present context, that would mean the federal government collecting payments on the loans it makes.

IS THERE A STUDENT DEBT CRISIS?

Student loan debt is lower than is widely perceived. Consider students who first enrolled in college in 2003–04. Six years later, in 2009, 44 percent had borrowed nothing, and another 25 percent had borrowed $10 000 or less (Figure 4.3). That is, 69 percent of undergraduates borrowed $10 000 or less. Another 29 percent had borrowed between $10 001 and $50 000. Only 2 percent had borrowed $50 001 or more. Based on limited data, today's students entering college appear to be on a similar path. While attention is focused on extreme cases, only a very small share of undergraduate borrowers hold the $100 000 loans that dominate the headlines. Using the Survey of Consumer Finances, a household survey, Akers and Chingos (2014) reach a similar conclusion.

While attention is focused on borrowers with high loan balances, most defaults occur on much smaller loans. For a cohort of undergraduates who borrowed in 2005, the loan balance of those in default in 2013 was

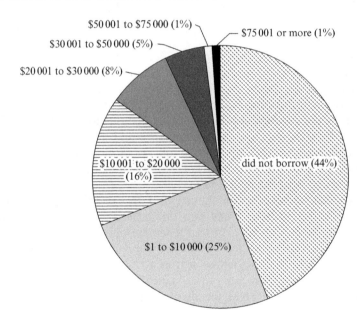

Note: Borrowing is measured for the six years following first-time college entry.

Source: College Board data, based on data from the National Postsecondary Student Aid Survey.

Figure 4.3   Total borrowing in 2009 by US undergraduates who first entered college in academic year 2003–04

smaller than among those who paid without adverse event: $6625 versus $8500.[13] Looking to the entire loan portfolio, including graduate students, the average loan in default was about $14000, while the average loan not in default was $22000.[14] Furthermore, the data indicate that more students experience temporary rough patches than default, but do not default: the delinquency rate (being behind on payments for 60 to 120 days) is much higher than the default rate. Most of these delinquent borrowers eventually manage to repay, but with damaged credit histories.

Graduate students borrow more than undergraduates. In fact, much of the recent growth in student debt is attributable to graduate borrowing. In recent years, 40 percent of federal loan dollars were disbursed to graduate students.[15] Even though graduate students' loan balances are much higher, their default rate is only 3 percent, compared with 21 percent among undergraduate borrowers.

THE COSTS AND BENEFITS OF INTEREST-RATE SUBSIDIES

Student loans correct a capital market failure: the private sector will not provide loans that are secured only by a borrower's future earnings. If enhanced liquidity were the only goal, loans would be offered at a market rate, with interest capitalized into principal while the student was in college. In the policy arena, it is frequently argued that low interest rates help students by encouraging college attendance and making loan payments more manageable. While an interest subsidy certainly reduces payments (which begin after students leave college), it is a blunt tool for increasing schooling and reducing loan defaults.

In the federal loan program, the interest rate is set to zero during college for low-income students; loans with this benefit are called "subsidized" loans. Assume for the moment that loans are offered at the market rate, and so the in-school payment of interest is the only subsidy. If a student borrows $1000 in their freshman year at a real rate of 4 percent, spends four years in college, and pays the loan off in ten years, the in-school subsidy saves them $200 over the life of the loan, or 20 percent of its face value.

All borrowers pay interest on federal loans after leaving school. This interest rate is set by Congress, varies across the federal loan programs, and is a hot topic of debate. At times the rate has been fixed in nominal terms, and generated large subsidies for borrowers. During the late 1970s and early 1980s, when interest rates on mortgages were in the double digits, the interest rate on student loans was fixed at 8 percent. Today, interest rates on federal student loans are tied to Treasury bills. The 2013 Student Loan Certainty Act links interest rates to the federal ten-year Treasury rate, plus a margin. For the 2013–14 academic year, interest rates were 3.86 percent for undergraduate Stafford loans and 4.41 percent for graduate loans.[16] They were set to be 80 basis points higher for the next academic year. Note that rates do not float for a given loan. Rather, they differ by the year in which the loan is initiated, but are then fixed over the life of a loan.

Can subsidized interest rates increase college enrollment? A lower interest rate reduces the lifetime costs of college, so a rational decisionmaker would include this price subsidy in a calculation of the lifetime, present-discounted value of schooling. However, the evidence from behavioral economics suggests that tangible and salient incentives at the moment of decisionmaking are most effective in changing behavior.[17] Interest-rate subsidies are not tangible when students are deciding whether to enroll in college: students are handed the same funds whether the loan's interest rate is 2 percent, 4 percent or 10 percent. The salience of an interest subsidy is an unsettled question; I know of no empirical study that estimates a causal relationship between college enrollment and the interest rate charged on student loans. While a field experiment would be most relevant for policy, even a lab experiment would reduce our ignorance about how interest rates affect student decisions.

Can subsidized interest rates reduce loan defaults? Here the answer is more straightforward. In a mortgage-style payment system, where payments are fixed at the beginning of the payment period, a lower interest rate reduces the monthly payments required to cover principal and interest. In this case, a lower interest rate will make loan payments more manageable for marginal borrowers and thereby reduce defaults. However, an across-the-board interest subsidy benefits every borrower, including those who have high earnings and no difficulty repaying loans. An interest subsidy is therefore a poorly targeted (and expensive) tool for reducing loan default in a mortgage-style repayment system. Tying payments to income, as discussed in the next section, is a more targeted mechanism for reducing default.

In an income-based repayment system (also discussed in the next section), payments are a fixed percentage of income. The interest rate does not enter into the calculation of the monthly payment and affects only the length of repayment. For a borrower with a given principal and lifetime income, a lower rate will reduce the time required to pay off the loan. This subsidy therefore arrives at the end of the repayment period: payments stop earlier than they would have otherwise. In a 20-year repayment plan, this would means that a borrower stops making payments (for example) when they are 42 rather than at age 43. These are peak earning years, and the risk of default in this period is likely to be relatively low; the effect of the subsidy on reducing defaults is also likely to be low. Further, this early cessation of payments equally benefits borrowers with very high incomes and those with typical incomes. An'interest subsidy is therefore a poorly targeted (and expensive) tool for reducing loan default in an income-based repayment system.

INCOME-BASED REPAYMENT PLANS ALIGN THE TIMING OF THE COSTS AND BENEFITS OF COLLEGE

A college education is an investment that pays off over many decades. Over a lifetime, the typical college graduate earns several hundred thousand dollars more than a high school graduate. For most types of borrowing, the life of a loan matches the life of the collateral. However, under the current system, the standard repayment period for a student loan is ten years. The mismatch between the timing of the costs and benefits of education is especially salient among young borrowers, who are most likely to default. Among borrowers under 21, for example, 28 percent default on their loan. The default rate drops sharply with age, to 18 percent of those 30 to 44, and 12 percent among those 45 and older (Cunningham and Kienzl 2011). This pattern of defaults matches the age profile of earnings. Earnings are lowest in the years right after college, when borrowers pay their loans. Among those with at least a Bachelor of Arts (BA) degree, median earnings are $32 000 for those ages 24 to 30, $48 000 for those 31 to 40, and $50 000 among those 41 through 48.[18]

An income-based repayment system determines loan payments based on income. Payments rise and fall with income, thereby reducing pressure on borrowers when they first graduate college (and whenever earnings are low). There are income-based loan programs in Australia, Chile, New Zealand, Thailand and the United Kingdom. In the United Kingdom, for instance, borrowers contribute 9 percent of any income that exceeds £21 000; any remaining student loan balance is forgiven after 30 years. These countries can be useful models as policymakers explore switching to an income-based repayment schedule. Dynarski and Kreisman (2013) describe one such model for the United States.

Policymakers can adjust the specific parameters of an income-based system to achieve alternative goals. Indeed, there are many contribution schedules that will work, with the choices affecting the length of payment, the level of payments and the share of loans forgiven. A lower contribution rate leads to a lower payment, a longer payment horizon, more interest paid by the borrower and more loans forgiven after 25 years. Higher contribution rates have the opposite effects.

The Pay As You Earn (PAYE) program, which US President Obama expanded in his June 2014 order, theoretically holds payments to 10 percent of income. The key limitations of PAYE, as well as all of the other income-based repayment plans in the United States, are that they are not the default option, and payments do not adjust automatically with earnings.

The default option for borrowers is a ten-year, mortgage-style, fixed payment. Borrowers must proactively apply to the income-based programs and demonstrate financial distress before being admitted. Eligibility must be renewed annually. As the theory and evidence of behavioral economics have demonstrated, defaults matter, and even small administrative hurdles can keep people from making beneficial choices. The Consumer Financial Protection Bureau has documented the difficulties that borrowers have in navigating this process.[19] The number of borrowers in these flexible repayment plans is much lower than the number in distress and default, which is evidence that the current system is not working to insure borrowers against risk.

Payments do not adjust automatically in the existing income-based payment programs. They are based on the previous year's income, and change only if the borrower submits evidence that income has changed. This backward-looking approach does not deal with shocks to income as they arrive. As a result, even a borrower enrolled in PAYE can see more than 10 percent of income consumed by loan payments, if their earnings drop while enrolled in the program. Or less than 10 percent of their income may go to payments, if their earnings rise.

To effectively buffer earnings shocks as they arrive, payments need to adjust dynamically with earnings. Such a framework has been advanced by several policy organizations.[20] How would such a system work in the United States? Social Security is a good model. Workers in the United States do little paperwork to make Social Security contributions: they complete an initial W-4 form and the employer handles the rest. Social Security contributions then automatically rise and fall with earnings. Loan payments can be handled the same way.

Some states are already moving toward income-based repayment. Michigan has now joined Oregon in proposing a "Pay It Forward" student lending system in which students pay no tuition up front and pay back a fixed percentage of their income after college. This sounds very similar to the income-based repayment system I describe above. However, a key distinction is that in a Pay It Forward program a borrower contributes a fixed percentage of income for a fixed number of years. The liability is not denominated in dollars, as in a standard loan, but as a fixed number of payments. Economists call this a graduate tax: a tax on earnings for those who have gone to college. It is called a tax, rather than a payment, because a borrower cannot buy their way out of the liability. The borrower is taxed for 25 years, even if they have repaid the principal (plus interest) after a few years.

In the proposed Pay It Forward systems, a graduate who does extremely well in the labor market will end up repaying many times over the cost of their education, while one who does poorly will pay much less. There is therefore cross-subsidization in this system, with the "winners" paying some of the college costs of the "losers." Economic theory suggests that loans funded by a graduate tax will not work, because those expecting high earnings will not participate. This is a classic case of adverse selection: borrowers who would be subsidized participate, while those who would subsidize stay away. This is unsustainable, as without the high earners the system does not get enough payments to cover tuition costs. Because of adverse selection, graduate tax can work only if participation is mandatory, with everyone forced into the borrowing pool.

This is similar to the dynamic in insurance markets, which collapse if sick people buy coverage and healthy ones go without. The young, healthy participants cross-subsidize the older, sicker participants, just as high earners subsidize low earners in a (mandatory) graduate tax. Neither the Oregon nor the Michigan plan requires all borrowers to participate in their programs. This suggests that the programs would be brought down by adverse selection.[21]

A minor change to Pay It Forward will maintain its positives (simplicity, insurance against bad draws in the labor market) while eliminating the negative (unsustainability caused by adverse selection). The change is this: denominate debt in dollars, and let borrowers pay off their debt. If a student borrows $25000 and earns enough that they have paid back the principal plus interest after just ten years, they will stop paying into the program. If a borrower instead runs into hard times and still owes money after 25 years, the balance is forgiven.

DATA ON STUDENT LOANS ARE INCOMPLETE

An evidence-based policy requires data. Data on student loans are remarkably thin, given the size of this market. They are particularly inadequate for modeling and costing out income-based repayment plans. Understanding the relationship between individual earnings and borrowing is critical for designing sound loan policy. If many former students carry debt beyond their capacity to repay, policymakers need to reconsider the parameters of student borrowing, such as eligibility, loan limits, loan forgiveness and repayment structures. All of these topics are currently under discussion in Washington, with little data to inform the debate.

To calculate the costs of an income-based repayment program, which typically includes a forgiveness provision after a certain number of years, we need to know about borrowers' lifetime earnings. Many data sources contain information on lifetime earnings. There are also comprehensive administrative data on borrowing through the federal loan programs. The two have not been linked, however, which leaves analysts unable to examine the covariance between lifetime earnings and borrowing. This is a critical parameter for designing a sustainable income-based repayment system.

An example will demonstrate the necessity of individual-level data on earnings and borrowing. The default rate on small loans is higher than that on large loans: the average loan in default in 2013 was $14000, while the average loan in good standing was $22000.[22] This pattern of defaults is consistent with two scenarios with very different implications for policy.

One scenario is that defaulters have temporarily low earnings and their loans fall into distress during these unusual bad times. At low cost to government, an income-based repayment program would insure borrowers against these temporary downturns by automatically reducing their payments. If lifetime earnings are sufficient to pay off the loans, this system can be self-funding.

An alternative scenario is that those who default have permanently low earnings that cannot support even moderate debt loads. An income-based repayment plan would still help these borrowers, but the ultimate cost to government would be much higher, since many of these loans will ultimately be forgiven. The cost of making, servicing and forgiving these loans could be so high that a grant program could be cheaper for taxpayers.

Distinguishing between these two scenarios requires individual-level, longitudinal data on student borrowing and earnings that follows former students for 25 years after college. Why 25 years? Income-based repayment plans have students paying back their loans within 20 to 25 years, after which any remaining balance is forgiven. Costing out these programs therefore requires tracking earnings for decades. Why individual-level, longitudinal data? Individual-level data are needed to capture the shocks to income that income-based repayment programs insure against. The payments required of borrowers with different earnings paths cannot be backed out from group averages. Any analysis that relies on averages will smooth away the within-person shocks that are needed to estimate the benefits and costs of income-based repayment.

How could this gap in the data be filled? The longitudinal surveys fielded by the US Department of Education's National Center for Educational Statistics (NCES) contain partial information on borrowing and earnings. They would be adequate for the task of guiding loan policy were they supplemented with administrative data.

The decadal NCES cohort surveys, which follow a high school class every ten years, follow respondents only to early adulthood, typically stopping when respondents are in their twenties.[23] The postsecondary surveys (fielded about every five years) stop following respondents about ten years after the start of college.[24]

To extend the borrowing data available for these surveys, they could be linked to the National Student Loan Data System (NSLDS), an administrative dataset that contains all federal student loans. These links would be updated annually; they are currently updated only a couple of times during the life of the surveys.

To extend the earnings data available for these samples, they could be linked to administrative data from the Social Security Administration (SSA) or Internal Revenue Service (IRS):

- The SSA maintains longitudinal records of individual earnings. These records are used to compute Social Security benefits, which, like income-based student loan repayments, are a function of lifetime earnings. Researchers have successfully linked SSA data to surveys, including the census (an example is Angrist et al. 2011).
- The IRS maintains household-level records of income tax returns and the informational returns that are used in the calculation of taxes. These data include information on college attendance, in the form of the 1098-T, which colleges send to the IRS to document tuition payments. In recent years, versions of these data have become available to outside researchers (for example, Chetty et al. 2011). Treasury employees can also conduct research with these data, and outside researchers have co-authored with them on studies (for example, Manoli and Turner 2014).

The merged versions of these surveys with administrative data would, by necessity, contain detailed, individual-level data from multiple government agencies. There are legal, political and administrative barriers to creating and releasing such sensitive data, but they can be overcome. The Census Bureau has been particularly aggressive and creative in matching administrative data to its surveys and finding new ways to distribute those data to researchers, and could provide a model for these purposes.

The Census Bureau has linked its Survey of Income and Program

Participation (SIPP) to data from the Internal Revenue Service and made it available in its secure Research Data Centers, which are located across the country and open to researchers who have undergone an extensive vetting process. The downside of this model is that a very limited number of researchers gain access to the data. A more promising approach is that taken by the SIPP Synthetic Beta. Through this pilot project, the Census Bureau publicly releases a version of its SIPP–SSA–IRS match that is "perturbed," with some variables statistically blurred to prevent identification. An unperturbed version of the matched data sits on the Census Bureau servers. Researchers run and refine their statistical models on the publicly available data, on their own computers. They can then upload the resulting code to the Census Bureau servers, where it is run on the original, unperturbed data. Results are returned to the researcher after being checked for compliance with data standards (for example, minimum cell sizes).

The SIPP Synthetic Beta is a promising model for NCES to distribute versions of its data that include variables sufficiently detailed that they threaten to reveal individual identities. This model could be used as the standard for mergers of NCES surveys with sensitive data from the IRS and SSA. Agencies reluctant to allow their data to be released to researchers may well cooperate when the SIPP Synthetic model is used, with public versions being statistically perturbed. This approach appears to have worked with the IRS and SSA, agencies that are notoriously protective of their data.

CONCLUSION

In this chapter, I provide an economic perspective on student debt in the United States. Governments across the world provide student loans, allowing students to borrow against the lifetime welfare gains created by a college education. While borrowing has risen over time in the United States, so too has the return to schooling. The typical student holds debt that is well below the lifetime benefits of a college education. The typical student borrower is not "under water," as were many homeowners during the mortgage crisis.

Rather, there is a mismatch in the timing of the arrival of the benefits of college and its costs, with payments due when earnings are lowest and most variable. Ironically, this mismatch is the very motivation for providing student loans in the first place. One solution is an income-based repayment structure for student loans, with payments automatically flexing with earnings over a longer horizon than the ten years that is currently standard.

There are income-based repayment options in the United States, but the administrative barriers to accessing them are considerable. Further, the existing options do not adjust loan payments quickly enough to respond to the high-frequency shocks that characterize young people's earnings, especially during a recession.

A well-structured repayment program would insure borrowers against both micro and macro shocks. With an interest rate that appropriately accounts for the government's borrowing and administrative costs, as well as default risk, this program could be self-sustaining. Designing such a program requires detailed data on individual earnings and borrowing, which are currently unavailable to researchers within and outside the government. If loan policy is to be firmly grounded in research, this gap in the data must be closed.

ACKNOWLEDGMENT

This research was partially supported by a grant from the Spencer Foundation.

NOTES

1. The US Department of Education, which administers the federal loan programs, defines default. This definition has varied over time, hindering the creation of a consistent measure of borrower distress. At present, default indicates that a borrower has not made a payment in 270 days; in the past, this window has been narrower.
2. There were 6.5 million borrowers in default as of the third quarter of 2013. See http://studentaid.ed.gov/sites/default/files/fsawg/datacenter/library/PortfoliobyLoanStatus.xls.
3. In part, this is because it is very difficult for private parties to place a lien on (or confirm) individual earnings. By contrast, governments, through the income tax system, have the ability to both measure and collect from income.
4. See Dynarski and Scott-Clayton (2013) for a review of this evidence.
5. Field (2009) studies an experiment in which loan repayment terms were randomly varied at a law school.
6. See Figure 6 in College Board (2012).
7. Total fall enrollment (undergraduate and graduate) rose from 15.9 to 21.0 million between 2001 and 2011. See Table 221 in US Department of Education (2012).
8. Besides Stafford, most other loans are also federal; just 7 percent of student loan volume was from private sources in 2011–12. PLUS loans to parents are the second-largest source of student borrowing (10 percent of volume), followed by PLUS loans to graduate students (6 percent). See Figure 6 in College Board (2012). The private and parental PLUS loans require a credit check or co-signer and so, as discussed earlier, are not classic student loans, which are secured only by the future earnings of the borrower.
9. Federal PLUS loans, which are made to the parents of college students, also require a minimum level of creditworthiness as defined by the US Department of Education.
10. This begs the question: why would anyone take out a private loan? One hypothesis is that demand is induced by schools that are trying to avoid sanctions from the federal government, which kicks out of the federal aid programs (including the Federal Pell Grant Program) any schools whose students default too frequently on their federal loans. Some

of these schools (community colleges, in particular) have withdrawn altogether from the federal loan program, so that their students have no alternative to the private market. Other schools still formally participate in the federal program, but may steer borrowers they perceive as poor risks toward the private loans rather than the public options. Another, related, hypothesis is that students are poorly informed about their borrowing options.

11. http://files.consumerfinance.gov/f/201310_cfpb_student-loan-ombudsman-annual-repo rt.pdf.
12. www.treasury.gov/initiatives/financial-stability/reports/Documents/March%202014%20 MHA%20Report%20Final.pdf.
13. See Table A-6 in Cunningham and Kienzl (2011). These numbers are based on a cohort of 1.7 million students who borrowed in 2005. The federal government does not make these statistics available. The authors of the cited study gathered data themselves from loan servicers.
14. Calculated from data in http://studentaid.ed.gov/sites/default/files/fsawg/datacenter/ library/PortfoliobyLoanStatus.xls. There were 6.5 million borrowers in default as of the third quarter of 2013, representing $89.3 billion in loans.
15. These figures are from Delisle (2014) and are based on calculations from the National Postsecondary Student Aid Survey.
16. www.staffordloan.com/stafford-loan-info/interest-rates.php.
17. Dynarski and Scott-Clayton (2013) discuss this evidence.
18. These statistics are from the 2012 March Current Population Survey (authors' calculations), and exclude full-time students but include former students who are out of the labor force or unemployed. The twenty-fifth percentiles for those with a BA were $14 000, $24 000 and $15 000, respectively. Among those with some college but no BA, median earnings were $24 000 for those ages 24 to 30, $30 000 for those in their thirties, and $34 000 for those ages 41 to 48. The twenty-fifth percentiles for this group were $6000, $15 000 and $12 000, respectively.
19. http://files.consumerfinance.gov/f/201310_cfpb_student-loan-ombudsman-annual-repo rt.pdf.
20. See Dynarski (2014) for a discussion of these proposals.
21. Yale attempted a graduate tax in the 1970s, lending money to its undergraduates and then having them pay back a fixed percentage of their income for a fixed number of years. The program collapsed, with Yale ultimately forgiving outstanding debt.
22. Calculated from data in spreadsheet "Direct Loan and Federal Family Education Loan Portfolio by Loan Status," accessed October 2013, http://studentaid.ed.gov/sites/ default/files/fsawg/datacenter/library/PortfoliobyLoanStatus.xls.
23. The National Longitudinal Survey of the High School Class of 1972 surveyed students until 1986, when they were about 32. High School and Beyond, which includes the high school class of 1982, stopped surveying students when they were in their twenties (in 1986, four years after high school). So did the National Education Longitudinal Study of 1988, which stopped surveying in 2000 (when respondents were about eight years out of high school). The surveys currently in the field (Education Longitudinal Study of 2002 and the High School Longitudinal Study of 2009) are not planned to survey any later in life than their predecessors. See http://nces.ed.gov/surveys/hsb.
24. The Baccalaureate and Beyond has varied in how long it tracks students. Graduates who started college in 1993 were followed for ten years, which would yield a typical exit age of late twenties. See http://nces.ed.gov/surveys/b&b/about.asp.

REFERENCES

Akers, Beth and Matthew Chingos (2014), *Is a Student Loan Crisis on the Horizon?*, Washington: Brown Center on Education Policy, Brookings Institution.

Angrist, Joshua D., Stacey Chen and Jae Song (2011), "Long-term consequences of Vietnam-era conscription: new estimates using Social Security data," *American Economic Review*, **101**(3), 334–38.

Chetty, Raj, John Friedman, Nathaniel Hilger, Emmanuel Saez, Diane Whitmore-Schanzenbach and Danny Yagan (2011), "How does your kindergarten class-room affect your earnings? Evidence from Project Star," *Quarterly Journal of Economics*, **126**(4), 1593–660.

College Board (2012), *Trends in Student Aid* 2012, New York: The College Board, available at http://trends.collegeboard.org/sites/default/files/student-aid-2012-full-report-130201.pdf.

Cunningham, Alisa F. and Gregory S. Kienzl (2011), *Delinquency: The Untold Story of Student Loan Borrowing*, Washington, DC: Institute for Higher Education Policy, available at www.ihep.org.

Delisle, Jason (2014), "The graduate student debt review," *Education Policy Papers*, Washington, DC: New America Foundation, available at www.newamerica.org.

Dynarski, Susan (2014), "Finding shock absorbers for student debt," *New York Times*, (June 15), BU8.

Dynarski, Susan and Daniel Kreisman (2013), *Loans for Educational Opportunity: Making Borrowing Work for Today's Students*, Washington, DC: Brookings Institution, available at www.brookings.edu.

Dynarski, Susan and Judith Scott-Clayton (2013), "Financial aid policy: lessons from research," *Future of Children*, **23**(1), 67–91.

Field, E. (2009), "Educational debt burden and career choice: evidence from a financial aid experiment at NYU Law School," *American Economic Journal: Applied Economics*, **1**(1), 1–21.

Gurgand, M., A. Lorenceau and T. Mélonio (2011), "Student loans: liquidity constraint and higher education in South Africa," Working Paper 117, Paris: Agence Française de Développement, available at http://papers.ssrn.com.

Lee, Donghoon (2013), "Household debt and credit: student debt," *Media Advisory*, New York: Federal Reserve Bank of New York, available at www.newyorkfed.org/medialibrary/media/newsevents/mediaadvisory/2013/Lee022813.pdf.

Manoli, Dayanand S. and Nicholas Turner (2014), "Cash-on-hand and college enrollment: evidence from population tax data and policy nonlinearities," NBER Working Paper 19836, Cambridge, MA: National Bureau of Economic Research.

Piketty, Thomas and Emmanuel Saez (2003), "Income inequality in the United States, 1913–1998," *Quarterly Journal of Economics*, **118**(1), 1–39.

Solis, Alex (2012), "Credit access and college enrollment," Department of Economics Working Paper 2013:12, Uppsala: Uppsala University, available at http://alexsolis.webs.com/CreditAccessSolis_v3.pdf.

US Department of Education (2012), *Digest of Education Statistics*, Washington, DC: Department of Education, available at http://nces.ed.gov/pubs2014/2014015.pdf.

5. Korea's college loan program

Sungmin Han

INTRODUCTION

It is not easy to maintain a stable lifestyle in Korea without a college degree. Changes in the social atmosphere have made it difficult to secure a good-quality job or even to take a low-salary job without a degree. Furthermore, getting a chance of promotion in the workplace is realistically tough. For these reasons, the majority of high school graduates recently have tried to continue on to college, and it has become common for students to receive tertiary education.

Table 5.1 shows trends of the university enrollment rates in seven countries of the Organisation for Economic Co-operation and Development (OECD) since 1995. The enrollment rates in Korea were 41 percent and 71 percent in 1995 and 2010, respectively. The rate has significantly increased and reached a high level compared with that of other countries. Students receiving higher education and thus accumulating human capital can be very helpful to the economic development of a country. In Korea, however, the fact should not be overlooked that obtaining tertiary education is due in part to change in the social environment rather than personal

Table 5.1   College enrollment rates in seven OECD countries, 1995–2011 (%)

Year	1995	2000	2005	2008	2009	2010	2011
Korea	41	45	51	71	71	71	69
Japan	31	40	44	48	49	51	52
Mexico	–	24	27	30	31	33	34
Sweden	57	67	76	65	68	76	72
Switzerland	17	29	37	38	41	44	44
England	–	47	51	57	61	63	64
United States	57	58	64	64	70	74	72
OECD average	39	48	54	56	58	61	60

Source: OECD (2013).

requirements, and that efforts toward change in social structure and environment are needed in order to alleviate this phenomenon. For example, if expertise in a particular field can be achieved and recognized on the basis of a high school diploma, a student may decide upon a curriculum best suited to personal aptitude before entering high school. Such an individual may then be able to develop to full potential as an expert earlier than other students can. Nationally, investment in education can be highly effective. However, changes in social awareness and environment need much time. Nevertheless, government efforts are required to change the social environment for a better society.

Another reason for the dramatic increase in the college enrollment rate in Korea is that the rate has been largely affected by changes in the government's education policy. Since 2005, the Korean government has implemented three different tuition supporting programs for the purpose of helping students with financial needs. The programs are mainly classified as scholarships and loans. The General Student Loan (GSL) program and the Income Contingent Loan (ICL) program were started in 2005 and 2009, respectively. The aim of these programs is to help students concentrate on their studies regardless of financial status. Moreover, a national scholarship program that provides students with tuition according to their income level was implemented in 2012. Although the scholarship and loan programs are fundamentally different, the underlying principle is similar. If low-income students decide not to go to college due to the burden of college cost, it seems difficult for them to get a good-quality job. If so, they will be trapped within a vicious cycle of poverty. In order to deal with this problem, the Korean government has implemented various tuition supporting programs. However, the national scholarship program, the world's only half-price tuition policy, has been expanded for political reasons. The total scholarship funding and the numbers of beneficiaries have been dramatically increased. If the government continues to try to expand the national scholarship, a serious fiscal crisis that leads to the depletion of the government budget will obviously be reached. Therefore, it should be operated by considering in depth the government budget and the effectiveness of the program.

Other countries have made various efforts to provide students access to higher education by meeting their financial needs. The supporting systems have been primarily operated as scholarships or student loan systems. The Nordic countries such as Sweden and Denmark provide students with full scholarships or make tuition free of charge for tertiary education. The United Kingdom and Japan provide income-contingent loans, which students repay after graduation. Many countries manage their supporting systems for college students differently according to the different characteristics of the country. This chapter seeks a desirable direction for a tuition supporting policy that will reflect the characteristics of Korea. Although it is natural that scholarship and loan programs should be analyzed together to develop the tuition supporting system, this study primarily focuses on analysis of the college loan program due to data restrictions.[1]

Considerable literature on the impact of college student loan programs has accumulated. Rau et al. (2013) analyze the effect of a Chilean state-guaranteed loan (SGL) program using a continuous academic decision model considering heterogeneity (a sequential schooling decision model). They find that the SGL program has a positive effect on the increase of the university enrollment rates and the reduction of dropout rates, and that it is particularly effective in lowering the dropout rates of less well-prepared students from low-income households. SGL beneficiaries of the program, however, are more likely to receive lower wages in the labor market. Thus, they suggest that the government should improve the quality of education. Glocker (2011) investigates whether a tuition supporting program has an effect on the length of study and the probability of graduation. Students who receive financial assistance complete their studies more quickly than those who do not receive it, but more financial aid does not significantly reduce the length of study. However, the probability of successful completion of study is high.

Using the propensity score matching method, Kim and Yi (2012) show the probability of getting a job and receiving a higher wage by comparing college loan programs. A college loan program does not have a statistically significant impact on getting a job and receiving a higher wage. However, because the recipients can find themselves in harsh conditions after graduation, efforts to improve the quality of their life are needed. Kim and Rhee (2009a, 2009b) report the impact of financial assistance on academic performance with a fixed-effects model. A student loan and scholarship program shows a positive impact on academic performance of college students. However, a discriminatory effect also occurs, depending on the income level. The scholarship program has an effect on relatively low-income students, but the student loan program has an effect on relatively higher-income students. These findings suggest that it is more efficient to provide high- and low-income students with loans and scholarships, respectively.

Previous studies on the effects of loan programs have mainly focused on the changes of college enrollment rates, dropout rates, graduation rates, employment rates and academic performance. The drawbacks of those studies are that they do not use data based on the type of loan or from a specific university. Accordingly, it is insufficient to generalize and apply the results to the Korean loan system. This study uses administrative data provided by the Ministry of Education, which operates the largest government student loan programs (GSL and ICL). The data contain detailed information on all recipients receiving loans from 2009 to 2012, which enables this study to derive more obvious implications.

In order to find a way to improve the college loan program, the research focus is twofold; the effect of a college loan program on students' academic performance, and the analysis of the characteristics of defaulters. The first channel – that a student loan program affects students' academic performance – is as follows. Most of the students borrow money to pay tuition. If there is no loan program for college students, they choose to work to raise the money. Conversely, when they can borrow money for this purpose, the time used to make money can be reduced. Then, they can spend more time learning, so their academic achievement can be improved. If students experience this effect, looking for ways to maximize this effect of the program will be preferable to any widespread reorganization of the current system.

With regard to the second channel, a student loan program can also have a negative impact on academic performance. In the case of the GSL, recipients must begin repaying the principal or interest from the time of receiving the loan. Although the repayment amount and period are flexible, they may choose to work if they have difficulty paying off the debt. As a result, a reduction of time for studies may cause their grades to fall. In addition, since students receiving a loan start a social life with debt, there is a high probability of selecting a low-quality job to pay off the debt earlier. In the case of the ICL, they may also feel the burden of loan repayments, even though the repayment period is delayed. However, the probability that students have an incentive to defer graduation in accordance with the delay of the repayment period is more problematic. This may cause a serious problem of government finance. Therefore, if students experience these negative effects, an overall review of the student loan program will be needed.

Finally, a way to reduce the default rate is also analyzed in this chapter, by identifying the characteristics of the defaulters. The total amount of delinquent loans increased from $300 million in 2010 to $500 million in 2012. A more serious problem is that a huge burden on the government budget is expected when the actual repayment time of the ICL arrives. It should be noted that delinquency can directly affect the financial health of the government and the system's sustainability. A comprehensive analysis of fiscal soundness, however, would be beyond the scope of the present study, which focuses primarily on the relative effects of student loan programs on students' academic performance.

BACKGROUND OF SUPPORT PROGRAMS

Support programs for college students in Korea can be largely divided into scholarships and student loans. The biggest difference between the two is whether or not the money received is repayable. If students receive a scholarship, they do not need to pay back the money. However, once they receive support through a loan, they must repay the borrowed money. Accordingly, whether or not to repay the money can affect students' school life. As the pressure to repay becomes high (when a student borrows more money), the negative impact becomes greater. Therefore, it can be expected that pending repayment may affect students' academic performance. As discussed above, this study investigates the relationship between borrowing restrictions and students' academic performance.

As shown in Table 5.2, there are seven government college loan programs in Korea. Five ministries operate one loan program each for their own purposes, and the Ministry of Education operates two (the GSL and ICL). Although it would be necessary to consider all loan recipients for a concrete analysis on the effect of the student loan program, the five individual programs operated by ministries are for the welfare of specific groups. An analysis of these programs would be inappropriate to this study, which examines the GSL and ICL, most of whose beneficiaries are college students.

The Korean government implemented the GSL in 2005 for the purpose of "creating an environment for students to dedicate to learning." However, there was a growing voice for alternatives to reduce students' financial burdens, because students who received the GSL often had difficulty in repaying the debt while still in school. For this reason,

Table 5.2   *Government budget for the college loan program by line ministry in Korea, 2011–14 (US$ million)*

Line ministry	2011	2012	2013	2014
Ministry of Education (GSL and ICL)	191.8	159.3	221.5	191.4
Ministry of Security and Public Administration	70.5	52.1	28.7	0.2
Ministry of Employment and Labor	5.1	6.7	4.4	2.9
Ministry of National Defense	68.0	60.7	51.2	47.4
Ministry of Agriculture and Forestry	60.5	35.5	31.1	20.8
Ministry of Patriots and Veterans	0.3	0.2	0.3	0.2
All ministries	396.2	314.5	337.2	262.9

Source: Ministry of Strategy and Finance data.

the ICL was introduced in 2009, so that the debt could be repaid after graduation.

The criteria for receiving the GSL and ICL loans are as follows:

- students in the top three deciles of household income for the GSL;
- students in the bottom seven deciles for the ICL;
- students obtaining 12 credits in the previous semester for both loans;
- students receiving grades above C and less than 55 years old for the GSL;
- students receiving grades above C and less than 35 years old for the ICL.

Once these conditions are met, students can borrow tuition and living expenses at a 2.9 percent annual interest rate; fixed for the GSL and adjustable for the ICL. In the case of the GSL, they can freely set the repayment period and amount within 20 years, but should repay the amount of the loan (interest, or principal and interest) from the time of setting the loan on a monthly basis. By contrast, in the case of the ICL, they do not have to repay the principal and interest of the loan until after graduation (with certain income criteria applying). Thus, the Korean government has been operating two different programs with different repayment systems.

College students can receive national scholarships as well as government loans. As mentioned above, the amount of the scholarship is determined according to the student's income level. The requirements are as follows:

- students must be in the bottom eight deciles of household income;
- students must obtain 12 credits in the previous semester;
- students must receive a grade above B.

In 2014, the national scholarship provided students in the bottom one and two deciles of household income with $4500 per academic year, and students in the top two deciles of household income with $675 per academic year.

Table 5.3 describes the requirements of grades and income level to qualify for the GSL, ICL and national scholarship programs. Almost all students (except for the two highest income groups) can receive national scholarships from the government. These scholarships provide only part support according to the income level and are insufficient to cover all tuition in many cases. The students must therefore use a loan program to cover the rest of their tuition.

Table 5.4 shows the total amount of loans paid to students and the

Table 5.3   *Grade and income requirements to qualify for loan and*
              scholarship programs in Korea

Income level	Grade			
	60+	70+	80+	90+
1	ineligible	ICL	NS and ICL	NS and ICL
2	ineligible	ICL	NS and ICL	NS and ICL
3	ineligible	ICL	NS and ICL	NS and ICL
4	ineligible	ICL	NS and ICL	NS and ICL
5	ineligible	ICL	NS and ICL	NS and ICL
6	ineligible	ICL	NS and ICL	NS and ICL
7	ineligible	ICL	NS and ICL	NS and ICL
8	ineligible	GSL	NS and GSL	NS and GSL
9	ineligible	GSL	GSL	GSL
10	ineligible	GSL	GSL	GSL

Note: ICL = Income Contingent Loan; NS = national scholarship; GSL = General
Student Loan. Income level 1 is the lowest and 10 is the highest. See text for exceptions
where ICL may be available for families with three children at income levels 8, 9 and 10.

number of recipients for the GSL and ICL from 2009 to 2013. The rapid
increase in amounts and recipients for the ICL from 2009 to 2012 is
attributed to the government's efforts to lessen the financial burden on
students. Nonetheless, beginning in 2012 the total number of loan beneficiaries was reduced due to the enlargement of the national scholarship
program.

THEORETICAL BACKGROUND

This section shows the theoretical relationship between borrowing constraints and human capital investment. If students have no borrowing
constraints, they can invest in human capital regardless of their wealth.
If borrowing constraints exist, however, they will invest less in human
capital. To compare the level of human capital investment in each case,
I set up a theoretical model using the general human capital investment
model (Lochner and Monge-Naranjo 2011). A simple two-period-lived
individuals model is as follows.

Individuals invest in schooling in the first period, and work in the second
period. Then, their utilities are:

$$\mathcal{U} = u(c_0) + \beta u(c_1) \tag{5.1}$$

*Table 5.4   Total loan amounts and numbers of beneficiaries of the loan
            programs in Korea, 2009–13*

Year and type	Total loan amount (US$ million)	Number of beneficiaries	Interest rate (%)
2009			
GSL	2521.9	675 900	7.3[a] and 5.8[b]
2010			
ICL	845.6	232 448	5.7[a] and 5.2[b]
GSL	1920.5	528 943	5.7[a] and 5.2[b]
Subtotal	2766.1	761 391	
2011			
ICL	1087.3	303 792	4.9
GSL	1598.0	429 742	4.9
Subtotal	2685.3	733 534	
2012			
ICL	1515.0	510 052	3.9
GSL	811.5	217 615	3.9
Subtotal	2326.5	727 667	
2013			
ICL	750.2	230 039	2.9
GSL	340.4	79 957	2.9
Subtotal	1090.6	309 996	

Notes:
a.   First semester.
b.   Second semester.

Source: Korea Student Aid Foundation data.

where c_t is consumption in period $t (t = 0$ or $1)$, $\beta > 0$ is a discount factor and $u(\cdot)$ is a positive, strictly increasing, strictly concave and twice continuously differentiable function. Each individual is endowed with financial wealth $w (w > 0)$ and ability $a (a > 0)$, and invests in human capital to increase future labor earnings. Labor earnings (y) at $t = 1$ are equal to $af(h)$. Here, h is human capital investment and $f(\cdot)$ is a positive, strictly increasing, strictly concave and twice continuously differentiable function that satisfies Inada conditions. The individual can borrow money $d (d < 0)$ to pay tuition while attending school at gross interest rate $\mathcal{R} (>1)$.

Without Borrowing Constraints

If an individual is not restricted by borrowing constraints, they maximize their utility (equation 5.1) under the consumption levels in each period:

$$C_0 = w + d - h$$

$$C_1 = af(h) - \mathcal{R}d \tag{5.2}$$

Then, the condition to determine the optimal level of human capital investment in order to maximize the present value of a net lifetime income is as follows:

$$\frac{u'(c_0)}{\beta u'(c_1)} = af'(h^u) = \mathcal{R} \tag{5.3}$$

where h^u indicates the optimal level of human capital investment without borrowing constraints.

With Borrowing Constraints: The ICL Program

In the case of the ICL, only one borrowing constraint exists. There is a limit to the amount of the loan that students can accumulate (up to tuition and living expenses). Now, consider a fixed upper limit on the amount of debt, with ICL constraints as follows:

$$C_0 = w + d - h$$

$$C_1 = af(h) - \mathcal{R}d$$

$$d \leq d_{max} \tag{5.4}$$

Then, the condition to determine the optimal level of human capital investment is as follows:

$$af'(h^i) = \mathcal{R} + \lambda^* \left(\lambda^* = \frac{\lambda}{\beta u'(c_1)} \right) \tag{5.5}$$

where λ is the LaGrange multiplier. It is strictly positive when the constraint binds, and $\lambda = 0$ otherwise. Here, h^i indicates the optimal level of human capital investment in the case of the ICL.

With Borrowing Constraints: The GSL Program

In the case of the GSL, two borrowing constraints exist. Once students borrow money in period 0, they should begin repayment of the money in period 0, and the rest of the money should be repaid in period 1. The same as above, another restriction is that a fixed upper limit of the loan amount exists. Therefore, the constraints can be expressed as:

$$C_0 = w + d - h - rd$$

$$C_1 = af(h) - (1-r)\mathcal{R}d$$

$$d \le d_{max} \tag{5.6}$$

where r $(0 < r < 1)$ is the ratio of the repayment to the total amount that students pay back. Under these constraints, the optimization problem is as follows:

$$af'(h^g) = \mathcal{R} + \lambda^{**} \left(\lambda^{**} = \frac{\lambda}{(1-r)\beta u'(c_1)} \right) \tag{5.7}$$

where h^g indicates the optimal level of human capital investment in the case of the GSL.

Comparing Levels of Human Capital Investment

Based on the optimal level of human capital investment in each case, this study considers how borrowing constraints affect human capital investment. Once equations 5.3 and 5.5 are compared, the latter is greater because λ is positive and $f(\cdot)$ is strictly concave and increasing. Therefore, h^u is greater than h^i.

$$af'(h^i) - af'(h^u) = \lambda^* > 0$$

$$h^u > h^i \tag{5.8}$$

Next, comparing equations 5.5 and 5.7, the latter is greater because r is less than 1 and $f(\cdot)$ is strictly concave and increasing. Therefore, h^i is greater than h^g.

$$af'(h^g) - af'(h^i) = \lambda^{**} > \lambda^* > 0 h^i > h^g \tag{5.9}$$

In conclusion, the magnitude of the optimal level of human capital investment in each case is listed as follows:

$$h^u > h^i > h^g \tag{5.10}$$

In short, if borrowing constraints exist, the optimal level of human capital investment is reduced. Compared with the two different loan programs, the optimal level of human capital investment of the GSL is lower than that of the ICL and can be related to the time of repayment. While the GSL should be partly repaid in period 0, the ICL is repaid in period 1. In the case of the GSL, students may work to pay the principal or interest. If so, time for study can be reduced, and that can negatively affect the students' academic performance. That is, the repayment burden of students may reduce the accumulating human capital investment.

DATA

This analysis uses the administrative data provided by the Ministry of Education to see how the student loan program affects the student's academic achievement. These data contain detailed information on the beneficiaries of the GSL and ICL from the second semester in 2009 to the first semester in 2012. However, the drawback of this dataset is that it includes only information of students who received the GSL or ICL. Thus, it is not possible to analyze the effectiveness of the student loan program through a comparison of students who did and did not receive a loan. Therefore, these data are used to examine the relative effectiveness of the GSL and ICL programs on students' performance.

The dataset includes information on students' educational attainments, socioeconomic background (such as household income, sex, age and college), and the loan (such as loan amount, repayment amount, type, overdue period and overdue amount). The main variables for the empirical analysis are summarized in Table 5.5. The total number of students who received loans is 917 509, and the number of observations in this analysis is 1 563 554. On average, students used loans about 1.7 times during the sample period. Loans are divided into three types: to cover living expenses, or tuition, or both. The dataset does not distinguish how much money is used for living expenses or tuition when students receive money to cover both living expenses and tuition. Women receive loans more often than men, and borrowers were 22 years old on average. Their grades were between 80 and 90 points out of a maximum of 100. Most students who borrowed money attend private schools. This suggests that the burden of tuition for students attending private schools is high. The average income decile of borrowers was about 4.7, and the average of loans and repayments was about $3300 and $500, respectively. With regard to default, since delinquency of the ICL had not yet occurred in the data, only the overdue amount (averaging about $3000) and period (averaging about 15 months) for the GSL borrowers are presented. While many students used the GSL for tuition, the ICL was used for both living expenses and tuition.

The loan program that students can use is mainly determined by household income. Low-income students can receive support through the

Table 5.5   *Summary statistics of the data in Korea, second semester 2009*
              to first semester 2012

Variables	Observations	Mean	Standard deviation	Min.	Max.
Sex	1 563 554	0.552	0.497	0	1
Age	1 563 554	22.274	3.620	14	57
Grade	1 563 554	2.199	0.694	0	3
Private universities	1 563 554	0.873	0.333	0	1
Income decile	1 563 554	4.658	2.966	0	10
Loan amount ($1000)	1 563 554	3.261	1.160	0.100	24.200
Reimbursement ($1000)	1 563 554	0.496	1.041	0	23.200
Overdue period (months)	58 165	15	22.8	2	59
Overdue amount ($1000)	58 133	3.016	1.209	1.694	9.977
GSL					
Tuition ($1000)	599 785	3.228	0.977	0.100	24.200
Living expenses ($1000)	20 678	1.119	0.848	0.500	15.000
Tuition and living expenses ($1000)	189 028	3.879	1.046	0.508	11.000
ICL					
Tuition ($1000)	295 050	3.029	1.015	0.100	24.200
Living expenses ($1000)	65 316	1.574	1.349	0.500	23.700
Tuition and living expenses ($1000)	393 697	3.578	1.113	0.600	15.900

Source: Ministry of Education data.

ICL program, whereas high-income students can receive it through the GSL program. There are exceptions for the latter, however: a student from a high-income family can receive the ICL if the household has more than three children, and the repayment amount can also be modified.

Table 5.6 indicates that the amounts of loans and repayments increase as income grows. The data can be interpreted in two ways. One is that lower-income students borrow less due to the burden of the repayment in the future. The other is that lower-income students borrow less because they are eligible for the national scholarship and therefore have to borrow only to pay for the balance of the tuition cost.

In the case of the ICL, in return for a loan of about $2900, lower-income students repay about $280 which, on average, represents about 10 percent of the principal. Other income groups, even high-income groups, have likewise experienced a 10 percent redemption rate. This is due to the characteristics of the program, which allow repayment after students become employed. On the other hand, in the case of the GSL, students repay about

Table 5.6 *Loan and reimbursement amounts of the GSL and ICL by income level in Korea*

Income level	GSL loan	Reimbursement		ICL loan	Reimbursement	
	won/person	won/person	%	won/person	won/person	%
1	3 035 120	541 234	18	2 871 737	284 498	10
2	3 264 490	587 618	18	3 150 357	236 921	8
3	3 266 552	595 989	18	3 247 283	224 676	7
4	3 318 929	673 301	20	3 414 173	228 029	7
5	3 351 937	706 612	21	3 433 377	237 260	7
6	3 380 629	799 779	24	3 473 031	254 683	7
7	3 405 782	822 511	24	3 533 618	265 655	8
8	3 386 342	722 184	21	3 561 521	343 940	10
9	3 458 363	824 989	24	3 631 950	369 213	10
10	3 495 731	790 017	23	3 744 954	306 834	8

Source: Korea Student Aid Foundation data.

$540 for a loan of about $3300 in lower-income groups, approximately representing an 18 percent reimbursement rate. In return for loans of about $3400, $720 has been repaid in higher-income groups, reflecting a 21 percent reimbursement rate.

In conclusion, the repayment rate of the GSL program is two times higher than that of the ICL. Moreover, in the case of the GSL, the reimbursement rate of the highest income students is 5 percent greater than that of lower-income students. The different repayment rates depend on the characteristics of each program and are related to household income.

EMPIRICAL METHODOLOGY

Effect of the Loan Program on Student Performance

As discussed above, it is not possible to estimate the effectiveness of the loan program through a comparison of students with and without loans. Therefore, this study examines the relative effectiveness of the programs through a comparison of the students who have received the GSL and ICL. Regressions of the following form are estimated for the empirical analysis:[2]

$$GPA_{it} = \alpha Loan_{it} + \beta X_{it} + c_i + y_t + \varepsilon_{it} \qquad (5.11)$$

where i indicates a student, t is a semester each year and *GPA* represents the grade point achieved. In this dataset, the *GPA* is presented as a range, in which a grade below 70 is 0; 70 and above but below 80 is 1; 80 and above but below 90 is 2; and 90 and above is 3. *Loan* equals 1 if a student receives the GSL and 0 otherwise (that is, they receive the ICL). X represents control variables that affect the grade such as sex, age, income, type of school, residence area, loan amount, repayment amount, overdue period and overdue amount. This analysis uses fixed effects including the year effect to control for the students' unobserved characteristics.

Characteristics of the Defaulters

Because data on defaults do not yet appear in the ICL, the analysis of delinquency is limited to the GSL program. The following equation is estimated by using a probit model:

$$Default_{it} = \alpha TuiLife_{it} + \beta Life_{it} + \gamma X_{it} + c_i + y_t + \varepsilon_{it} \quad (5.12)$$

where i indicates a student, t is a semester each year, and *Default* is a dummy variable indicating whether the repayment is overdue. *TuiLife* and *Life* are indicators for whether a student uses the loan for tuition and living expenses, or living expenses alone. X represents control variables that affect the probability of default (as above, such as sex, age and so on). Also as above, fixed effects control for the students' unobserved characteristics.

RESULTS

Effect of the Loan Program on Students' Performance

This section examines whether the loan program causes any differences in students' performance. Equation 5.11 is used for this analysis. Table 5.7 shows the results of the relationship between student academic performance and the loan program.

Using the ordinary least squares method, the first column is analyzed without considering the region, major and year effects. The second column takes them into account, using the same method as the first column. The third column provides analysis using the fixed effects to account for the students' unobserved characteristics. Overall, the results are similar, so those of the third column are described here.

The grades received by GSL students are relatively lower than those of ICL students. The greater the loan amount, overdue period and overdue

Table 5.7 *Regression results for the effect of college loan program on student academic achievement in Korea*

Variable	(1)	(2)	(3)
GSL	−0.204***	−0.513***	−0.334***
	(0.001)	(0.003)	(0.0026)
Loan balance	−0.008***	−0.009***	−0.007***
	(0.000)	(0.000)	(0.000)
Overdue period	−0.002***	−0.003***	−0.0005***
	(0.000)	(0.000)	(0.000)
Overdue amounts	−0.006***	−0.005***	−0.001***
	(0.000)	(0.000)	(0.000)
Age	0.011***	0.016***	−0.002***
	(0.000)	(0.000)	(0.002)
Income decile	0.025***	0.030***	0.019***
	(0.000)	(0.000)	(0.000)
Residence area	no	yes	yes
Private school	no	yes	yes
Major	no	yes	yes
School area	no	yes	yes
Year effect	no	yes	yes
Observations	1 563 554	1 563 554	1 563 554

Note: Numbers in parentheses are standard deviations. * $p < 0.1$; ** $p < 0.05$; *** $p < 0.01$.

Source: Ministry of Education data.

amount, the lower the academic performance is. In addition, student performance improves as the income level grows.

The reason for the greater effect in the case of the ICL can be explained by the difference between the two systems. Whereas the GSL recipient repays the principal and interest from the time of receiving the loan, the ICL recipient does not repay the principal until after graduation. Thus, it is generally assumed that students may experience psychological or financial pressure from the outset for repaying the debt in the case of the GSL. Or, they may resume working in order to pay back the money. It is possible to draw conclusions from those circumstances. It is obvious that the ICL imposes a lower financial burden than the GSL while the student is still in school. Therefore, the GSL program can negatively impact a student's academic performance through any channel. In conclusion, it seems that the ICL program achieves the government's goal of "creating an environment for students to dedicate to study" more closely than the GSL does.

Table 5.8   Regression results for the characteristics of defaulters in Korea

Variable	(1)
Loan balance	0.009***
	(0.0001)
Grade	−0.2345***
	(0.003)
Sex	0.005***
	(0.005)
Age	−0.002**
	(0.000)
Income decile	0.031*
	(0.001)
Living expenses	0.100
	(0.006)
Tuition and living expenses	−0.052**
	(0.018)
Number of observations	809 491

Note: Numbers in parentheses are standard deviations. * $p < 0.1$; ** $p < 0.05$;
*** $p < 0.01$.

Source: Ministry of Education data.

Characteristics of the Defaulters

Under the ICL, which began operation in 2009, the principal is redeemed only after graduation, and therefore insufficient data for analyzing defaults had not yet accumulated in the study database. By contrast, the GSL program began five years earlier, and enough data had become available to show that GSL delinqency had occurred and had increased rapidly. A way to manage it is obviously needed. Empirical analysis is performed here using equation 5.12 to find out the characteristics of the defaulters in the case of the GSL. Table 5.8 presents the main findings on the characteristics of the delinquents.

A higher loan amount and a lower grade lead the probabilities of an increase in defaults. Moreover, an interesting finding is that the probability of delinquency becomes higher when students receive a loan for living expenses and tuition. Naturally, the probability of default increases as the loan amount that students borrow increases. Nonetheless, the characteristics of the type of loan should be carefully considered.

If a student receives a loan for living expenses, there is greater likelihood of some difficulty in the student's financial situation. In other words, financing for living expenses may mean that the student has more serious economic problems than others do. Thus, it is necessary for the government to help students in serious financial trouble. This result suggests that efforts are needed to reduce the financial burden at least for the students borrowing money for living expenses. That is, even in the case of the GSL, it is necessary for students to select a repayment scheme such as the ICL. As shown above, if the economic burden can affect the student's academic achievement, conversion to the ICL would be the best education policy. Caution has to be applied, however, in the event of any rapid change in the loan program, due to the restrictions of the government budget.

CONCLUSION

This chapter studies the effect of the college loan program on students' performance and the characteristics of defaulters. Since the dataset does not include information about students who do not receive loans, this study examines the relative effects between the GSL and ICL program. In addition, this study tries to find a way to improve the Korean loan program by investigating the defaulters' characteristics. The main findings are as follows.

First, the grades of students receiving the GSL are relatively lower than those of ICL students. The reason for this greater effect on the GSL students appears to be that GSL borrowers have a more serious sense of the psychological or financial burden for repaying the debt. Thus, improvement of the loan program so that it reduces this burden is needed.

Second, the probability of delinquency is higher in the case of students who receive a loan for living expenses and tuition than for students who receive a loan only for tuition. This result suggests that students seeking financing for living expenses have more serious economic burdens than those who do not. Thus, the repayment system should be improved depending on the purpose of the loan.

In short, these findings suggest that the ICL program is more effective in reducing the students' financial burden and that the repayment system should be diverse. Nonetheless, a rapid change of the program to the ICL system would place a financial burden on the government budget. Thus, taking the government budget into consideration, gradual change is needed.

NOTES

1. A further restriction on data is the absence of research on the various effects of the college loan programs with information about full-loan beneficiaries.

2. The relationship between income and eligibility can be nonlinear. Thus, omitting nonlinear functions in income from the regressions could induce bias in the estimates. Therefore, this study considers dummies for each income decile, and the results are almost similar. They are available from the author upon request.

REFERENCES

Glocker, Daniela (2011), "The effect of student aid on the duration of study," *Economics of Education Review*, **30**(1), 177–90.

Kim, JiHa and ByungShik Rhee (2009a), "Examining the differential impacts of financial aid on college GPA by income level," *Journal of Educational Administration*, **27**(3), 447–70 (in Korean).

Kim, JiHa and ByungShik Rhee (2009b), "Who needs college student loans? Exploring the characteristics of student loans recipients," *Journal of Economics and Finance of Education*, **18**(1), 27–58 (in Korean).

Kim, KyungNyun and Pilnam Yi (2012), "The effects of reliance on student loan on early-career labor market outcomes of four year college graduates," *Journal of Economics and Finance of Education*, **21**(2), 87–115 (in Korean).

Lochner, Lance and Alexander Monge-Naranjo (2011), "Credit constraints in education," NBER Working Paper 17435, Cambridge, MA: National Bureau of Economic Research.

Organisation for Economic Co-operation and Development (OECD) (2013), *Education at a Glance 2013*, Paris: Organisation for Economic Co-operation and Development.

Rau, Tomás, Eugenio Rojas and Sergio Urzúa (2013), "Loans for higher education: does the dream come true?" NBER Working Paper 19138, Cambridge, MA: National Bureau of Economic Research.

PART III

Human capital inputs and outcomes

6. Parental information and human capital formation

Flávio Cunha

INTRODUCTION

Inequalities in skills are fundamentally linked to economic and social inequalities. A substantial fraction of the residual variance in log wages is due to the stock of human capital that accumulates long before individuals begin to work (Keane and Wolpin 1997; Cunha et al. 2005). Gaps in college enrollment among young men classified by the household income of their respective parents are substantively explained by gaps in skills as measured during the teenage years of the subjects' lives (Cameron and Heckman 1998; Carneiro and Heckman 2003). The same is true for the notable black–white gap in wages earned by men (Neal and Johnson 1996).

Low investments in young children in part explain the emergence of gaps in skills (Cunha and Heckman 2007). The technology of skill formation – the process that maps current stocks of skills and investments in future stocks of skills – is such that large investments in later stages of the life cycle are necessary to compensate for early neglect (Cunha et al. 2010). This partially explains why it is more difficult to reduce inequalities with interventions made during the adult stages of the life cycle. The evidence from experimental as well as nonexperimental data shows that increasing investments made during early ages for children from disadvantaged backgrounds has significant economic benefits with respect both to labor market outcomes (for example, higher labor income, stronger attachment to the labor force, less dependence on welfare) and with respect to indicators of high performance in other dimensions of life, such as higher educational attainment for females and lower probability of participation in criminal activities for males (Karoly et al. 2005; Ludwig and Miller 2007; Campbell et al. 2008; Hoddinott et al. 2008; Maluccio et al. 2009; Reynolds and Temple 2008; Behrman et al. 2009; Heckman et al. 2010).

Low investments in children are more common in low socioeconomic status (SES) families. A vast literature on language development has shown that the quantity (for example, number of words) and quality (for example, variety of words and greater syntactic complexity) of verbal interaction between parents and children increases with SES (Brody 1968; Dunn et al. 1977; Field and Pawlby 1980; Hoff-Ginsberg 1991; Hess and Shipman 1965; Ninio 1980; Tulkin and Kagan 1972). Parents with high SES engage in more explicit teaching (for example, teaching about object labels or teaching about causality) than do parents with low SES (Brophy 1970; Hammer and Weiss 1999; Lawrence and Shipley 1996). The analysis of time-use data by Bianchi et al. (2007) demonstrates that higher-SES mothers spend more time on teaching activities with their children than do lower-SES mothers. Kalil et al. (2012) show that they not only spend more time with their children, but are also more likely to dedicate time to activities that best suit their children's developmental needs. There is evidence that investments, measured either directly by specific maternal actions or indirectly by Home Observation for Measurement of the Environment (HOME) scores, increase with one important determinant of family SES: maternal schooling. Currie and Moretti (2002) explore exogenous variations in college attendance costs to show that maternal schooling raises investments in the health of children in the form of more frequent prenatal care and reduced smoking. Carneiro et al. (2013) use a similar strategy and conclude that, as maternal schooling increases, so does the respective mother's provision of appropriate play materials and daily stimulation for her child.

There are at least four nonmutually exclusive explanations for the pattern between investments and family SES. First, differences in parental permanent income and credit constraints would lead low-SES families to invest less in their children (Becker and Tomes 1986; Dahl and Lochner 2012; Duncan et al. 2010).

Second, differences in maternal preferences about two (or more) distinct dimensions of human capital can also explain the observed pattern of investments (for example, Lynd and Lynd 1929, 1937).

Third, marginal returns to investments and, consequently, levels of investments, may be affected by the characteristics of the parents or those of the child. For example, the mothers' skills may affect how much schooling they obtain and the productivity of their investments (Behrman and Rosenzweig 2002).

Fourth, and the focus of this chapter, parental information as modeled through maternal subjective beliefs about the technology of skill formation may be correlated with SES. These beliefs partially determine maternal expectations about returns for investments, which, in turn, determine investment choices. If markets are complete and if low-SES mothers' beliefs generate low expectations for returns to investments, then low-SES mothers will invest too little in their children (for example, Cunha et al. 2013).

The next section summarizes the evidence on the socioeconomic gap in investments in children. This evidence is used to construct a model in which parents are rational, but may not have up-to-date information on how to invest in their children, which is done in the third section. The informational constraints have implications for the types of policies that can be adopted in order to reduce the investment gap in children. The fourth section shows that preliminary evidence from small randomized controlled trials is suggestive of promising programs that can substantially improve parental investments and child welfare.

INEQUALITY IN INVESTMENTS IN HUMAN CAPITAL

According to the evidence presented in Cunha et al. (2010), the socioeconomic gaps in human capital accumulation are partly caused by socioeconomic discrepancies in investments in the human capital of children. In their study, the authors use the Children of the National Longitudinal Survey of Youth 1979 (CNLSY/79) which is a national longitudinal study that follows children from birth to adulthood. In the CNLSY/79 dataset, investments in children are measured by the Home Observation for the Measurement of the Environment, Short Form (HOME-SF) (Bradley and Caldwell 1980). The HOME-SF scale is based on interviewer observation and parental reports of the home environment that the children are exposed to. For example, the interviewers observe whether there are books to be read to the child, educational toys to be used, as well as whether the environment is clean and safe for the child to explore and play. The interviewers ask parents about time spent with children, such as whether the parents usually have a daily meal together with the child or not, and the frequency that parents take children to outings, to museums or to visit friends and relatives.

What makes the HOME so compelling for researchers is the fact that there is evidence from experimental studies showing that exogenous manipulation of the quality of the environment that children receive leads to improvement in human capital formation. An important example of such a program is the Nurse–Family Partnership home visitation program, which provides families with a nurse home visitor during pregnancy and until the child is two years old. These nurses visit the families once every two weeks, and each visit lasts 1 hour and 15 minutes. The program is designed to improve three aspects of maternal and child functioning: (1) the outcomes of pregnancy; (2) qualities of parental caregiving (including reducing associated child health and developmental problems); and (3) maternal life course development (helping women return to school, find work and practice family planning).

The analysis by Heckman et al. (2010) documents that the program improves the environment in which children grow (as measured by the HOME score) and has positive impacts on the children's human capital. Together with the quasi-experimental evidence in Carneiro et al. (2013), the Heckman et al. finding is important because it not only validates the use of the HOME scale as a measure of investment, but it also reinforces the results obtained from the observational studies that estimate the parameters of the technology of skill formation.

Given the importance of the home environment in producing skills, it is worrisome to see the large socioeconomic inequality in the HOME score reported by Reeves and Howard (2013), who also analyze the CNLSY/79 data. According to these authors, approximately 40 percent of the high school dropout parents are in the bottom quartile of the distribution of the HOME scores. In contrast, they find that about the same fraction of the parents with a college education were in the highest quartile. Reeves and Howard estimate that moving the home environment that disadvantaged children experience to the "average level" would lead to 9 percent more of the kids graduating from high school, 6 percent fewer becoming teen parents, and 3 percent fewer being convicted of a crime by the age of 19. To the extent that these authors do not account for "dynamic complementarity," it is arguable that their estimates underestimate the true impact of an improvement in the home environment.

Unfortunately, socioeconomic inequality in investments is present irrespective of the way that investments are measured. For example, the analysis of the American Time Use Survey data by Guryan et al. (2008) reveals that mothers with a college education spend six more hours per week interacting with their children than do mothers who did not finish high school. This difference already takes into account other confounding factors such as labor supply, marital status and other demographic characteristics. By the time that children are five years old, this weekly difference in attention translates into a gap of over 1500 hours of parent–child interaction.

The discrepancy in time spent with children becomes even more important because, according to Kalil et al. (2012), there is a socioeconomic discrepancy in the quality of time. The issue at hand here is that the activities that define effective parenting naturally evolve according to the age of the child. For example, basic care (such as feeding and bathing) and parent–child play (such as "peek-a-boo") are especially important for development until the child reaches two years old, and become less important after that period. In contrast, when children are three to five years old, active teaching (such as teaching letter recognition and counting) can really make a difference in promoting human capital development. According to the analysis of the Child Development Supplement from the Panel Study of Income Dynamics data by Kalil et al. (2012), the socioeconomic gap in basic care and play peaks at age zero to two, and in teaching time it peaks at age three to five. Thus, differences in school readiness arise not only because of the home environment and the quantity of time, but also because of how parental time is distributed according to activities that are appropriate for the child's age.

Similar findings are reported in the ethnographic study by Lareau (2003). In her influential study, middle-class families (that is, those whose parents are likely to have a college degree) adopt a parental style of "concerted cultivation" of the child's human capital. These parents are prone to actively organize activities that are designed to develop different dimensions of human capital. They enroll their children in music lessons, tutoring classes and sport clubs. They interact with teachers and other school officials to obtain feedback about their child's academic weaknesses and to provide important information about their child's needs. They make sure that the activities that take place in school are coordinated with those that are executed as part of the child's after-school programs. In other words, it is not only that highly educated parents tend to invest a lot in their children, it is also that they actively manage the interaction of the different organizations that help their child accumulate human capital.

In contrast, Lareau's data show that working-class parents (that is, those parents who are likely not to have a college degree) assume a more passive role in organizing the child's activities. This attitude partly arises because of the formidable constraints that the working-class parents face. They have unstable and unforecastable work schedules; they depend on time-consuming public transportation, which makes enrollment in music lessons or sport clubs prohibitively inconvenient. However, this parenting style also partly arises because working-class parents believe that their duty is "to put food on the table, arrange for housing, negotiate unsafe neighborhoods, take children to the doctor (often waiting for city buses that do not come), clean children's clothes, and get children to bed and have them ready for school the next morning" (Lareau 2003: 2). For this reason, Lareau (2003) classifies the parenting style adopted by working-class families as "accomplishment of natural growth." It is important to emphasize that the evidence described by Lareau is confirmed from the time-use data in Kalil et al. (2012), who report that the socioeconomic time gap in "management" is largest precisely when children are at school-going ages.

Differences in the quality of time that parents spend with children are also well captured by the heterogeneity in the language environment that children experience in their homes. The pioneering longitudinal study by Hart and Risley (1995) observes the language environment of 42 families in Kansas City, from the time that the children were nine months old until the time that the same children reached 36 months old. These families were divided into three socioeconomic groups (professional, working class and welfare) and observed for one hour per month. The data collected through tape recorders and laboriously transcribed by research assistants provided, at the time, unique understanding of the socioeconomic differences in investments in language. The results were astonishing: in professional families, children heard an average of 2153 words per hour, while children in welfare-recipient families heard an average of 616 words per hour.

Technological innovations in recording and transcription have allowed researchers to replicate the Hart and Risley study by recording the language environment for a period of ten hours or more per day. Using electronic recording with computer processing, Greenwood et al. (2011) show that the children from high school dropout parents heard about 950 words per hour. In contrast, the children whose parents had a college degree were exposed to around 1250 words per hour. If we use those figures and extrapolate until children are five years old, we estimate that the socioeconomic gap in language environment corresponds to nearly 5.5 million words.

The evidence is clear: disadvantaged children grow up in home environments that offer little opportunities for development, they spend far less time with their parents and the quality of the time is remarkably lower. The next section proposes a simple model that provides some discipline in terms of understanding why gaps in investments in children arise.

THE MODEL

The model has few components. First, a child's human capital is determined by the interaction between inputs that parents directly determine (which I call investments), and inputs that parents have little control over (which I call organizations). Investments, for example, consist of the amount and the quality of interaction between parent and child. Organizations are represented, for example, by the quality of the schools in the neighborhood where the family resides.

Second, a parenting style is a way to combine investments with organizations. Inspired by the research of Lareau (2003), I assume that parents can choose between two types of parenting styles. The "concerted cultivation" parenting style is one in which the parent actively engages with organizations for the benefit of their child's human capital development.

In contrast, the "natural growth" parenting style is the one in which the parent takes a more passive role. For each of these parenting styles, there is an equation that specifies how investments and organizations are combined to produce the child's human capital. This equation is called the technology of human capital formation.

Third, the parent chooses investments and a parenting style that will maximize the parent's preferences subject to three constraints: (1) the budget constraint; (2) the technology of human capital formation; and (3) the parental information constraint. In what follows, I provide a mathematical description of the model.

Parenting Styles and Investments

Let h_i and x_i denote, respectively, the child's human capital and the parent's investment in the child's human capital. Let e_i denote the organizations that affect the child's human capital but are not directly controlled by the parents.

I distinguish investments from parenting styles. A parenting style p_i is a technology of human capital formation. One technology, which I refer to as concerted cultivation, is very efficient in combining organizations and investments into the child's human capital. The other, which I call natural growth, is less efficient in doing so:

$$h_i = \begin{cases} e_i^\alpha x_i^\beta & \text{if } p_i = concerted\ cultivation \\[2mm] e_i^\gamma x_i^\delta & \text{if } p_i = natural\ growth \end{cases} \tag{6.1}$$

The parameters β and δ in equation 6.1 determine the responsiveness of human capital to investments under concerted cultivation and natural growth, respectively. The interpretation of these parameters is straightforward. Suppose that the parent increases investments x_i by 100 percent (say, from one to two hours per day). Then h_i will increase by β percent if the parent chooses the concerted cultivation approach and δ percent if the parent chooses natural growth. Similar interpretations apply to the parameters α and γ.

The research by Kalil et al. (2012) shows that high-SES parents not only spend more time with their children, but they are also more likely to dedicate time to activities that best suit their children's developmental needs. In other words, the high-SES parents – the ones that, according to Lareau (2003), are more prone to adopt a concerted cultivation approach – invest in skills when these skills undergo sensitive periods of development. Thus, a mathematical interpretation of the findings by Kalil et al. (2012) is that $\beta > \delta$.

In this model, parenting styles are technologies of skill formation. As illustrated by Lareau (2003), parents who follow the concerted cultivation approach are present in their child's education: they make sure that the child is doing homework, and they exert a major monitoring effort for the child to do so; they also make sure that the teachers and school principals understand and work around any limitations the child has; they actively search for information about the best teachers in the school, and they do not hesitate to contact the school if they believe their child is not receiving the necessary attention. In the context of equation 6.1, these observations imply that $\alpha > \gamma$.

Preferences, Budget Constraint

The parent's utility function has three arguments. First, the parent cares about the goods and services that satisfy the basic needs of the family (such as housing, food and heating). I refer to such expenditures as household consumption, and they are represented by c_i. Second, the parent cares about the child's human capital h_i. Third, the parent cares about the parenting style. In particular, I assume that there is a behavioral cost of adopting the concerted cultivation parenting style. For simplicity, I denote by η_i this utility cost, and I assume that it is normally distributed with mean μ_η and variance σ_η^2. The utility function is:

$$U(c_i, h_i, p_i) = \ln c_i + \theta_i \ln h_i - \eta_i \mathbf{1}(p_i = concerted\ cultivation). \quad (6.2)$$

The parameter θ_i describes how the parent values the child's human capital relative to current household consumption. Heterogeneity in θ_i arises because of differences in altruism toward the child or in future discounting. Clearly, parents who are more altruistic and/or have lower discount rates value the child's human capital more and, thus, are more likely to choose parenting styles and investments that produce high stocks of the child's human capital.

Let y_i and π denote, respectively, the parent's income and the relative price of the investment in the child's human capital. The budget constraint is:

$$c_i + \pi x_i = y_i. \quad (6.3)$$

The Parent's Information Set

At the time that the parent is choosing investments and parenting style, I assume that the parent knows their valuation of the child's human capital

θ_i, the behavioral cost η_i, the price of investment π and the income y_i. In this model, the benefits of investments and parenting styles are determined by the parameters α, β, γ and δ. If we observe investments, organizations, parenting styles and the child's human capital, it is possible (although challenging) to estimate the values of these parameters (for example, Cunha et al. 2010). In the model in this chapter, I assume that parents do not know the estimated value of these parameters. Instead, I assume that parents have their own subjective expectations about the value of these parameters. I denote by $\mu_{\alpha,i}, \mu_{\beta,i}, \mu_{\gamma,i}$ and $\mu_{\delta,i}$, respectively, parent i's subjective expectation of α, β, γ and δ. Note that the parent's subjective expectations can be different from the value of the parameters estimated by social scientists.

Thus, parent i's information set is represented by $\Omega_i = (\mu_{\alpha,i}, \mu_{\beta,i}, \mu_{\gamma,i}, \mu_{\delta,i}, \theta_i, \eta_i, y_i, \pi)$. The parent's problem is to choose a parenting style p_i and to decide how to allocate income y_i between consumption c_i and investment x_i to maximize the parent's expected utility conditional on the information set Ω_i. In what follows, I discuss the empirical evidence for the model presented in this section. Then, I characterize the solution of the problem.

Subjective Rationality

In the model described above, parents are rational, that is, they choose investments in children and parental styles that maximize a well-defined objective function under constraints. At the same time, I do not assume that parents know the "true" technology of skill formation. Instead, I assume that parents have their own subjective beliefs about the (parameters of the) technology of skill formation. Thus, in my model, parents are subjectively rational; that is, parents choose a parenting style that is optimal given their subjective beliefs of the constraints under which they operate. As I document next, a large literature in anthropology, sociology and psychology presents evidence that parents are subjectively rational in their choice of parenting styles and investments in children.

A major insight by anthropologists is that it is possible to learn a lot about a people's culture by studying the way that parents rear their children.[1] Consider, for example, the San, a group of very mobile hunters and gatherers who inhabit the Kalahari Desert in Africa. San parents believe that motor skills, such as sitting, standing and walking, must be taught and that children should be encouraged to practice these skills (Konner 1977). As a result, San parents invest time and effort in making sure that their babies develop appropriate motor skills early on. As a consequence of this training, San children perform better in motor coordination tests because their physical development is more advanced than their Western peers (Konner 1973). A possible interpretation of this finding is that San children are genetically predisposed to learn motor skills from an early age. However, experimental evidence shows that it is possible to accelerate motor development in typical Western children by providing them with a regimen of physical exercises similar to the ones San children are exposed to from an early age (Zelazo et al. 1972).

In contrast, consider the Ache Indians who live in Paraguayan forests in which children can fall prey to jaguars, poisonous snakes or other dangers. In such an environment, early mobility could endanger a child's survival. Indeed, Ache parents act to postpone motor development: their babies ride in slings early on and are carried piggyback by fathers at later ages. Research shows that Ache children walk over a year later when compared with the San children (Kaplan and Dove 1987; Hill and Hurtado 1996).

Since the early twentieth century, sociologists have been interested in how parents of different SES raise their children. In the United States, Lynd and Lynd (1929, 1937) observed that working-class mothers ranked "strict obedience" as their most important goal more frequently than higher-SES mothers did. Their findings have been replicated in more recent studies and in other contexts as well (for example, Alwin 1984; Harwood 1992; Luster et al. 1989; Pearlin and Kohn 1966; Tudge et al. 2000; Wright and Wright 1976). The data on language interaction partially support this view (Hart and Risley 1995). Low-SES parents tend to use more directives in their speech, while high-SES parents are more likely to use reasoning. Kohn (1963) argues that the stronger preferences toward socio-emotional skills by lower-SES mothers reflect those mothers' forecasts for their children choosing occupations in which obedience and conformity have relatively higher returns.

There is evidence that parents differ in their information about the process of child development. For example, a large literature in child development shows that the lower the parents' SES, the lower their expectation about cognitive development (for example, Epstein 1979; Hess et al. 1980; Ninio 1988; Ninio and Rinott 1988; Mansbach and Greenbaum 1999). More-educated mothers embrace important information sooner than less-educated ones. The smoking habits of educated and uneducated pregnant women were tracked before and after the release of the 1964 Surgeon General's Report on Smoking and Health (Aizer and Stroud 2010).[2] Before the release of the report, educated and uneducated pregnant women smoked at roughly the same rates. After the report, the smoking habits of educated women decreased immediately, and suddenly a 10 percentage point gap in smoking arose between educated and uneducated pregnant women.

Differences in parental information about the importance of the language environment that children experience may explain the finding of the path-breaking study by Hart and Risley (1995). Their results were reproduced by Rowe (2008), whose aim was to understand why some parents spoke so little to their children. According to Rowe's data, poor and uneducated women were simply unaware that it was important to talk to their babies. This is persuasive evidence that parents may not know the importance of investments and parenting styles in fostering their child's human capital development.

In essence, the evidence briefly summarized above supports the assumption that parents are rational: in settings where early mobility is desired, parents act to accelerate motor development, and the opposite happens when early mobility is a disadvantage for survival. Parental expectations about the child's future occupations partly determine the types of skills that parents choose to foster in their children. At the same time, not all parents have up-to-date information about the process by which the child's human capital accumulation can be fostered. Parents make rational choices based on subjective assessments of the constraints they face. Next, I characterize the solution of the model.

SOLUTION OF THE MODEL, POLICY RECOMMENDATIONS AND PRELIMINARY EVIDENCE

To solve the model, I break down the problem into two stages. In the first stage, the parent chooses a parenting style. In the second stage, the parent chooses the investment conditional on the parenting style chosen in the first stage. Once the problem is broken down in this fashion, I solve the problem by backward induction. That is, I start by deriving the optimal investment for each parenting style. Then, I derive the optimal parenting style in the first stage.

So, starting from the second stage, it is possible to show that optimal investments for a parent who chooses concerted cultivation (*CC*) in the first stage are given by:

$$x_i^{CC} = \left(\frac{\theta_i \mu_{\beta,i}}{1 + \theta_i \mu_{\beta,i}} \right) \frac{y_i}{\pi} \text{ if } p_i = concerted\ cultivation. \qquad (6.4a)$$

Alternatively, if the parent chooses the natural growth (*NG*) approach in the first stage, then the optimal investments in the second stage are given by:

$$x_i^{NG} = \left(\frac{\theta_i \mu_{\delta,i}}{1 + \theta_i \mu_{\delta,i}} \right) \frac{y_i}{\pi} \text{ if } p_i = natural\ growth. \qquad (6.4b)$$

The empirical literature shows that high-SES parents tend to invest more in their children. According to equations 6.4a and 6.4b, this can happen for different reasons. First, high-SES parents have higher income, which is consistent with the evidence from Dahl and Lochner (2012). Second, if we compare parents who have chosen the same parenting style, the gap between high- and low-SES parents could be explained by differences in expectations about the parameters β and δ. Third, the gaps in investments could also be explained by differences in parenting styles if the expectations about β of the high-SES parents who choose the concerted cultivation approach are higher than the expectations about δ of the low-SES parents who choose the natural growth approach.

As I show below, the parents who choose the concerted cultivation approach are a selected sample of parents. In particular, they tend to have higher income and access to higher-quality organizations. Under the assumption that $\eta_i \sim N(\mu_\eta, \sigma_\eta^2)$, the probability that parent i chooses concerted cultivation, which I denote by $Pr(p_i = CC \mid \Omega_i)$, is:

$$Pr(p_i = CC \mid \Omega_i) = \Phi\left(\frac{\kappa_i - \mu_\eta + \theta_i(\mu_{\beta,i} - \mu_{\delta,i})\ln\left(\dfrac{y_i}{\pi}\right) + \theta_i(\mu_{\alpha,i} - \mu_{\gamma,i})\ln e_i}{\sigma_\eta}\right).$$

The model states that the following four factors determine the choice of parenting observed in the data. The first factor is the behavioral cost associated with the concerted cultivation parenting style. The model implies that the higher the behavioral cost, which is denoted by μ_η, the less likely that parents are going to choose concerted cultivation.

The second factor that affects the choice of parenting style is family resources. In the empirical literature, the higher the parental income, the more likely that the parent chooses the concerted cultivation approach. A sufficient condition for the model to generate this implication is that $\mu_{\beta,i} > \mu_{\delta,i}$. In this case, the relationship between family resources and parenting style arises because investments are an increasing function of family income. The higher the parental income is, the higher the difference between the child's human capital under concerted cultivation and natural growth. In other words, the higher the family income, the higher the benefit of choosing the concerted cultivation parenting style.

The third factor that determines the choice of parenting style is the quality of the organizations. The findings by Lareau (2003) show that middle-class parents have access to organizations of higher quality and are also more likely to take a more active role in their child's school activities. These actions are indicative of parents who choose the concerted cultivation parenting style. A sufficient condition for the model to generate this prediction is that $(\mu_{\alpha,i} - \mu_{\gamma,i}) > 0$. Under this condition, the implication that parenting styles are affected by the quality of organizations is similar to the relationship between parenting style and income. When the quality of the organizations is higher, the benefit of choosing concerted cultivation over natural growth is larger.

Interestingly, there is evidence that low-SES parents respond to exogenous changes in the quality of the organizations. Bergman (2013) studied whether changes in the frequency and mode of communication to parents could change parental involvement in the child's education. In order to do so, Bergman randomly assigned parents to a treatment or control group. Parents in the control group received the default amount of information that the school provided. Parents in the treatment group received not only the default information but also text messages about their child's missing assignments, grades and upcoming exams. As Bergman (2013) shows, this experiment changed parental relationships with the school. Parents in the treatment group were 85 percent more likely to initiate contact with the school than parents in the control group. Parents in the treatment group also increased their attendance at conferences with teachers. These are actions usually taken by parents who follow the concerted cultivation approach. The children of parents in the treatment group were more likely to submit their work on time, to improve their work habits and to cooperate in school. Consequently, there was improvement in the child's human capital formation: the students of parents in the treatment group had higher GPA scores and higher scores on state standardized tests.

The fourth factor in the choice of parenting style is the expectation that parents have about the benefits of concerted cultivation (measured by $\mu_{\alpha,i}$ and $\mu_{\beta,i}$) versus natural growth (measured by $\mu_{\gamma,i}$ and $\mu_{\delta,i}$). In particular, the larger the differences $\mu_{\beta,i} - \mu_{\delta,i}$ or $\mu_{\alpha,i} - \mu_{\gamma,i}$, the more likely it is that parents will adopt the concerted cultivation style. As described above, Rowe (2008) shows that low-SES parents may talk little to their children because they are unaware of the role of child-directed speech in the child's language development. A small-scale intervention to improve parental knowledge about the importance of talking to young children was conducted by Suskind and Leffel (2013). The intervention, known as the Thirty Million Words Project, is based on three components. The first component is communicating to parents the scientific evidence on how the early language environment experienced by children affects children's brain development. The second component is providing parents with suggestions on how to easily and very cheaply improve the language environment at home. The third component is supplying parents with information about the quality of the language environment at their home, and encouraging them to reach for higher levels of hourly word counts and daily conversational turns. As a result of the intervention, the parents in the treatment group increased the amount of conversation turns per hour by around 50 percent, and the children's language development (measured in number of vocalizations per hour) also increased by 50 percent.

Another similar intervention was conducted in Africa. In the context of poor countries, researchers often equate parental investments to feeding practices that young children experience on a day-to-day basis. Indeed, this is an important topic of study, because it is known that early malnourishment has detrimental consequences for longer-term outcomes such as schooling, adult health and productivity (Glewwe et al. 2001; Maluccio et al. 2009). Consider, for example, Malawi, an African country where 48 percent of children younger than five are stunted and 22 percent of them are underweight. It is very likely that poor feeding practices are partly responsible for these extreme indicators. For example, over half of all infants below six months of age are given food and/or unsterilized water (Malawi Demographic and Health Survey 2004), which is contrary to World Health Organization (WHO) recommendations.

Fitzsimons et al. (2012) study whether the provision of information about the impact of these poor feeding practices on child development leads Malawi parents to become more careful with the food they give their children. In the context of the model above, this is essentially informing parents about values of β and δ. A randomized counseling intervention was used to impart information and advice on infant feeding to mothers of young children. Counseling visits not only encouraged exclusive breast-feeding up to the age of six months, but also provided information about weaning, locally available nutritious foods, the importance of a varied diet (particularly, the inclusion of protein and micronutrient-rich foods such as eggs), and instructions on how to prepare foods so as to conserve nutrients and ease digestion. Three years after the beginning of the intervention, it was found that mothers in treated localities exhibited superior knowledge about infant feeding best practices. Children in treatment localities experienced a more varied diet, richer in protein. By age three, the children in the treatment group were 20 percent of a standard deviation (for age) taller than the children in the control group.

The findings from the Thirty Million Words Project (Suskind and Leffel 2013) and the nutrition counseling intervention by Fitzsimons et al. (2012) are persuasive evidence that beliefs have a causal effect on child development. An important design in the Thirty Million Words Project is that the parent was provided feedback about the child's vocalizations in response to an increase in parental child-directed speech. The feedback may have been key to changing parents' beliefs about the importance of the home language environment for the child's language development. In the Malawi experiment, Fitzsimmons et al. (2012) showed that the intervention generated interest in child nutrition within the village, beyond just the households directly affected, making child health- and nutrition-related issues more salient in these communities. This finding suggests that parents not only updated their beliefs, but they also communicated their updated beliefs to other parents who were not directly treated.

CONCLUSION

In this chapter, I summarize the literature on socioeconomic inequality in investments in children. I show that the evidence is consistent with a model in which parents are subjectively rational. Although parents act to maximize a well-defined objective function, they lack information about the constraints that link parenting style and investments to child development. I then show that empirical implications of the model have been validated in recent experiments that provide parents with important information to foster child development. These findings provide useful guidance for the design of new policies that can close the human capital gap that opens up long before children reach school.

NOTES

1. A helpful survey of the literature I present in the next two paragraphs is provided by Small (1999).
2. The thesis that information dissemination impacted cigarette smoking is also analyzed by de Walque (2010). See also de Walque (2007) for the impacts of information campaigns on HIV contamination.

REFERENCES

Aizer, A. and L. Stroud (2010), "Education, medical knowledge and the evolution of disparities in health," NBER Working Paper 15840, Cambridge, MA: National Bureau of Economic Research.

Alwin, D.F. (1984), "Trends in parental socialization values: Detroit, 1958–1983," *American Journal of Sociology*, **90**, 359–82.

Becker, G. and N. Tomes (1986), "Child endowments and the quantity and quality of children," *Journal of Political Economy*, **84**, S143–S162.

Behrman, J.R., M.C. Calderon, S. Preston, J. Hoddinott, R. Martorell and A.D. Stein (2009), "Nutritional supplementation of girls influences the growth of their children: prospective study in Guatemala," *American Journal of Clinical Nutrition*, **90**, 1372–79.

Behrman, J.R. and M.R. Rosenzweig (2002), "Does increasing women's schooling raise the schooling of the next generation?" *American Economic Review*, **92**, 323–34.

Bergman, P. (2013), "The more you know: evidence from a field experiment on parent–child information frictions and human capital investment," Columbia University Working Paper, New York: Columbia University, available at http://peterlsb.bol.ucla.edu/PBergmanJMP3-13.pdf.

Bianchi, S., J.P. Robinson and M.A. Mylkie (2007), *Changing Rhythms of American Family Life*, New York: Russell Sage.

Bradley, R.H. and B.M. Caldwell (1980), "The relation of home environment, cognitive competence, and IQ among males and females," *Child Development*, **51**, 1140–48.

Brody, G.F. (1968), "Socioeconomic differences in stated maternal child-rearing practices and in observed maternal behavior," *Journal of Marriage and Family*, **30**, 656–60.

Brophy, J.E. (1970), "Mothers as teachers of their own preschool children: the influence of socioeconomic status and task structure on teaching specificity," *Child Development*, **41**, 79–94.

Cameron, S.V. and J.J. Heckman (1998), "Life cycle schooling and dynamic selection bias: models and evidence for five cohorts of American males," *Journal of Political Economy*, **106**, 262–333.

Campbell, F.A., B.H. Wasik, E. Pungello, M. Burchinal, O. Barbarin, et al. (2008), "Young adult outcomes of the Abecedarian and CARE early childhood educational interventions," *Early Childhood Research Quarterly*, **23**, 452–66.

Carneiro, P. and J.J. Heckman (2003), "Human capital policy," in J.J. Heckman and A. Krueger (eds), *Inequality in America: What Role for Human Capital Policy?*, Cambridge, MA: MIT Press, pp. 77–240.

Carneiro, P., C. Meghir and M. Parey (2013), "Maternal education, home environments and child development," *Journal of European Economic Association*, **11**, 123–60.

Cunha, F., I. Elo and J. Culhane (2013), "Eliciting maternal expectations about the technology of skill formation," NBER Working Paper 19144, Cambridge, MA: National Bureau of Economic Research.

Cunha, F. and J.J. Heckman (2007), "The technology of skill formation," *American Economic Review: Papers and Proceedings*, **97**(2), 3147.

Cunha, F., J.J. Heckman and S. Navarro (2005), "Separating heterogeneity from uncertainty in life cycle earnings," *Oxford Economic Papers*, **57**, 191–261.

Cunha, F., J. Heckman and S. Schennach (2010), "Estimating the technology of cognitive and noncognitive skill formation," *Econometrica*, **78**, 883–931.

Currie, J. and E. Moretti (2002), "Mother's education and the intergenerational transmission of human capital: evidence from college openings and longitudinal data," NBER Working Paper 9360, Cambridge, MA: National Bureau of Economic Research.

Dahl, G. and L. Lochner (2012), "The impact of family income on child achievement: evidence from the Earned Income Tax Credit?" *American Economic Review*, **102**, 1927–56.

de Walque, Damien (2007), "How does the impact of an HIV/AIDS information campaign vary with educational attainment? Evidence from rural Uganda," *Journal of Development Economics*, **84**, 686–714.

de Walque, Damien (2010), "Education, information and smoking decisions:

evidence from smoking histories, 1940–2000," *Journal of Human Resources*, **45**, 682–717.

Duncan, G.J., K. Ziol-Guest and A. Kalil (2010), "Early-childhood poverty and adult attainment, behavior, and health," *Child Development*, **81**, 306–25.

Dunn, J., C. Wooding and J. Hermann (1977), "Mothers' speech to young children: variation in context," *Developmental Medicine and Child Neurology*, **19**, 629–38.

Epstein, A.S. (1979), "Pregnant teenagers' knowledge of infant development," Ypsilanti, Michigan: High/Scope Educational Research Foundation working paper, available at www.eric.ed.gov/PDFS/ED176875.pdf.

Field, T. and S. Pawlby (1980), "Early face-to-face interactions of British and American working- and middle-class mother-infant dyads," *Child Development*, **51**, 250–53.

Fitzsimons, E., B. Malde, A. Mesnard and M. Vera-Hernández (2012), "Household responses to information on child nutrition: Experimental evidence from Malawi," IFS Working Paper W12/07, London: Institute for Fiscal Studies, available at www.ifs.org.uk.

Glewwe, P., H. Jacoby and E. King (2001), "Early childhood nutrition and academic achievement: a longitudinal analysis," *Journal of Public Economics*, **81**, 345–68.

Greenwood, C.R., K. Thiemann-Bourque, D. Walker, J. Buzhardt and J. Gilkerson (2011), "Assessing children's home language environments using automatic speech recognition technology," *Communication Disorders Quarterly*, **32**, 83–92.

Guryan, J., E. Hurst and M. Kearney (2008), "Parental education and parental time with children," *Journal of Economic Perspectives*, **22**, 23–46.

Hammer, C.S. and A.L. Weiss (1999), "Guiding language development: how African American mothers and their infants structure play interactions," *Journal of Speech, Language, and Hearing Research*, **42**, 1219–33.

Hart, B. and T. Risley (1995), *Meaningful Differences in the Everyday Experience of Young American Children*, Baltimore, MD: Paul H. Brooks.

Harwood, R.L. (1992), "The influence of culturally derived values on Anglo and Puerto Rican mothers' perceptions of attachment behavior," *Child Development*, **63**, 822–39.

Heckman, J.J., S.H. Moon, R. Pinto, P.A. Savelyev and A.Q. Yavitz (2010), "Analyzing social experiments as implemented: a reexamination of the evidence from the High Scope Perry Preschool Program," *Quantitative Economics*, **1**, 1–46.

Hess, R.D., K. Kashiwagi, H. Azuma, G. Price and W.P. Dickson (1980), "Maternal expectations for mastery of developmental tasks in Japan and the United States," *International Journal of Psychology*, **15**, 259–71.

Hess, R.D. and V.C. Shipman (1965), "Early experience and the socialization of cognitive modes in children," *Child Development*, **36**, 869–86.

Hill, K. and A.M. Hurtado (1996), *Ache Life History: The Ecology and Demography of a Foraging People*, Hawthorne, NY: Aldine de Gruyter.

Hoddinott, J., J.A. Maluccio, J.R. Behrman, R. Flores and R. Martorell (2008), "The impact of nutrition during early childhood on income, hours worked, and wages of Guatemalan adults," *Lancet*, **371**, 411–16.

Hoff-Ginsberg, E. (1991), "Mother–child conversation in different social classes and communicative settings," *Child Development*, **62**, 782–96.

Kalil, A., R. Ryan and M. Corey (2012), "Diverging destinies: maternal education and the developmental gradient in time with children," *Demography*, **49**, 1361–83.

Kaplan, H. and H. Dove (1987), "Infant development among the Ache of Paraguay," *Developmental Psychology*, **23**, 190–98.

Karoly, L.A., M.R. Kilburn and J.S. Cannon (2005), *Early Childhood Interventions: Proven Results, Future Promise*, Santa Monica, CA: RAND Corporation.

Keane, M.P. and K.I. Wolpin (1997), "The career decisions of young men," *Journal of Political Economy*, **105**, 473–522.

Kohn, M.L. (1963), "Social class and parent–child relationships: an interpretation," *American Journal of Sociology*, **68**, 471–80.

Konner, M.J. (1973), "Newborn walking: additional data," *Science*, **179**(4070), 307.

Konner, M.J. (1977), "Infancy among the Kalahari Desert San," in P.H. Leiderman, S.R. Tulin and A. Rosenfeld (eds), *Culture and Infancy: Variations in the Human Experience*, New York: Academic Press, pp. 287–327.

Lareau, A. (2003), *Unequal Childhoods: Class, Race, and Family Life*, Berkeley, CA: University of California Press.

Lawrence, V.W. and E.F. Shipley (1996), "Parental speech to middle- and working-class children from two racial groups in three settings," *Applied Psycholinguistics*, **17**, 233–55.

Ludwig, J. and D.L. Miller (2007), "Does Head Start improve children's life chances? Evidence from a regression discontinuity design," *Quarterly Journal of Economics*, **122**, 159–208.

Luster, T., K. Rhoades and B. Haas (1989), "The relation between parental values and parenting behavior: a test of the Kohn hypothesis," *Journal of Marriage and Family*, **51**, 139–47.

Lynd, R.S. and H.M. Lynd (1929), *Middletown: A Study in Contemporary American Culture*, New York: Harcourt, Brace & Company.

Lynd, R.S. and H.M. Lynd (1937), *Middletown in Transition: A Study in Cultural Conflicts*, New York: Harcourt, Brace & Company.

Malawi Demographic and Health Survey (2004), *Malawi Demographic and Health Survey: Preliminary Report 2004*, Zomba, Malawi: National Statistics Office, available at www.nsomalawi.mw/index.php/publications/malawi-demographic-and-health-survey/17-2004-mdhs.html.

Maluccio, J., J. Hoddinott, J.R. Behrman, R. Martorell, A. Quisumbing and A.D. Stein (2009), "The impact of improving nutrition during early childhood on education among Guatemalan adults," *Economic Journal*, **119**, 734–63.

Mansbach, I.K. and C.W. Greenbaum (1999), "Developmental maturity expectations of Israeli fathers and mothers: effects of education, ethnic origin, and religiosity," *International Journal of Behavioral Development*, **23**, 771–97.

Neal, D.A. and W.R. Johnson (1996), "The role of premarket factors in black–white wage differences," *Journal of Political Economy*, **104**, 869–95.

Ninio, A. (1980), "Picture-book reading in mother–infant dyads belonging to two subgroups in Israel," *Child Development*, **51**, 587–90.

Ninio, A. (1988), "The effects of cultural background, sex, and parenthood on beliefs about the timetable of cognitive development in infancy," *Merrill-Palmer Quarterly*, **34**, 369–88.

Ninio, A. and N. Rinott (1988), "Fathers' involvement in the care of their infants and their attributions of cognitive competence to infants," *Child Development*, **59**, 652–63.

Pearlin, L.I. and M.L. Kohn (1966), "Social class, occupation, and parental values: a cross-national study," *American Sociological Review*, **31**, 466–79.

Reeves, R.V. and K. Howard (2013), *The Glass Floor: Education, Downward Mobility, and Opportunity Hoarding*, Washington, DC: Brookings Institution.

Reynolds, A.J. and J.A. Temple (2008), "Cost-effective early childhood development programs from preschool to third grade," *Annual Review of Clinical Psychology*, **4**, 109–39.

Rowe, M.L. (2008), "Child-directed speech: relation to socioeconomic status, knowledge of child development, and child vocabulary skill," *Journal of Child Language*, **35**, 185–205.

Small, M.F. (1999), *Our Babies, Ourselves: How Biology and Culture Shape the Way We Parent*, New York: Anchor Books.

Suskind, D. and K. Leffel (2013), "Parent-directed approaches to enrich the early language environments of children living in poverty," *Seminars in Speech and Language*, **34**, 267–77.

Tudge, J.R.H., D.M. Hogan, I.A. Snezhkova, N.K. Kulakova and K.E. Etz (2000), "Parents' child-rearing values and beliefs in the United States and Russia: the impact of culture and social class," *Infant and Child Development*, **9**, 105–21.

Tulkin, S.R. and J. Kagan (1972), "Mother–child interaction in the first year of life," *Child Development*, **43**, 31–41.

Wright, J.D. and S.R. Wright (1976), "Social class and parental values for children: a partial replication and extension of the Kohn thesis," *American Sociological Review*, **41**, 527–37.

Zelazo, P.R., N.A. Zelazo and S. Kolb (1972), "Walking in the newborn," *Science*, **176**(4032), 314–15.

7. US charter schools as a test of the theory of school choice

Julian R. Betts

INTRODUCTION

The provision of high-quality education is surely one of the most important goals of any society. Schooling prepares young people to contribute to the labor market and to society more broadly. Numerous studies suggest that the average level of skills in a country positively influences national income and perhaps economic growth (for example, Hanushek et al. 2008; Hanushek and Woessmann 2008).

From an economic standpoint, the market that provides educational services is worth studying, because the structure of the market can have a huge influence on the quality and cost of education. Economic theory suggests that a more competitive market is likely to produce better outcomes for consumers. In the case of education, the implication is that families can obtain a better education for their children if many independent school operators compete against each other.

In the United States, public school systems, funded through property and income taxes, provide education to the vast majority of students between kindergarten and grade 12 (K–12). For instance, in fall 2009, private schools accounted for only 10 percent of K–12 student enrollment (Snyder and Dillow 2013: 108). As for the public school districts themselves, they often do not compete against each other for students. In many cities, one dominant school district enrolls the majority of K–12 students, becoming close to a monopoly provider of education.

Partly as a reaction to the lack of competition in K–12 education, a number of innovative forms of school choice have emerged over the last several decades. Open enrollment programs allow students to apply to schools outside their local attendance area, although typically to schools that are in the same district. Magnet schools are public schools that attempt to integrate districts demographically by attracting students from a variety of neighborhoods. They often do this by adopting special curricular or pedagogical themes. In a limited number of cities private funds or, in Washington, DC, public funds are used to pay for vouchers, allowing students to attend private schools.

Another less obvious form of school choice is that a family's residential choice determines the type of school the family's children will attend. In Tiebout's (1956) theory, like-minded individuals gather together in communities and assess taxes and spend on public schooling and other public amenities according to their preferences and ability to pay.

More recently, charter schools have emerged as a new type of public school choice in the United States. These schools receive their name from the charter they receive to operate, typically provided by a local school district. Although they are public schools, charter schools are given freedom to adopt innovative curricula and teaching approaches. The laws enabling charter schools differ from state to state, but to varying degrees they free charter schools from much of the education regulations to which traditional public schools must adhere. Typically, this means that charter schools have greater freedom to hire teachers from nontraditional sources. Charter schools can have unionized teacher staffs, but typically teachers are not unionized. Lack of a collective bargaining agreement further enhances charter schools' freedom to hire teachers from nontraditional sources and to determine how the school day should be set up. As detailed in the next section, charter schools are now one of the most important and quickest-growing forms of school choice in the United States.

The goal of this chapter is to provide an overview of what is known about charter schools and their impact. Are students who attend charter schools gaining more academically than they would have, had they attended traditional public schools? Do the impacts vary by the type of charter school, the characteristics of the students enrolled, or of their neighborhoods or the traditional public schools in their neighborhoods? Do charter schools create competitive pressure on the traditional public schools with which they compete for students to improve the quality of education they provide? Are there peer effects induced in traditional public schools as they lose potential students to charter schools?

This chapter provides an overview of a small but growing literature on these questions. The next section distills lessons from the theory of markets for the likely impact of school choice. The third section discusses the history and growth of charter schools. The fourth and fifth sections analyze what we know about the impact of charter schools on the educational achievement and other outcomes of attendees. The sixth addresses the important but difficult question of whether the presence of charter schools induces nearby traditional public schools to improve. The final section concludes by summarizing the key policy issues, from which a research agenda for future work emerges.

THE THEORY OF SCHOOL CHOICE

The case for creating markets that are "competitive," in which no buyer or seller is large relative to the market as a whole, is a general one that applies to the markets for all goods and services.[1] Economists have developed a formal mathematical theory showing that if prices are allowed to adjust, then under certain conditions markets will be "Pareto-efficient," which means that no party could be made better off without making another party worse off. This efficiency result is known as the first fundamental theory of welfare economics. It is very difficult for a centrally planned market to reach this first-best result. For example, the theory would contend that if a large number of school operators competed for students, the schools would adjust what they provide to match as best as possible the demand from families for the educational services they believe best serve their children. The genius of decentralized markets is that no resources go wasted, because suppliers listen closely to the needs of consumers, in this case parents. It would be very difficult for a large district to replicate the result from a decentralized market, in part because a centralized administration cannot gather the requisite information about the individual needs of students and respond nimbly. At the same time, a monopolist would not feel compelled to provide the same level of educational services for a given level of funding.

A second important aspect of the theory of competitive markets is that it does not assume that all suppliers are equally efficient. Parents understand in a very deep way that not all teachers are equally effective, and that not all schools are equally effective. In a highly competitive market, schools that are relatively unproductive in terms of the amount of learning they promote for a given amount of funding per pupil will lose students to more effective competitors. If the inefficient schools do nothing to improve, they will lose students and will eventually close, while the more efficient schools will expand. In this way market competition raises the average productivity of schools. Alternatively, schools that begin to lose students will study how the more effective schools function, and then reform themselves. Competition, by inducing emulation of the best ways of running schools, promises to make all schools better.

So, we have efficiency if there is a high degree of competition ("perfect competition" in the parlance of economists). However, an efficient market need not be a just or equitable market. To make this problem more concrete, consider the most extreme form of school choice, in which education is completely privatized, and families must pay for education on their own. The result would probably be a highly segregated education system, in which the affluent segregated themselves into well-funded schools, and the less affluent settled for whatever educational services they could afford. This would be a much more inequitable system than we have today, because the public school system redistributes tax dollars more evenly than in this hypothetical example just given.

The second fundamental theorem of welfare economics comes to the rescue here. It states that any Pareto-efficient outcome can be attained merely by redistributing resources among consumers. In our case, if policymakers disliked the thought of families segregating themselves into private schools based entirely on income, then public subsidies that favored the less affluent families would lead to a new Pareto-efficient outcome in which there was a greater degree of socioeconomic mixing. One form for this would be a voucher system in which the size of the voucher were larger for less affluent families. In essence, it is possible to have both efficiency and equity if resources are redistributed.

In the case of charter schools, which as public schools do not charge tuition, it is not obvious that concerns about differences in purchasing power across families would influence the families' access to a given charter school. However, one cost of attending a charter school is that it may be some distance from the family's home. For this reason, decisions by charter school operators on where to open up new schools have the potential to create unequal access due to differential transportation costs among families.

The above summary of the benefits of perfect competition applies if certain assumptions, such as a large number of suppliers and consumers, apply to the market in question. Many of these conditions can be questioned in the case of the market for schooling. Betts (2005) describes these conditions and also discusses both the possible exceptions to these conditions in the context of schooling, and policy prescriptions to implement as partial antidotes to each exception.

AN OVERVIEW OF CHARTER SCHOOLS

Early History and the Growth of the Charter School Movement

Since Minnesota passed the first state law allowing for the creation of charter schools in 1991, charter schools have grown rapidly in number. Figure 7.1 shows charter schools' steady growth in their share of all public schools and public school enrollment. In 2010–11, charter schools enrolled almost 1.8 million students. With enrollment growth of over 100 000 students in each of the preceding five years, charter schools were poised to overtake magnet schools in enrollment, which bounced erratically around

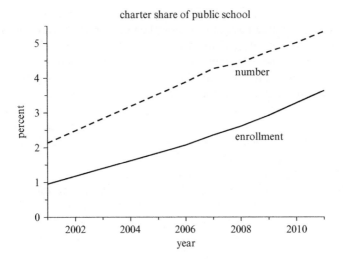

charter share of public school

Source: Author's calculations based on Snyder and Dillow (2013: 175).

Figure 7.1 Charter school shares of number of public schools and of public school enrollment in the United States, 2001–11

2 million in the five years up to 2010–11. This comparison is meaningful given the much longer history of magnet schools, which trace their history back to court desegregation orders in the 1970s.

Currently, 42 states and the District of Columbia have laws allowing for the creation of charter schools (Christie et al. 2014). Charter schools typically have greater freedom than do traditional public schools over important choices such as curriculum, textbooks, pedagogical methods and whom to hire. But charter schools are not unregulated by any stretch of the imagination. They must conform to the same health and safety regulations as traditional public schools, for example.

Ironically, the regulations that remain in place for charter schools may hinder the degree to which they can innovate. For example, Loveless and Field (2009) point out that under the federal No Child Left Behind law, all public school students in certain grades must take state-mandated tests in math and English language arts. As such, charter schools must hew to the state curriculum standards fairly closely in order for their students to perform reasonably well.

Further, states have issued regulations that apply only to charter schools. Christie et al. (2014) tabulate some of these regulations. Most notably, 11 states and the District of Columbia have minimums for school achievement performance, and charters are apt not to be renewed if the charter schools fall below these minimums. Also, Christie et al. report that 20 states and the District of Columbia have put caps on the number of charter schools and/ or the total number of students who can enroll in charter schools.

It is natural to ask why some states have more liberal charter school laws and others have more restrictive laws. The extent of lobbying by teachers' unions to restrict charter schools may play a role. Stoddard and Corcoran (2007) analyze the passage of charter school laws across different states and conclude that "Teachers unions have been particularly effective in slowing or preventing liberal state charter legislation; however, conditional on law passage and strength, local participation in charter schools rises with the share of unionized teachers."

Setting aside regulations, funding is the most important form of control for state government and the local school districts that typically grant charters to new charter schools. Wong and Klopott (2009) conclude that, as part of the political compromise when states passed charter school laws, charter schools were typically funded at lower levels than traditional public schools. Speakman et al. (2005) surveyed funding mechanisms in 16 states and the District of Columbia, which together at that time accounted for 84 percent of charter schools, and found that charter schools routinely received less funding than traditional schools. A particular problem is that charter schools must pay for their facilities, yet few states provide support explicitly for this need. Wong and Klopott (2009) cite a study by Balboni et al. (2007) which found that only 11 states provided funds specifically earmarked to pay for facilities.

In a similar vein, Betts et al. (2005) discuss the main constraints limiting the supply of schools of choice. They pay particular attention to the difficulties that charter schools have in obtaining loans that they often need to secure land and build school facilities. One of the central problems is that lenders understandably balk at making such loans to a charter school that can be closed after a few years if the host district opts not to renew its charter. Against this backdrop, the quick growth rate of the charter school movement seems all the more impressive.

IMPACT OF CHARTER SCHOOLS ON OUTCOMES FOR ENROLLED STUDENTS: EDUCATIONAL ACHIEVEMENT

Most studies of the impact of charter schools on student outcomes have focused on measures of achievement, typically as measured through test scores.

Methodological Concerns

Many supposed evaluations of charter schools' impact on achievement are in truth nothing more than descriptive reports that take a snapshot of student performance at one point in time. Such studies compare achievement at charter schools and nearby traditional public schools, but they fail utterly to explain why achievement may differ. Such studies do not take into account students' past academic achievement. For example, if a charter school opens in a less affluent area, it is likely to attract students from less affluent families, and on average these students will have lower achievement before entering the charter school. It is difficult to account for "selection effects" of this sort, especially if the study does not follow individual students over time. In a literature review, Betts and Tang (2008) reported that two-thirds of the charter school studies they could find did not meet minimum standards of quality, typically because they did not take account of students' past achievement.

What, then, constitutes a high-quality study? The gold standard is a study that exploits lotteries at oversubscribed charter schools. The advantage of using lotteries is that one can compare lottery winners and lottery losers. On average the only difference between those who win and lose the lottery is the luck of the draw. A well-conducted lottery analysis is essentially an experiment, with well-defined treatment and comparison groups whose members on average should differ across groups only in the random numbers they were assigned in a lottery.

There are still very few of these studies. In a meta-analysis of the literature, Betts and Tang (2014) found only eight studies that used lotteries.[2] However, they found another 43 studies that used other approaches which made suitable attempts to control for students' past academic history and their personal characteristics.

These other studies have used a variety of methods, but in every case the studies take into account a student's past achievement. Such studies are often referred to as "value-added" studies because they assess how a student's achievement grows while attending the current school. Taking into account each student's learning trajectory is a major improvement over the "snapshot" studies that simply compare achievement in a given year between students at charter schools and students at traditional public schools. Each of the nonexperimental methods takes a different approach to finding a comparison group with which charter school students can be compared. Each of these methods has pluses and minuses.

Fixed-effect models do away with the need to compare charter school students to noncharter school students, by instead comparing the progress of a given charter school student to their own progress when attending a traditional public school. This method has its own "selection on observables" problem, though, because we cannot know for sure whether the student's motivation, home life and so on were the same during the years they attended charter school and when they attended traditional public school. A second problem is that many students, especially in elementary grades, enter charter schools at kindergarten or grade 1 and never attend traditional public schools. Their data do not contribute to the fixed-effect estimates. A third issue is that if the impact of attending a charter school persists even after a student switches to a traditional public school, we will understate the impact of attending the charter school, because we are overstating the gain in achievement the student would have had if they had enrolled in the traditional public school in all grades.

Propensity score matching is an approach in which the researcher first estimates a model; in this case, to predict whether the student enters a charter school. For each student in a charter school, this model will produce a predicted probability of entering the charter school. The researcher then identifies, for each charter school student, one or more noncharter school students with the most similar probability of entering the charter school. This method is a clever way of matching, which reduces the problem of trying to match on every possible characteristic – such as gender, race, ethnicity, initial test scores and socioeconomic status – to the simpler problem of matching based on a single number: the predicted probability of enrolling. The main weakness of the method is that it assumes "selection on observables." Put simply, if there are any factors that determine whether a student enrolls in a charter school that are not in the researcher's dataset, the researcher will probably end up with a biased estimate of attending a charter school, because they will attribute the impact of those unobserved variables on achievement to the charter school.

One of the most prolific contributors to the charter school achievement literature is the Center for Research on Education Outcomes (CREDO) at Stanford, California. CREDO's studies use a method that is closest in spirit to the propensity score approach, in that they match each charter school student to one or more students at traditional public schools. A potentially major issue in the CREDO approach is that some charter school students in their sample lack test score data available prior to their entry to the charter school. The CREDO approach matches these students to students at traditional public schools using achievement that is the result of having attended the charter school. If the charter school has large (positive or negative) causal effects on achievement, then matching the charter school's students to those at traditional public schools is risky, because it is matching apples to oranges. For instance, suppose a charter school has a positive causal impact on achievement. A grade 4 student at that school would be matched with a student with a similar test score at a traditional public school who had managed to obtain a similar score without the benefit of having attended the charter school. We are thus matching this charter school student with an innately higher-achieving student, and thus may understate the positive impact of attending the charter school. Conversely, if the charter school has a negative causal impact on achievement, a student with no test scores available prior to enrolling at the charter school would likely be matched with a student whose test scores were quite low, and whose trajectory was lower to start with. This could bias upward (toward zero) the estimated impact of attending that school. Davis and Raymond (2012) compare the CREDO approach to some other nonexperimental approaches and find broadly similar results.

Findings

Betts and Tang (2014) perform a meta-analysis of the studies that use value-added student-level methods to assess the relation between attending a charter school and achievement in math and English language arts. Table 7.1 summarizes the patterns Betts and Tang (2014) found. The sign of the average estimated effect is shown. (Signs in parentheses indicate that the overall estimated effect was not significantly different from zero at the 5 percent level.) Different studies have combined grade levels in different ways. Although many studies report results separately for charter schools that are elementary, middle and high schools, a number of studies provide one overall estimate for elementary and middle charter schools combined

Table 7.1   Effect sizes and significance from meta-analysis, by grade span and subject area

Grade span	Reading tests	Math tests
Elementary	(+)	+*
Middle	(+)	+*
High	(+)	(+)
Combined elementary and middle studies	(−)	(−)
Elementary, middle and combined elementary/middle	(+)	+*
All grade spans	(+)	+*

Note: Signs + and − indicate the sign of the overall estimated effect. An asterisk (*) indicates that the estimated overall effect across studies is statistically significant at the 5 percent level or less. A sign in parentheses indicates that the overall estimated effect is not significantly different from zero.

or, less frequently, elementary, middle and high schools combined. (The last-named is the "all grade spans" row at the bottom of the table.)

The patterns are slightly different for reading and math tests. For all but one of the grade spans for which results are reported in the literature, the overall reading effect is positive but it is never statistically significant (in the sense of there being a probability of 5 percent or less that the true effect is zero). The pattern is not strong enough to be conclusive, but it is clear that most estimates are positive. For math achievement, the pattern of signs is identical: as for reading, in math the estimated effects are positive for all grade spans except for the studies that combine elementary and middle schools. But in four of six cases the math achievement effect is statistically significant and positive. Thus the evidence of positive effects is much more persuasive for mathematics than for reading.

What about the magnitude of the estimated effects? The two largest estimated effects are for math achievement in elementary schools and middle schools. In those studies Betts and Tang (2014) estimate overall effect sizes of 0.045 and 0.084, respectively. (This means that after attending a charter school for one year, a student is predicted to gain 4.5 percent and 8.4 percent of a standard deviation in math achievement relative to the achievement that student would have had if they had attended a traditional public school.) For many readers, a more transparent way of describing the size of the elementary school effect is to say that if a student started at the fiftieth percentile of the test score distribution, after one year of attending an elementary charter school they are predicted to rise to percentile 51.8, meaning that this student would now have achievement equal to or higher than 51.8 out of every 100 students on average. The middle school effect is bigger: one year in a charter middle school is predicted to boost a student from the fiftieth percentile to percentile 53.3. After several years in a charter school, these gains would presumably grow.

It is becoming quite clear that charter school impact estimates vary dramatically across studies. Betts and Tang (2014) estimate that typically over 90 percent of the variation in effect sizes across studies reflects genuine differences in impacts, rather than statistical noise. Figure 7.2, from Betts and Tang, provides one illustration of this point. This histogram shows that, although math effect sizes in elementary school studies are generally positive, they are sometimes negative, and the range is high. This is an intriguing finding because it suggests that charter schools themselves can vary dramatically in their effectiveness. I return to this issue in the next two sections.

Betts and Tang (2014) test for patterns in the effect sizes across studies. Particularly interesting is the possibility that the analysis methods could lead to different effect sizes. They compare effect sizes for lottery studies,

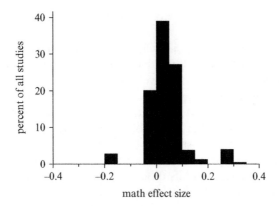

Note: Studies are weighted by the weights resulting from a random-effects meta-analysis.

Source: Adapted from Betts and Tang (2014).

Figure 7.2   Histogram of math effect sizes from elementary school studies

propensity score studies, fixed-effect studies and other studies (mostly consisting of the CREDO studies that use a method somewhat similar to propensity score matching). Betts and Tang find for math, but not reading, that lottery-based and propensity score studies tend to have higher effect sizes than studies using the default "other" methods, mostly consisting of the CREDO studies. Betts and Atkinson (2012) note the relatively high estimates from lottery-based studies and conjecture that these arise because only in areas where charter schools outperform traditional public schools are charter schools popular enough to be oversubscribed, and therefore use admission lotteries. In this way, lottery-based studies may focus on areas where charter schools outperform traditional public schools by a greater degree than is true nationally. Betts and Atkinson show three cases in which lottery-based and nonexperimental estimates have been obtained for the same sets of schools. The results are similar, although the latter are sometimes slightly lower.[3]

Evidence on Types of Charter Schools That Outperform, or Settings in Which Charter Schools Outperform

Beyond attempting to find the overall average effect of attending a charter school, researchers have shown some interest in looking for heterogeneity of effects across types of charter schools or types of students. This is an extremely important question, because it helps policymakers to focus on which types of charter schools to replicate, and which to either improve or close, as well as which types of students to recruit based on observed benefits.

We are nowhere near the point where we can make nuanced delineations about types of charter schools that have the largest impact on achievement. The first obstacle is that we still have relatively few studies that describe the curriculum or pedagogical approach of individual charter schools. More generally, we lack broad-based qualitative studies that describe characteristics of large groups of charter schools. The second obstacle is simply that the literature is still far too small.

There are two exceptions to the rule that we lack evidence on whether major types of charter schools differ in their impact. First, a number of studies have examined the Knowledge is Power Program (KIPP) middle schools. KIPP is an example of a charter management organization (CMO), a nonprofit organization that manages multiple charter schools. The KIPP schools have emphasized very high expectations, character development and a "no excuses" approach. Betts and Tang (2011, 2014) perform the first two meta-analyses of the rapidly growing set of KIPP achievement studies. Betts and Tang (2014) estimate an overall effect across all the studies, and find that a student who was initially at the 50th percentile when enrolling in a KIPP charter school is predicted to rise within a single year to percentiles 56.9 and 64.6 in reading and math, respectively. These are impressive effects, based on papers that use either quite good quasi-experimental approaches or gold standard approaches that use lottery winners to create a valid control group against which to compare those admitted in the lottery. The KIPP studies from which these estimates were obtained are Woodworth et al. (2008), Tuttle et al. (2010, 2013) and Angrist et al. (2010).

The second exception to the earlier conclusion that we lack studies of specific types of charter schools is that a multi-year study of CMOs more broadly has been conducted by Furgeson et al. (2012). This study has been of great policy interest because in a sense it indicates whether we should be looking toward these management organizations to expand the charter school sector, or whether the estimated effects are similar to those of studies that include all charter schools, including the many one-of-a-kind locally managed charter schools. On average, the authors find a positive effect of attending a charter school, but this is not significantly different from zero. They also report substantial variation across CMOs. The tentative conclusion seems to be that CMOs, as a management style, are not a magic bullet; but, as shown convincingly for KIPP in other studies, they can be quite effective in some cases.

What about variations in the estimated effect of charter schools across different groups of students? Again, the literature on subgroups of students is surprisingly sparse. But two patterns seem to be emerging: black students appear to gain more from attending charter schools than do students from other racial or ethnic groups. And, in a pattern that may be closely related, charter schools in urban areas appear to outperform charter schools as a whole. Betts and Tang (2014) find evidence in favor of both these patterns. Again, we need to be cautious, because the literature on these subgroups of charter schools and subgroups of students is small.

All Studies Estimate Relative, Not Absolute, Performance

One way of understanding the significant variations in findings across studies is to conclude that charter schools, which vary in pedagogical and curricular approaches, must surely vary in quality. This explanation undoubtedly has merit.

Less well understood, but perhaps equally important, is that no matter the statistical method used, researchers are estimating the relative effectiveness of charter schools compared with nearby traditional public schools. Much of the variation in estimated effects of charter schools could very well reflect variations in the quality of local traditional public schools. This possibility seems quite likely. For instance, the relatively high effect sizes for charter schools in urban areas could mainly reflect relatively low effectiveness of traditional public schools in these locations, rather than a particularly high absolute quality of charter schools serving those areas.

IMPACT ON OUTCOMES OTHER THAN TEST SCORES

A number of papers have modeled educational attainment (such as graduation or college enrollment), and a smaller number have started to examine behavioral outcomes. Parents, and society, should care about these outcomes at least as much as test scores.

Educational Attainment

A central problem in analyzing years of education, whether a student graduates from high school or enters college, is that we observe a person's (final) level of education only once. Lottery data are especially useful in this instance, because we cannot use student fixed-effects to compare a student with themselves in such a case.

Angrist et al. (2013a) use lottery data from Boston schools to examine a range of outcomes related to postsecondary success, and they find strong evidence of a positive impact of attending any of the six charter schools in their study. Lottery winners, compared with lottery losers, were more likely to pass the high school exit examination in Massachusetts, were more likely to take an advanced placement exam and scored higher on the advanced placement calculus exam. Although lottery winners were not more likely to take the Scholastic Aptitude Test, they scored higher on it than did lottery losers. Overall postsecondary enrollment did not rise much, but there was a pronounced shift away from two-year colleges and toward four-year colleges. For instance, in two-stage least-squares models with lottery winning as the instrumental variable, the authors found that the probability of enrollment in a four-year college within 18 months of high school graduation was 17 percent higher for charter attendees than nonattendees. The estimated impacts on two-year college enrollment and any college enrollment were negative and positive, respectively, but neither effect was significant.

Dobbie and Fryer (2013) use lottery data to study impacts of winning a lottery to attend the Promise Academy in the Harlem Children's Zone. They examine a number of outcomes in addition to test scores. Lottery winners were 14 percent more likely to enroll in college than lottery losers.

The first lottery-based study of the effects of charter schools on educational attainment examines one California charter school. McClure et al. (2005) utilize admission lotteries at the Preuss School at the University of California, San Diego, to examine the effect of winning a lottery on student achievement and educational attainment. They did not find big differences in test scores between lottery winners and losers, but they did observe large differences in a variety of measures of educational attainment. First, they studied how many college preparatory courses the students completed, and found large differences emerging as early as grade 10, in favor of lottery winners.

The authors also surveyed lottery losers in the graduating class of 2005 (who had enrolled in traditional public schools in San Diego) when they reached grade 12. The survey found a striking gap in planned college attendance. Among the Preuss School attendees (the lottery winners), 90.3 percent were set to enroll in a four-year college in the fall, and 9.7 percent were planning to enroll in community college. Only 66.7 percent of respondents from the group of lottery losers planned to attend a four-year college in the fall, a gap of about 23 percent.

The remaining studies of educational attainment do not use lottery data and so potentially suffer from bias caused by omitted variables.

Zimmer et al. (2009) examine the association between educational attainment and charter school attendance in a variety of locations. One of the approaches they take to reduce potential self-selection among charter students is to focus on students who attend a charter school in grade 8, then comparing educational attainment within this subsample between students who later attend high school charter schools and those who attend traditional public high schools.

In Chicago, the authors estimate that attending a charter high school is associated with a 7 percent increase in the probability of graduating from high school and a 10 percent increase in the probability of attending a community college or four-year college. The corresponding figures for Florida are 12–15 percent and 8 percent. The limitations of this method are that we cannot be sure that limiting the analysis to students who attended charter schools in grade 8 removes unobserved variations among students who, after all, come to different decisions about whether to attend charter public high schools.

Another perhaps more convincing approach implemented by these same authors uses measures of proximity to charter schools as instrumental variables to take into account students' endogenous choice of whether to attend a charter school. These models produced even larger estimates. The probability of graduating from high school is predicted to rise when attending a charter high school by about 15 percent in Florida and about 32 percent in Chicago. The estimated changes in probability of attending a two- or four-year college are 18 percent and 14 percent in Florida and Chicago, respectively.

Furgeson et al. (2012) study charter schools in various CMOs. They find mixed results for high school graduation but strong positive effects on college enrollment for two of four CMOs for which college data were available, with 21 percent and 23 percent boosts in college enrollment relative to the matched comparison group and statistically insignificant effects for the two other CMOs.

These papers on the whole produce large positive estimated effects on educational attainment. But they cover a very limited area: a fairly large number of CMO-run charter schools, six schools in Boston, one in New York City, one school in San Diego and charter schools in Chicago and Florida.

Evidence on Attendance and Behavior

Imberman (2011) studies two behavioral outcomes: attendance and suspensions from school (combined with more serious disciplinary actions). Using data from an anonymous large urban school district, he finds significant reductions in student disciplinary infractions among those who attend charter high schools. Imberman also models the percentage attendance rate. He finds zero or positive impacts on attendance depending on the model specification.

Dobbie and Fryer (2013) use lottery data to study impacts of winning a lottery to attend the Promise Academy in the Harlem Children's Zone on a number of behavioral outcomes in addition to the college attendance outcome mentioned earlier. Lottery winners who were female were 12 percent less likely than lottery losers to become pregnant in their teens than females who lost the lottery, and lottery winners who were male were 4 percent less likely to go to jail relative to males who lost the lottery.

Conversely, Tuttle et al. (2013) use a student survey of KIPP lottery winners and losers and find some evidence that lottery winners may engage in undesirable behavior such as lying or fighting with parents more often than lottery losers. However, this finding involves self-reports, and the authors point out that KIPP students may simply be trained to be more open about admitting such behaviors.

This literature is obviously very small, but the first two papers outlined above both find evidence that charter school attendance is associated with better noncognitive outcomes.

ARE THERE COMPETITIVE EFFECTS OR PEER EFFECTS ON TRADITIONAL PUBLIC SCHOOLS?

This section considers two separate but related questions. First, it considers the concerns of some critics of charter schools that charter schools will "skim off" the highest-achieving students from traditional public schools. This matters because if peers influence each other in schools, as evidence suggests they might, then charter schools could aggravate inequality by reducing average peer achievement for those students left behind in traditional public schools.[4] Second, as mentioned earlier, the economic theory of markets suggests that competition boosts efficiency. Applying that idea to charter schools, the theory implies that traditional public schools, facing new competition, will work harder to educate students well, for fear of losing students to charter schools.

This section begins with a review of the skimming question and then turns to the broader question of whether there is evidence that traditional public schools have higher achievement when faced with competitive pressures from charter schools.

Do Charter Schools Skim Off the Highest-Achieving Students?

Booker et al. (2005) examine students who moved into charter schools in Texas and in several districts in California, and compare these students' achievement before their moves to those of students in the schools they left. They find that in the California districts they study, students leaving traditional public schools have achievement very close to the average at those schools. In Texas, they find that those leaving traditional public schools have markedly lower achievement than the average at their schools. Thus, in one case they find no skimming, and in the other they find the opposite of skimming taking place.

A few papers have instead examined race. Dee and Fu (2004) examine school-level trends in Arizona and conclude that the introduction of charter schools in that state was associated with a 2 percent drop in white non-Hispanic students in traditional public schools in that state. Ross (2005) finds that 47 percent of Michigan's charter school students are African-American, compared with only 17 percent statewide. She further shows that this discrepancy is wholly due to the decision of charter school operators to locate charter schools in communities with high African-American populations.

There are more papers that consider a related but distinct question: are charter school students more or less likely to be eligible for meal assistance than are traditional public school students? Not only does this question not yield a direct answer to the issue of ability skimming, but the literature suffers from the problem that some charter schools do not participate in the federal meal assistance program due to the paperwork involved. See Loveless and Field (2009) for a brief review of this inconclusive literature.

Overall, the literature is very limited, but studies in two states suggest that charter schools attract students whose achievement is the same as or below that of traditional public school students. There is no evidence in these papers of skimming the top achievers. Two papers on race, which is a separate issue, find varying results in two different states.

Evidence on the Competitive Effects of Charter Schools on Traditional Public Schools

The literature has used one of three techniques to measure whether the presence of charter schools hastens improvements at traditional public schools. This section summarizes those methods and the findings of papers that have each method. For a more detailed review of this literature, see Betts (2009).

First, studies have used the number of charter schools within a certain distance of each traditional public school as the measure of charter competition facing each traditional public school. This approach assumes that charter schools that are relatively close to the traditional school impose far greater competitive pressure to improve than do charter schools that are further away. Sass (2006) finds in Florida that the presence of charter schools nearby was associated with gains in math achievement for individual students in traditional public schools, but no effects emerged for reading. Bifulco and Ladd (2006) find no effects using a similar approach in North Carolina. Buddin and Zimmer (2005) examine five California school districts, again using a similar approach, and find no competitive effects. Bettinger (2005) studies the same question in Michigan, and finds no effects. But a weakness of this last study is that it does not follow individual students over time. Suppose that charter schools attract relatively high-performing students from a local school, which lowers average test scores at the local school in a mechanical way. This would bias down the estimated impact on the local school. Of course, the bias could go the other way.

A second approach involves measuring the net number of students who have left a given traditional public school to enroll in charter schools, expressed as a proportion of current attendance. A carefully executed example of this work, by Booker et al. (2004), finds significant increases in both math and reading achievement at the traditional public school as the net outflow of students rises.

A third approach involves comparing districts with high shares of students enrolled in charter schools against districts with low shares. There is obviously an apples and oranges issue here, in that the district that is more welcoming to charters may differ in unobserved ways that might directly affect achievement. The aforementioned paper by Booker et al. (2004) also employs this approach using Texas school districts. It finds, using student-level data, that charter school enrollment share in the given district is correlated with gains in achievement among individual students in traditional public schools. Two papers using slightly weaker research designs, due to data limitations, point roughly in the same direction. Hoxby (2003) finds positive competitive effects on traditional public schools in Michigan. Eberts and Hollenbeck (2001) also study Michigan schools and find mixed, but more often than not positive, competitive effects.

Betts (2009) studies this "competitive effects" literature in greater detail. That review article notes a number of empirical challenges that each of the three methods described above must deal with, but concludes that overall this small but growing literature suggests that there may indeed be positive competitive effects of charter schools on nearby traditional public schools. The literature is far from conclusive, though, at the current time.

KEY RESEARCH NEEDS RELEVANT TO POLICY

In almost two decades of research, we have learned a great deal about the contributions charter schools are making to student learning. The effects clearly vary dramatically across charter schools and host districts. The research and policy communities could significantly improve both the base of research knowledge and the governance of charter schools by working together more closely. Here is a selective list of suggestions that, if taken, could improve both our understanding of the impact of charter schools and policymakers' ability to discern between charter school models that are working and should be replicated, and models that should either be reformed or curtailed.

Research Suggestions

The small but growing literature on the impact of charter schools on educational attainment and behavioral outcomes shows quite promising results. This area of research deserves much more attention.

There remains some uncertainty about whether the statistical method used can influence the outcomes of the study. A number of studies have tried to compare two or more methods (for example, Betts et al. 2010; Tuttle et al. 2013; Davis and Raymond 2012). We need more of these studies to learn more definitively whether biases in some nonexperimental studies are small or large, and whether the biases tend to be positive or negative.

The evidence of large variations in charter school impacts on achievement is growing. This undoubtedly partly reflects variations in the effectiveness of traditional public schools in the charter school's immediate area. But more interestingly from a policy perspective, it also probably reflects variation in the absolute quality of charter schools as well. The research community is still struggling to find a concise yet insightful way of cataloguing the many flavors of charter schools. KIPP and other "no excuses" schools are one emergent theme. Researchers could do much to learn what makes some charter schools outperform others. But to do so will require mixed methods that combine rigorous quantitative research with surveys and observational studies of how charter schools work on a day-to-day basis.

Policy Suggestions

Deciding whether to renew a school's charter based on test score levels, rather than student-level gains, does not make much sense. But many districts are taking precisely such an approach. Researchers and policymakers could work together so that districts and other organizations overseeing charter schools would begin to use student value-added measures to evaluate charter schools.

As called for by Betts and Atkinson (2012), states could amend laws to require charter schools to provide details of school choice lotteries to the chartering authority. This simple policy change would make lottery data more widely collected, and could make lottery-based studies possible for a far wider set of charter schools than is currently the case.

NOTES

1. For a more detailed development of the ideas in this section, see Betts (2005).
2. These include Hoxby and Rockoff (2005), Chicago; McClure et al. (2005), one school in San Diego; Hoxby et al. (2009), New York City; Abdulkadiroglu et al. (2009), Boston; Gleason et al. (2010), a national sample of middle schools; Angrist et al. (2010), one school in Massachusetts; Dobbie and Fryer (2011), one school in New York City; and Angrist et al. (2013b), 23 schools in Massachusetts.
3. The other main pattern Betts and Tang (2014) find is that, for both reading and math achievement, effect sizes tend to be higher for middle school studies than for studies that combine elementary and middle schools.
4. See Sacerdote (2011) for a review of the evidence that students can influence each others' educational outcomes.

REFERENCES

Abdulkadiroglu, Atila, Josh Angrist, Sarah Cohodes, Susan Dynarski, Jon Fullerton, et al. (2009), *Informing the Debate: Comparing Boston's Charter, Pilot and Traditional Schools*, Boston, MA: Boston Foundation.

Angrist, Joshua D., Sarah R. Cohodes, Susan M. Dynarski, Parag A. Pathak and Christopher R. Walters (2013a), "Stand and deliver: effects of Boston's charter high schools on college preparation, entry and choice," NBER Working Paper 19275, Cambridge, MA: National Bureau of Economic Research.

Angrist, Joshua D., Susan M. Dynarski, Thomas J. Kane, Parag A. Pathak and Christopher R. Walters (2010), "Inputs and impacts in charter schools: KIPP Lynn," *American Economic Review*, **100**, 1–5.

Angrist, Joshua D., Parag A. Pathak and Christopher R. Walters (2013b), "Explaining charter school effectiveness," *American Economic Journal: Applied Economics*, **5**(4), 1–27.

Balboni, E., E. Rainer, C. Chae and K. Olsen (2007), *2007 Charter School Facility Finance Landscape*, New York: Local Initiatives Support Corporation, available at www.issuelab.org/resources/8090/8090.pdf.

Bettinger, Eric P. (2005), "The effect of charter schools on charter students and public schools," *Economics of Education Review*, **24**(2), 133–47.

Betts, Julian R. (2005), "The economic theory of school choice," in Julian R. Betts and Tom Loveless (eds), *Getting Choice Right: Ensuring Equity and Efficiency in Education Policy*, Washington, DC: Brookings Institution Press, pp. 14–39.

Betts, Julian R. (2009), "The competitive effects of charter schools on traditional public schools," in Mark Berends, Matthew G. Springer, Dale Ballou and

Herbert Walberg (eds), *Handbook of Research on School Choice*, New York: Routledge, pp. 195–208.

Betts, Julian R. and Richard C. Atkinson (2012), "Better research needed on the impact of charter schools," *Science*, **335**(6065), 171–72.

Betts, Julian R., Dan Goldhaber and Larry Rosenstock (2005), "The supply side of school choice," in Julian R. Betts and Tom Loveless (eds), *Getting Choice Right: Ensuring Equity and Efficiency in Education Policy*, Washington, DC: Brookings Institution Press, pp. 61–84.

Betts, Julian R. and Y. Emily Tang (2008), *Value-Added and Experimental Studies of the Effect of Charter Schools on Student Achievement: A Literature Review*, Bothell, WA: National Charter School Research Project, Center on Reinventing Public Education, available at www.crpe.org.

Betts, Julian R. and Y. Emily Tang (2011), *The Effect of Charter Schools on Student Achievement: A Meta-Analysis of the Literature*, Bothell, WA: National Charter School Research Project, Center on Reinventing Public Education, available at www.crpe.org.

Betts, Julian R. and Y. Emily Tang (2014), *A Meta-Analysis of the Literature on the Effect of Charter Schools on Student Achievement*, Bothell, WA: National Charter School Research Project, Center on Reinventing Public Education, available at www.crpe.org.

Betts, Julian R., Y. Emily Tang and Andrew C. Zau (2010), "Madness in the method? A critical analysis of popular methods of estimating the effect of charter schools on student achievement," in Paul T. Hill and Julian R. Betts (eds), *Taking Measure of Charter Schools: Better Assessments, Better Policymaking, Better Schools*, Lanham, MD: Rowman & Littlefield Publishers, pp. 15–32.

Bifulco, Robert and Helen F. Ladd (2006), "The impacts of charter schools on student achievement: evidence from North Carolina," *Education Finance and Policy*, **1**(1), 50–90.

Booker, Kevin, Scott M. Gilpatric, Timothy Gronberg and Dennis Jansen (2004),"The effect of charter competition on traditional public school students in Texas," unpublished paper, Private Enterprise Research Center at Texas A&M University.

Booker, Kevin, Ron Zimmer and Richard Buddin (2005), "The effect of schools on school peer composition," Working Paper WR-306-EDU, Santa Monica, CA: RAND Corporation.

Buddin, Richard and Ron Zimmer (2005), "Is charter school competition in California improving the performance of traditional public schools?" Working Paper WR-297-EDU, Santa Monica, CA: RAND Corporation.

Christie, Kathy, Maria Millard, Jennifer Thomsen and Micah Wixom (2014), *Trends in State Charter School Laws: Authorizers, Caps, Performance-Based Closures and Virtual Schools*, Denver, CO: Education Commission of the States, available at www.ecs.org.

Davis, Devora H. and Margaret E. Raymond (2012), "Choices for studying choice: assessing charter school effectiveness using two quasi-experimental methods," *Economics of Education Review*, **31**, 225–36.

Dee, Thomas and Helen Fu (2004), "Do charter schools skim students or drain resources?" *Economics of Education Review*, **23**(3), 259–71.

Dobbie, Will and Roland Fryer, Jr (2011), "Are high quality schools enough to close the achievement gap? Evidence from a social experiment in Harlem," *American Economic Journal: Applied Economics*, **3**(3), 158–87.

Dobbie, Will and Roland Fryer, Jr (2013), "The medium-term impacts of high-achieving charter schools on non-test score outcomes," NBER Working Paper 19581, Cambridge, MA: National Bureau of Economic Research.

Eberts, Randall W. and Kevin M. Hollenbeck (2001), "An examination of student achievement in Michigan charter schools," Staff Working Paper 01-68, Kalamazoo, MI: Upjohn Institute.

Furgeson, Joshua, Brian Gill, Joshua Haimson, Alexandra Killewald, Moira McCullough, et al. (2012), *Charter-School Management Organizations: Diverse Strategies and Diverse Student Impacts*, Princeton, NJ: Mathematica Policy Research, available at www.mathematica-mpr.com.

Gleason, Philip, Melissa Clark, Christina Clark Tuttle and Emily Dwoyer (2010), *The Evaluation of Charter School Impacts: Final Report (NCEE 2010-4029)*, Washington, DC: National Center for Education Evaluation and Regional Assistance, Institute of Education Sciences, US Department of Education.

Hanushek, E., D. Jamison, E. Jamison and L. Woessmann (2008), "Education and economic growth," *Education Next*, **8**(2), 62–70.

Hanushek, E.A. and L. Woessmann (2008), "The role of cognitive skills in economic development," *Journal of Economic Literature*, **46**(3), 607–68.

Hoxby, Caroline M. (2003), "School choice and school productivity: could school choice be a rising tide that lifts all boats?" in Caroline Hoxby (ed.), *The Economics of School Choice*, Chicago, IL: University of Chicago Press, pp. 287–341.

Hoxby, Caroline M., Sonali Murarka and Jenny Kang (2009), *How New York City's Charter Schools Affect Achievement*, Cambridge, MA: New York City Charter Schools Evaluation Project.

Hoxby, Caroline M. and Jonah E. Rockoff (2005), "Findings from the city of big shoulders: younger students learn more in charter schools," *Education Next*, **5**(4), 52–58.

Imberman, Scott (2011), "Achievement and behavior in charter schools: drawing a more complete picture," *Review of Economics and Statistics*, **93**(2), 416–35.

Loveless, Tom and Katharyn Field (2009), "Perspectives on charter schools," in Mark Berends, Matthew G. Springer, Dale Ballou and Herbert Walberg (eds), *Handbook of Research on School Choice*, New York: Routledge, pp. 99–114.

McClure, Larry, Betsy Strick, Rachel Jacob-Almeida and Christopher Reicher (2005), *The Preuss School at UCSD: School Characteristics and Students' Achievement*, La Jolla, CA: University of California, San Diego, Center for Research on Educational Equity, Assessment and Teaching Excellence, available at http://create.ucsd.edu/_files/publications/PreussReportDecember2005.pdf.

Ross, Karen E. (2005), "Charter schools and integration: the experience in Michigan," in Julian R. Betts and Tom Loveless (eds), *Getting Choice Right: Ensuring Equity and Efficiency in Education Policy*, Washington, DC: Brookings Institution Press, pp. 146–75.

Sacerdote, Bruce (2011), "Peer effects in education: how might they work, how big are they and how much do we know thus far?" in Erik A. Hanushek, Stephen Machin and Ludger Woessmann (eds), *Handbook of the Economics of Education, Volume 3*, Amsterdam: North-Holland, pp. 249–77.

Sass, Tim R. (2006), "Charter schools and student achievement in Florida," *Education Finance and Policy*, **1**(1), 91–122.

Snyder, Thomas S. and Sally A. Dillow (2013), *Digest of Education Statistics 2013 (NCES 2014-015)*, Washington, DC: National Center for Education Statistics, Institute of Education Sciences, US Department of Education.

Speakman, Sheree, Chester E. Finn Jr. and Bryan Hassel (2005), *Charter School Funding: Inequity's Next Frontier*, Washington, DC: Thomas B. Fordham Foundation, available at http://edexcellence.net/publications/charterschoolfund ing.html.
Stoddard, Christina and Sean P. Corcoran (2007), "The political economy of school choice: support for charter schools across states and school districts," *Journal of Urban Economics*, **62**(1), 27–54.
Tiebout, Charles M. (1956), "A pure theory of local expenditures," *Journal of Political Economy*, **64**(5), 416–24.
Tuttle, Christina Clark, Brian Gill, Philip Gleason, Virginia Knechtel, Ira Nichols-Barrer and Alexandra Resch (2013), *KIPP Middle Schools: Impacts on Achievement and Other Outcomes. Final Report*, Washington, DC: Mathematica Policy Research.
Tuttle, Christina Clark, Bing-ru Teh, Ira Nichols-Barrer, Brian P. Gill and Philip Gleason (2010), *Student Characteristics and Achievement in 22 KIPP Middle Schools*, Washington, DC: Mathematica Policy Research.
Wong, Kenneth K. and Shayna Klopott (2009), "Politics and governance in charter schools," in Mark Berends, Matthew G. Springer, Dale Ballou and Herbert Walberg (eds), *Handbook of Research on School Choice*, New York: Routledge, pp. 115–35.
Woodworth, Katrina R., Jane L. David, Roneeta Guha, Haiwen Wang and Alejandra Lopez-Torkos (2008), *San Francisco Bay Area KIPP Schools: A Study of Early Implementation and Achievement, Final Report*, Menlo Park, CA: SRI International.
Zimmer, Ron, Brian Gill, Kevin Booker, Stephane Lavertu, Tim R. Sass and John Witte (2009), *Charter Schools in Eight States: Effects on Achievement, Attainment, Integration, and Competition*, Santa Monica, CA: RAND Corporation.

8. Does private school make a difference? Evidence from autonomous private high school policy in Korea

Yoonsoo Park

INTRODUCTION

Are private schools more effective in educating students? Ever since Coleman et al. (1982) reported a large performance gap between students in private schools and those in public schools, this question has long been discussed among empirical researchers in the social sciences. However, a clear answer to this question has not been reached yet. For example, Evans and Schwab (1995) and Neal (1997) report large positive effects of attending private schools, while Altonji et al. (2005a, 2005b) cast doubt on the validity of the empirical strategy of those two studies and conclude that the evidence is limited.

Recently, the long-standing academic debate has arisen again among education policymakers and interest groups in Korea. After the High School Equalization Act of 1974, the Korean government equalized curricula, teachers and facilities of high schools in most cities. Under the equalization policy, private high schools were required to operate in a way very similar to public high schools. In 2010, the government partially deregulated the equalization policy by granting a certain level of autonomy to some selected private high schools. These schools are called "autonomous private high schools" (APH schools), which are essentially the first "real private" high schools in Korea since 1974. Over the years since their introduction, there has been continued public interest as to whether the APH schools are more effective in improving student outcomes than regular "equalized" (private or public) high schools.

This chapter contributes to both the economic literature and the education policy in Korea by examining the effectiveness of APH school attendance on educational outcomes of students. In order to isolate a causal effect of the APH schools, I use birth order of students as an instrumental variable for APH school attendance, under the assumptions that first-born students have a higher chance of attending the APH schools than their later-born peers, and that birth order does not affect educational outcomes of students directly, other than through affecting parental educational investment decision. Applying this idea to the three-year panel data, following students who entered high schools in 2010 over the period 2010–12, I find that the APH school attendance substantially improves levels of student satisfaction compared with those of regular high schools. However, I do not find any clear evidence that APH school attendance improves achievement test scores, suggesting that the observed large academic performance gaps between APH school students and regular high school students are largely driven by sample selectivity.

INSTITUTIONAL BACKGROUND AND RELATED STUDIES

In 1974 the Korean government introduced the regulation to equalize high schools in large cities, in order to reduce the excessive competition to enter prestigious high schools and to enhance educational equity. Virtually all high schools, either private or public, were subject to this regulation. Consequently, there was virtually no difference between private high schools and public high schools in Korea after 1974, which raised serious public concerns over the limited diversity of education in the schools and lack of incentives to produce high-quality educational service among schools. To resolve these issues, the government partially deregulated the equalization policy by introducing the APH schools in 2010. As the name suggests, the APH schools are allowed to manage their own affairs autonomously, including developing school curricula and recruiting students, similar to typical private high schools in the United States. Over the years after the establishment of the APH schools, however, there was heated debate as to whether the APH schools should be maintained or not. Advocates argue that the APH schools can improve the overall quality of education by guaranteeing students more school choice opportunities and thus providing non-APH schools with greater incentives to compete with APH schools. On the other hand, opponents argue that the introduction of APH schools will extend the education gap between those who can afford the relatively high tuition costs of the APH schools and those who cannot.

In spite of these heated debates, during the first four years after their introduction only one study attempted to evaluate the effectiveness of attending APH schools in terms of educational outcomes. Kim et al.

(2012) compare changes in test scores of APH school students between the first year and second year of high school with those of regular high school students over the same period. They find that the effect of attending the APH schools on test scores is modest. They name this approach a "difference-in-differences" strategy, although it actually is not because the baseline period of their strategy is the first year of high school, when the treatment of interest (entering the APH schools) has already been assigned.

This chapter helps to remedy the lack of empirical evidence on the effectiveness of the APH schools, by estimating the causal effect of attending the APH schools on educational outcomes.

DATA

The data used for this study are from the 2010 Seoul Education Longitudinal Study (or SELS 2010), which surveys 5200 fourth-graders, 4600 seventh-graders, and 6600 tenth-graders within the Seoul area annually starting in 2010. The basic structure of this survey is similar to that of the Education Longitudinal Study of 2002 in the United States (US). Like the US study, SELS 2010 surveys not only students but also their parents, teachers and school principals to measure cognitive, emotional and physical changes of students from various perspectives. Data from the baseline survey (collected in 2010) and the two follow-up surveys (collected in 2011 and 2012) are available.

There are two advantages of using SELS 2010 rather than other surveys for this study. First, more APH schools were introduced in Seoul than in other regions: 25 out of 49 in 2013 were in Seoul. SELS 2010 focuses on students within the Seoul area and is therefore a useful source of data for studying the effect of the APH schools. Second, students from the baseline year (2010, which was the first year when the APH schools started recruiting students) had completed their high school education by the end of the study. Their data allow me to investigate the effect of APH school attendance over the entire high school years for the first cohort of the APH school entrants.

I exclude students who are enrolled in vocational high schools and special-purpose high schools from my sample. Such schools differ considerably from regular high schools, as they pursue specific objectives: the former providing vocational education, and the latter training students in specialized areas such as arts, foreign languages and sciences. For a similar reason, I exclude students receiving special education (students with disabilities) or gifted education. Since the main objective of this study is to evaluate school effect, I also exclude students who moved to different schools.[1] Finally, I restrict my sample to students who have at least one sibling in order to make use of birth order as an instrumental variable for APH school attendance. Consequently, my estimation sample consists of 9315 observations from the three-year (2010–12) surveys of 3642 students.

Table 8.1 summarizes the descriptive statistics of my sample. Test scores are standardized by subtracting means and dividing by standard deviations. The top rows of the table reveal that students attending the APH schools tend to score substantially higher than their peers in regular high schools by 0.500, 0.646 and 0.589 standard deviations in Korean, math and English, respectively. However, APH students were already performing better than regular high school students even before they entered high school. For example, 20.7 percent of APH students reported that their math grades before entering high school were "excellent," whereas only 10 percent of the regular high school students did so. This indicates that any empirical approach that fails to account for differences in cognitive abilities between the two groups would not successfully evaluate the causal effect of APH school attendance.

Table 8.1 also shows that students in APH schools are more satisfied with their schools than those in regular high schools. The student satisfaction index in Table 8.1 is computed by averaging students' answers to five-scale questionnaires about the following points: (1) school enhances students' ability to study; (2) school identifies and develops students' specialty and aptitude; (3) teachers are eager to teach students; (4) school curricula are tailored to each student for their level; (5) school provides individual consultation and career guidance for each student; (6) school provides comfortable facilities and environment for students to study; and (7) school makes efforts to ensure the safety of students. In order to easily compare the student satisfaction index with the achievement test scores, I standardize the student satisfaction index by subtracting means and dividing by standard deviations.

The proportion of female students is substantially different between regular high schools (47.8 percent) and APH schools (23.7 percent). This is largely because most APH schools in Seoul are male-only. Among 13 APH schools established in 2010 within the Seoul area, only one was female-only, three were co-educational and the other nine were male-only. Additionally, first-born students are more prevalent in APH schools (52.0 percent) than in regular high schools (38.0 percent). Given that tuition levels of the APH schools are about 2.5 to 3 times more expensive than those of regular high schools, the prevalence of first-born children in the APH schools could be explained by the well-known empirical regularity that Korean parents tend to invest more on educating their first-born

Table 8.1 Summary statistics

Variable	Regular high school			APH school		
	N	Mean	SD	N	Mean	SD
Test score (Z score)						
Korean	9247	−0.143	0.955	1034	0.357	0.871
Math	9002	−0.199	0.888	1010	0.448	0.972
English	9265	−0.203	0.904	1036	0.386	0.873
Student satisfaction index (Z score)	9310	−0.142	0.932	1039	0.398	1.022
Predetermined grade (yes = 1)						
Korean						
Excellent	9264	0.097	0.296	1033	0.181	0.385
Good	9264	0.282	0.450	1033	0.378	0.485
Average	9264	0.441	0.497	1033	0.351	0.478
Fair	9264	0.143	0.350	1033	0.072	0.258
Poor	9264	0.037	0.189	1033	0.018	0.134
Math						
Excellent	9279	0.100	0.300	1039	0.207	0.405
Good	9279	0.203	0.402	1039	0.306	0.461
Average	9279	0.300	0.458	1039	0.301	0.459
Fair	9279	0.252	0.434	1039	0.119	0.324
Poor	9279	0.145	0.352	1039	0.066	0.249
English						
Excellent	9271	0.116	0.320	1039	0.225	0.418
Good	9271	0.240	0.427	1039	0.268	0.443
Average	9271	0.317	0.465	1039	0.340	0.474
Fair	9271	0.223	0.416	1039	0.133	0.340
Poor	9271	0.104	0.305	1039	0.035	0.183
Female (yes = 1)	9311	0.478	0.500	1037	0.237	0.426
Number of siblings	9272	2.211	0.476	1040	2.148	0.401
First-born (yes = 1)	9276	0.380	0.485	1040	0.520	0.500
Disabled (yes = 1)	9281	0.035	0.183	1037	0.024	0.153
Single parent (yes = 1)	9288	0.123	0.329	1039	0.113	0.316
Father's education (yes = 1)						
Less than high school	8951	0.041	0.199	989	0.015	0.122
High school graduate	8951	0.341	0.474	989	0.207	0.406
Some college	8951	0.101	0.301	989	0.059	0.235
College graduate	8951	0.412	0.492	989	0.508	0.500
Graduate school or more	8951	0.105	0.306	989	0.211	0.408
Mother's education (yes = 1)						
Less than high school	9130	0.052	0.222	1017	0.009	0.094
High school graduate	9130	0.510	0.500	1017	0.349	0.477
Some college	9130	0.103	0.304	1017	0.107	0.309
College graduate	9130	0.300	0.458	1017	0.445	0.497
Graduate school or more	9130	0.035	0.184	1017	0.089	0.286

Table 8.1 (continued)

Variable	Regular high school			APH school		
	N	Mean	SD	N	Mean	SD
Father's age (yes = 1)						
49 or younger	8927	0.010	0.101	992	0.000	0.000
50 to 59	8927	0.697	0.460	992	0.674	0.469
60 or older	8927	0.293	0.455	992	0.326	0.469
Mother's age (yes = 1)						
49 or younger	9185	0.041	0.199	1026	0.026	0.160
50 to 59	9185	0.855	0.352	1026	0.846	0.361
60 or older	9185	0.104	0.305	1026	0.128	0.334
Free lunch (yes = 1)	9315	0.106	0.308	1040	0.084	0.277
Monthly income (in 10 000 Korean won)	8578	471.1	516.4	971	615.3	657.8
Parents' employment (yes = 1)						
Only father employed	9264	0.397	0.489	1032	0.468	0.499
Only mother employed	9264	0.087	0.282	1032	0.067	0.250
Both employed	9264	0.505	0.500	1032	0.454	0.498
Neither employed	9264	0.010	0.101	1032	0.011	0.103
Hours of self-directed study (weekly, hours)						
Korean	8578	3.119	2.203	991	3.928	2.394
Math	8724	3.893	2.675	1006	5.485	2.616
English	8718	3.609	2.381	998	4.584	2.459
Type of math exam (science major = 1)	9282	0.250	0.433	1039	0.360	0.480
School characteristics						
Private school (yes = 1)	9315	0.607	0.488	1040	0.000	0.000
Autonomous public school (yes = 1)	9315	0.066	0.248	1040	0.000	0.000
Co-educational school (yes = 1)	9315	0.314	0.464	1040	0.380	0.486
Grade enrollment size	9315	455.6	117.4	1040	353.7	72.78
Class size	9315	36.05	4.135	1040	32.81	2.846
Survey year (yes = 1)						
Year 1 (2010)	9315	0.352	0.478	1040	0.348	0.477
Year 2 (2011)	9315	0.332	0.471	1040	0.330	0.470
Year 3 (2012)	9315	0.316	0.465	1040	0.322	0.468

Notes: Test scores and student satisfaction index are standardized by subtracting means and dividing by standard deviations.

than on later-born children (Ryu and Kang 2013). Using this tendency of parental educational investment decisions, I try to isolate a causal effect of attending APH schools, which will be discussed in the next section. Finally, the remaining part of the table clearly shows that students in APH schools tend to have better family backgrounds than those in regular high schools. For example, parents of APH school students tend to have higher levels of educational attainment and monthly income than those of the regular school students.

EMPIRICAL ANALYSIS

Effects on Test Scores

I begin by estimating the following equation:

$$Y_{ist} = \beta_0 + \beta_1 APH_s + X_{it}\beta_2 + W_{st}\beta_3 + \rho_t + \varepsilon_{ist} \qquad (8.1)$$

where Y_{ist} indicates test scores of student i of school s in year t, which is standardized by subtracting the mean and dividing by the standard deviation. APH_s denotes a dummy variable that takes 1 if school s is an APH school and 0 otherwise. X_{it} refers to individual characteristics of student i in year t, such as dummies for female, being physically challenged, free lunch recipients, being raised by a single parent, self-reported academic performance before entering high schools (five categories), parents' age (three categories), parents' employment status (four categories), parents' educational attainment (five categories), hours of self-directed learning (right-censored at eight hours per week; spent on the subject for which test scores are measured), and household monthly income. W_{st} refers to school characteristics of school s in year t such as dummies for private schools,[2] autonomous public schools, co-educational schools, class size and grade enrollment size. Finally, ρ_t and ε_{is} represent the year fixed effect and an error term, respectively. I estimate equation 8.1 by the ordinary least squares (OLS) method, clustering standard errors at school level.[3]

Tables 8.2, 8.3 and 8.4 summarize the estimation results of equation 8.1 for Korean language, math and English language test scores, respectively. In each of the three tables, column (1) shows the simple mean difference in standardized test scores between APH school students and regular school students, while columns (2) and (3) report the estimated OLS coefficients when individual and school characteristics are controlled, respectively.

These three tables show in common that students in the APH schools outperform their peers in regular high schools across all subjects. The simple mean differences in test scores between APH school students and regular high school students are larger in math (0.646) than in Korean (0.500) and English (0.589). However, when all the observable

Table 8.2   OLS estimation results for Korean test score in Korea

Dependent variable: Korean test score (Z score)	Specification		
	(1)	(2)	(3)
APH school attendance	0.500***	0.315***	0.536***
	(0.089)	(0.083)	(0.085)
Pregrade for Korean = poor		−0.486***	−0.474***
		(0.068)	(0.070)
Pregrade for Korean = fair		−0.366***	−0.371***
		(0.031)	(0.030)
Pregrade for Korean = good		0.360***	0.363***
		(0.035)	(0.035)
Pregrade for Korean = excellent		0.555***	0.567***
		(0.051)	(0.051)
Female		0.362***	0.399***
		(0.052)	(0.045)
Number of siblings		0.012	0.009
		(0.028)	(0.028)
Disabled		−0.112	−0.112*
		(0.070)	(0.066)
Having single parent		−0.008	−0.003
		(0.047)	(0.047)
Father's education < high school graduate		−0.066	−0.051
		(0.057)	(0.055)
Father's education = some college		−0.001	−0.013
		(0.040)	(0.040)
Father's education = college graduate		0.097**	0.073*
		(0.041)	(0.037)
Father's education > college graduate		0.188***	0.155***
		(0.060)	(0.058)
Mother's education < high school graduate		−0.084	−0.085
		(0.065)	(0.061)
Mother's education = some college		0.078	0.069
		(0.049)	(0.048)
Mother's education = college graduate		0.080**	0.069*
		(0.038)	(0.037)
Mother's education > college graduate		0.149*	0.123*
		(0.077)	(0.073)
Father's age < 50		0.110	0.106
		(0.165)	(0.164)
Father's age ≥ 60		−0.054*	−0.041
		(0.032)	(0.030)
Mother's age < 50		−0.159**	−0.136**
		(0.070)	(0.066)

Table 8.2   (continued)

Dependent variable: Korean test score (Z score)	Specification		
	(1)	(2)	(3)
Mother's age ≥ 60		0.053	0.048
		(0.047)	(0.047)
Free lunch recipient		−0.045	−0.041
		(0.045)	(0.046)
Family income (monthly, in million won)		−0.003	−0.004
		(0.003)	(0.003)
Only mother employed		0.032	0.052
		(0.051)	(0.050)
Mother and father employed		0.017	0.029
		(0.029)	(0.027)
Neither mother nor father employed		−0.381***	−0.374***
		(0.124)	(0.122)
Hours of self-study for Korean		0.044***	0.041***
		(0.006)	(0.006)
Science-oriented track		0.182***	0.171***
		(0.038)	(0.036)
Year 2011		−0.121***	−0.087***
		(0.030)	(0.030)
Year 2012		−0.174***	−0.131***
		(0.044)	(0.043)
Private school			0.131**
			(0.063)
Autonomous public school			0.381***
			(0.109)
Co-educational school			−0.130*
			(0.071)
Grade enrollment (in 1000 students)			0.136
			(0.335)
Class size			0.021**
			(0.009)
Observations	10 281	8120	8120
R-squared	0.025	0.220	0.237

Note: Huber–White robust standard errors allowing for unrestricted error correlation within schools are in parentheses. *** $p < 0.01$, ** $p < 0.05$, * $p < 0.1$.

characteristics are controlled for, the test score gaps are larger in Korean (0.536) and English (0.557) than in math (0.381).

Of course, it is hard to justify that the OLS estimation results in the three tables suggest that APH school attendance has a positive effect on

Table 8.3   OLS estimation results for math test score in Korea

Dependent variable: math test score (Z score)	Specification		
	(1)	(2)	(3)
APH school attendance	0.646***	0.251*	0.381***
	(0.165)	(0.127)	(0.125)
Pregrade for math = poor '		−0.358***	−0.351***
		(0.033)	(0.034)
Pregrade for math = fair		−0.245***	−0.245***
		(0.029)	(0.030)
Pregrade for math = good		0.347***	0.352***
		(0.037)	(0.038)
Pregrade for math = excellent		0.594***	0.609***
		(0.048)	(0.048)
Female		0.036	0.060
		(0.043)	(0.040)
Number of siblings		−0.004	−0.006
		(0.024)	(0.024)
Disabled		−0.084*	−0.085
		(0.050)	(0.051)
Having single parent		0.037	0.041
		(0.039)	(0.040)
Father's education < high school graduate		−0.044	−0.040
		(0.055)	(0.056)
Father's education = some college		0.013	0.010
		(0.038)	(0.037)
Father's education = college graduate		0.078**	0.061**
		(0.031)	(0.029)
Father's education > college graduate		0.262***	0.246***
		(0.051)	(0.052)
Mother's education < high school graduate		0.016	0.025
		(0.054)	(0.056)
Mother's education = some college		0.002	0.001
		(0.047)	(0.046)
Mother's education = college graduate		0.117***	0.108***
		(0.038)	(0.036)
Mother's education > college graduate		0.133*	0.113
		(0.075)	(0.075)
Father's age < 50		−0.042	−0.046
		(0.141)	(0.140)
Father's age ≥ 60		−0.004	−0.003
		(0.022)	(0.021)
Mother's age < 50		−0.071	−0.051
		(0.060)	(0.060)

Table 8.3   (continued)

Dependent variable: math test score (Z score)	Specification		
	(1)	(2)	(3)
Mother's age ≥ 60		0.018	0.022
		(0.035)	(0.035)
Free lunch recipient		−0.059*	−0.056
		(0.034)	(0.035)
Family income (monthly, in million won)		0.003	0.002
		(0.002)	(0.002)
Only mother employed		−0.065	−0.056
		(0.048)	(0.049)
Mother and father employed		−0.050**	−0.042*
		(0.025)	(0.024)
Neither employed		−0.157	−0.151
		(0.122)	(0.120)
Hours of self-study for math		0.078***	0.076***
		(0.005)	(0.005)
Science-oriented track		0.213***	0.207***
		(0.033)	(0.033)
Year 2011		−0.147***	−0.125***
		(0.028)	(0.030)
Year 2012		−0.195***	−0.169***
		(0.031)	(0.030)
Private school			0.054
			(0.052)
Autonomous public school			0.073
			(0.081)
Co-educational school			−0.031
			(0.064)
Grade enrollment (in 1000)			0.462*
			(0.260)
Class size			0.008
			(0.009)
Observations	10012	8075	8075
R-squared	0.045	0.352	0.359

Note: Huber–White robust standard errors allowing for unrestricted error correlation within schools are in parentheses. *** $p < 0.01$, ** $p < 0.05$, * $p < 0.1$.

academic performance of students. Since students choose to apply for the APH schools by themselves, there would be a number of unobserved differences between APH school students and regular high school students. For example, students who choose to enter the APH schools might have

Table 8.4   OLS Estimation results for English test score in Korea

Dependent variable: English test score (Z score)	Specification		
	(1)	(2)	(3)
APH school attendance	0.589***	0.312***	0.557***
	(0.153)	(0.116)	(0.129)
Pregrade for English = poor		−0.445***	−0.435***
		(0.041)	(0.040)
Pregrade for English = fair		−0.270***	−0.265***
		(0.032)	(0.031)
Pregrade for English = good		0.372***	0.375***
		(0.037)	(0.036)
Pregrade for English = excellent		0.612***	0.631***
		(0.047)	(0.048)
Female		0.260***	0.298***
		(0.053)	(0.046)
Number of siblings		−0.005	−0.009
		(0.027)	(0.027)
Disabled		−0.092	−0.093*
		(0.057)	(0.054)
Having single parent		0.036	0.039
		(0.043)	(0.044)
Father's education < high school graduate		−0.069	−0.053
		(0.054)	(0.052)
Father's education = some college		0.041	0.030
		(0.040)	(0.039)
Father's education = college graduate		0.139***	0.114***
		(0.032)	(0.030)
Father's education > college graduate		0.325***	0.295***
		(0.058)	(0.059)
Mother's education < high school graduate		−0.030	−0.027
		(0.060)	(0.059)
Mother's education = some college		0.072	0.066
		(0.045)	(0.044)
Mother's education = college graduate		0.171***	0.159***
		(0.039)	(0.036)
Mother's education > college graduate		0.208***	0.180**
		(0.071)	(0.071)
Father's age < 50		−0.086	−0.086
		(0.118)	(0.111)
Father's age ≥ 60		0.013	0.019
		(0.027)	(0.025)
Mother's age < 50		−0.043	−0.029
		(0.056)	(0.053)

Table 8.4   (continued)

Dependent variable: English test score (Z score)	Specification		
	(1)	(2)	(3)
Mother's age ≥ 60		0.036	0.036
		(0.042)	(0.041)
Free lunch recipient		−0.039	−0.038
		(0.036)	(0.037)
Family income (monthly, in million won)		0.004	0.003
		(0.003)	(0.003)
Only mother employed		−0.100**	−0.081*
		(0.050)	(0.048)
Mother and father employed		−0.038*	−0.026
		(0.021)	(0.020)
Neither employed		−0.207*	−0.204*
		(0.112)	(0.110)
Hours of self-study for English		0.059***	0.055***
		(0.005)	(0.005)
Science-oriented track		0.107***	0.096***
		(0.037)	(0.036)
Year 2011		−0.105***	−0.065**
		(0.027)	(0.030)
Year 2012		−0.148***	−0.099**
		(0.036)	(0.037)
Private school			0.151**
			(0.070)
Autonomous public school			0.351***
			(0.101)
Co-educational school			−0.025
			(0.079)
Grade enrollment (in 1000)			0.236
			(0.369)
Class size			0.024**
			(0.010)
Observations	10 301	8244	8244
R-squared	0.037	0.342	0.359

Note: Huber–White robust standard errors allowing for unrestricted error correlation within schools are in parentheses. *** $p < 0.01$, ** $p < 0.05$, * $p < 0.1$.

better cognitive abilities than those in regular high schools. If this were the case, the OLS estimates for β_1 in equation 8.1 would not reflect a causal effect of attending the APH schools.

In order to figure out whether the observed strong correlations between the type of school attended and the academic performance reflect any causal relationship, I use the birth order of students as an instrumental variable for APH school attendance. There is some empirical evidence suggesting that Korean parents tend to invest more on the education of their first-born than on later-born children (Ryu and Kang 2013). To the extent that Korean parents give higher priority to educational investment for their first-born, such students would have a higher chance of attending the APH schools than their later-born peers because tuition levels for the APH schools are about 2.5–3 times more expensive than those of regular high schools (first stage). On the other hand, conditional on the number of siblings, the birth order is randomly determined by nature and hence is not likely to affect the academic performance of students other than through affecting parental educational investment behaviors (exclusion restriction).

To test whether first-born students have a higher chance of attending APH schools than the later-born, I estimate the following linear probability model:

$$APH_s = \gamma_0 + \gamma_1 First_{is} + X_{it}\gamma_2 + W_{st}\gamma_3 + \phi_t + \varepsilon_{ist} \qquad (8.2)$$

where $First_{is}$ denotes a dummy variable that takes 1 if student i in school s is a first-born child and 0 otherwise. All the other variables are defined in the same way as in equation 8.1. As in equation 8.1, I estimate equation 8.2 by the OLS method, allowing for unrestricted correlation among error terms within each school. Table 8.5 summarizes the estimation results of equation 8.2. Across all model specifications and choice of samples, first-born students are about 4–5 percentage points more likely to attend the APH schools than their later-born peers.

Given that first-born students have a higher chance of attending the APH schools than their later-born peers do, I estimate the causal effect of attending the APH schools on test scores using students' first-born status as an instrumental variable for the type of school that they attend. In particular, I estimate Equation 8.1 by the two-stage least squares (2SLS) method instrumenting APH attendance (APH_s) of students with their first-born status ($First_{is}$).

Tables 8.6, 8.7 and 8.8 summarize the estimation results of the 2SLS model. In column 1 of the tables, I do not control for any covariate, which results in the conventional Wald estimates for the APH school effect. The Wald estimates (2.76, 1.42, 2.25 in Korean, math and English, respectively) tend to be much larger than their corresponding simple mean differences (0.500, 0.646, 0.589, respectively) presented in column 1 of Tables 8.2, 8.3 and 8.4. However, when both individual and school

Table 8.5   OLS estimation results for first-stage relationship

Dependent variable: APH school attendance	Specification		
	(1)	(2)	(3)
First-born	0.053***	0.053***	0.039***
	(0.019)	(0.018)	(0.011)
Pregrade for all subjects = poor		−0.024	−0.019
		(0.020)	(0.016)
Pregrade for all subjects = fair		−0.033*	−0.024*
		(0.017)	(0.012)
Pregrade for all subjects = good		0.018	0.017
		(0.023)	(0.020)
Pregrade for all subjects = excellent		0.033**	0.013
		(0.016)	(0.012)
Female		−0.094*	−0.103**
		(0.051)	(0.041)
Number of siblings		−0.022*	−0.007
		(0.013)	(0.009)
Disabled		−0.024	−0.011
		(0.022)	(0.018)
Having single parent		0.003	0.003
		(0.026)	(0.018)
Father's education < high school graduate		0.000	−0.021
		(0.023)	(0.023)
Father's education = some college		−0.025	−0.009
		(0.016)	(0.016)
Father's education = college graduate		−0.004	0.018
		(0.014)	(0.013)
Father's education > college graduate		0.021	0.036
		(0.038)	(0.028)
Mother's education < high school graduate		−0.043	−0.033
		(0.027)	(0.025)
Mother's education = some college		0.022	0.025
		(0.018)	(0.016)
Mother's education = college graduate		0.034*	0.033**
		(0.019)	(0.015)
Mother's education > college graduate		0.102**	0.095***
		(0.042)	(0.027)
Father's age < 50		−0.067**	−0.048
		(0.031)	(0.038)
Father's age ≥ 60		0.039*	0.024*
		(0.022)	(0.014)
Mother's age < 50		−0.018	−0.016
		(0.027)	(0.027)

Table 8.5   (continued)

Dependent variable: APH school attendance	Specification		
	(1)	(2)	(3)
Mother's age ≥ 60		0.013	0.001
		(0.025)	(0.019)
Free lunch recipient		0.018	0.015
		(0.028)	(0.025)
Family income (monthly, in million won)		0.002	0.002*
		(0.002)	(0.001)
Only mother employed		−0.005	−0.028
		(0.021)	(0.018)
Mother and father employed		−0.014	−0.021*
		(0.014)	(0.011)
Neither employed		0.065	0.060
		(0.060)	(0.045)
Hours of self-study for all subjects		0.005**	0.006***
		(0.002)	(0.002)
Science-oriented track		0.024	0.029*
		(0.023)	(0.016)
Year 2011		−0.021*	−0.044***
		(0.012)	(0.014)
Year 2012		−0.034**	−0.063***
		(0.015)	(0.018)
Private school			−0.265***
			(0.076)
Autonomous public school			−0.393***
			(0.105)
Co-educational school			−0.072
			(0.092)
Grade enrollment (in 1000)			−0.487*
			(0.268)
Class size			−0.015*
			(0.008)
Observations	10316	8074	8074
R-squared	0.007	0.087	0.366

Note: Huber–White robust standard errors allowing for unrestricted error correlation within schools are in parentheses. *** $p < 0.01$, ** $p < 0.05$, * $p < 0.1$.

characteristics are controlled for, the two-stage least squares (2SLS) estimates for the effects of attending the APH schools are only marginally significant in Korean, and statistically insignificant from zero in math and English. Given that the first-stage F statistics tend to be large enough

Table 8.6   2SLS estimation results for Korean test score

Dependent variable: Korean test score (Z score)	Specification		
	(1)	(2)	(3)
APH school attendance	2.755***	0.859*	1.214*
	(0.961)	(0.508)	(0.619)
Pregrade for Korean = poor		−0.486***	−0.469***
		(0.064)	(0.067)
Pregrade for Korean = fair		−0.348***	−0.365***
		(0.038)	(0.035)
Pregrade for Korean = good		0.343***	0.351***
		(0.034)	(0.034)
Pregrade for Korean = excellent		0.524***	0.543***
		(0.059)	(0.058)
Female		0.414***	0.469***
		(0.074)	(0.079)
Number of siblings		0.024	0.015
		(0.031)	(0.031)
Disabled		−0.099	−0.102
		(0.071)	(0.068)
Having single parent		−0.009	−0.005
		(0.049)	(0.047)
Father's education < high school graduate		−0.071	−0.041
		(0.056)	(0.056)
Father's education = some college		0.009	−0.010
		(0.046)	(0.043)
Father's education = college graduate		0.094**	0.055
		(0.041)	(0.038)
Father's education > college graduate		0.170***	0.123*
		(0.062)	(0.063)
Mother's education < high school graduate		−0.060	−0.063
		(0.070)	(0.066)
Mother's education = some college		0.060	0.047
		(0.050)	(0.050)
Mother's education = college graduate		0.057	0.042
		(0.045)	(0.045)
Mother's education > college graduate		0.090	0.057
		(0.092)	(0.092)
Father's age < 50		0.145	0.138
		(0.164)	(0.168)
Father's age ≥ 60		−0.066**	−0.048
		(0.033)	(0.032)
Mother's age < 50		−0.152**	−0.127*
		(0.070)	(0.066)

Table 8.6 (continued)

Dependent variable: Korean test score (Z score)	Specification		
	(1)	(2)	(3)
Mother's age ≥ 60		0.049	0.049
		(0.046)	(0.045)
Free lunch recipient		−0.055	−0.051
		(0.047)	(0.049)
Family income (monthly, in million won)		−0.005	−0.006*
		(0.003)	(0.003)
Only mother employed		0.038	0.074
		(0.050)	(0.052)
Mother and father employed		0.024	0.042
		(0.031)	(0.032)
Neither employed		−0.429***	−0.423***
		(0.132)	(0.127)
Hours of self-study for Korean		0.038***	0.032***
		(0.010)	(0.011)
Science-oriented track		0.161***	0.142***
		(0.048)	(0.050)
Year 2011		−0.107***	−0.054
		(0.035)	(0.041)
Year 2012		−0.152***	−0.085
		(0.051)	(0.061)
Private school			0.312*
			(0.183)
Autonomous public school			0.643**
			(0.259)
Co-educational school			−0.080
			(0.107)
Grade enrollment (in 1000)			0.487
			(0.537)
Class size			0.030**
			(0.012)
Observations	10 242	8110	8110
R-squared	−0.480	0.191	0.206
F statistics of excluded instrument	8.031	8.640	12.04

Note: Huber–White robust standard errors allowing for unrestricted error correlation within schools are in parentheses. *** $p < 0.01$, ** $p < 0.05$, * $p < 0.1$.

Table 8.7   2SLS estimation results for math test score

Dependent variable:	Specification		
Math test score (Z score)	(1)	(2)	(3)
APH school attendance	1.417**	−0.367	−0.443
	(0.606)	(0.396)	(0.531)
Pregrade for math = poor		−0.360***	−0.372***
		(0.036)	(0.038)
Pregrade for math = fair		−0.266***	−0.267***
		(0.035)	(0.036)
Pregrade for math = good		0.360***	0.364***
		(0.034)	(0.034)
Pregrade for math = excellent		0.625***	0.618***
		(0.053)	(0.050)
Female		−0.022	−0.024
		(0.063)	(0.072)
Number of siblings		−0.018	−0.012
		(0.025)	(0.023)
Disabled		−0.096*	−0.090*
		(0.051)	(0.052)
Having single parent		0.033	0.036
		(0.043)	(0.044)
Father's education < high school graduate		−0.047	−0.062
		(0.058)	(0.061)
Father's education = some college		0.000	0.004
		(0.039)	(0.038)
Father's education = college graduate		0.076**	0.080**
		(0.033)	(0.035)
Father's education > college graduate		0.277***	0.282***
		(0.056)	(0.061)
Mother's education < high school graduate		−0.013	0.000
		(0.061)	(0.061)
Mother's education = some college		0.016	0.021
		(0.051)	(0.051)
Mother's education = college graduate		0.141***	0.136***
		(0.044)	(0.045)
Mother's education > college graduate		0.201**	0.191**
		(0.091)	(0.097)
Father's age < 50		−0.086	−0.081
		(0.148)	(0.146)
Father's age ≥ 60		0.008	0.006
		(0.025)	(0.023)
Mother's age < 50		−0.072	−0.056
		(0.066)	(0.069)

Table 8.7 (continued)

Dependent variable: Math test score (Z score)	Specification		
	(1)	(2)	(3)
Mother's age ≥ 60		0.025	0.022
		(0.043)	(0.040)
Free lunch recipient		−0.047	−0.044
		(0.039)	(0.040)
Family income (monthly, in million won)		0.004	0.004
		(0.003)	(0.003)
Only mother employed		−0.071	−0.081
		(0.051)	(0.054)
Mother and father employed		−0.060**	−0.061*
		(0.029)	(0.032)
Neither employed		−0.102	−0.088
		(0.137)	(0.137)
Hours of self-study for math		0.087***	0.087***
		(0.008)	(0.010)
Science-oriented track		0.215***	0.213***
		(0.033)	(0.033)
Year 2011		−0.155***	−0.156***
		(0.030)	(0.037)
Year 2012		−0.206***	−0.208***
		(0.031)	(0.037)
Private school			−0.165
			(0.161)
Autonomous public school			−0.254
			(0.232)
Co-educational school			−0.089
			(0.108)
Grade enrollment (in 1000)			0.059
			(0.406)
Class size			−0.004
			(0.012)
Observations	9973	8064	8064
R-squared	−0.020	0.313	0.311
F statistics of excluded instrument	8.038	9.619	13.40

Note: Huber–White robust standard errors allowing for unrestricted error correlation within schools are in parentheses. *** $p < 0.01$, ** $p < 0.05$, * $p < 0.1$.

Table 8.8 2SLS estimation results for English test score

Dependent variable: English test score (Z score)	Specification		
	(1)	(2)	(3)
APH school attendance	2.251***	0.313	0.468
	(0.823)	(0.405)	(0.529)
Pregrade for English = poor		−0.447***	−0.441***
		(0.041)	(0.043)
Pregrade for English = fair		−0.271***	−0.268***
		(0.030)	(0.031)
Pregrade for English = good		0.370***	0.371***
		(0.036)	(0.036)
Pregrade for English = excellent		0.611***	0.630***
		(0.048)	(0.047)
Female		0.260***	0.289***
		(0.058)	(0.065)
Number of siblings		−0.005	−0.010
		(0.028)	(0.027)
Disabled		−0.092	−0.094*
		(0.059)	(0.055)
Having single parent		0.036	0.038
		(0.042)	(0.044)
Father's education < high school graduate		−0.070	−0.056
		(0.053)	(0.053)
Father's education = some college		0.039	0.028
		(0.041)	(0.038)
Father's education = college graduate		0.138***	0.116***
		(0.032)	(0.031)
Father's education > college graduate		0.325***	0.298***
		(0.058)	(0.062)
Mother's education < high school graduate		−0.031	−0.031
		(0.066)	(0.063)
Mother's education = some college		0.071	0.067
		(0.048)	(0.047)
Mother's education = college graduate		0.170***	0.162***
		(0.045)	(0.044)
Mother's education > college graduate		0.207**	0.188**
		(0.091)	(0.096)
Father's age < 50		−0.086	−0.090
		(0.117)	(0.110)
Father's age ≥ 60		0.012	0.019
		(0.028)	(0.025)
Mother's age < 50		−0.044	−0.030
		(0.056)	(0.053)

Table 8.8 (continued)

Dependent variable: English test score (Z score)	Specification		
	(1)	(2)	(3)
Mother's age ≥ 60		0.036	0.037
		(0.043)	(0.042)
Free lunch recipient		−0.040	−0.037
		(0.036)	(0.037)
Family income (monthly, in million won)		0.004	0.003
		(0.003)	(0.003)
Only mother employed		−0.099**	−0.083
		(0.050)	(0.051)
Mother and father employed		−0.038*	−0.029
		(0.022)	(0.023)
Neither employed		−0.207*	−0.199*
		(0.116)	(0.117)
Hours of self-study for English		0.059***	0.056***
		(0.006)	(0.007)
Science-oriented track		0.108***	0.100***
		(0.038)	(0.037)
Year 2011		−0.105***	−0.070**
		(0.027)	(0.035)
Year 2012		−0.148***	−0.105**
		(0.036)	(0.043)
Private school			0.128
			(0.153)
Autonomous public school			0.316
			(0.219)
Co-educational school			−0.031
			(0.086)
Grade enrollment (in 1000)			0.201
			(0.439)
Class size			0.022*
			(0.012)
Observations	10 262	8232	8232
R-squared	−0.262	0.342	0.358
F statistics of excluded instrument	7.961	9.146	13.35

Note: Huber–White robust standard errors allowing for unrestricted error correlation within schools are in parentheses. *** $p < 0.01$, ** $p < 0.05$, * $p < 0.1$.

(12.04, 13.40 and 13.35 in Korean, math and English, respectively) to precisely estimate the 2SLS models, these findings suggest that the OLS estimation results in Tables 8.2, 8.3 and 8.4 are largely driven by unobserved heterogeneity between the APH school students and the regular school students rather than reflecting causal effects of attending the APH schools.

Effects on Student Satisfaction

As discussed in the first section above, one of the policy objectives that the Korean government pursued by introducing the APH schools is to resolve the problem of limited diversity of educational services under the high school equalization policy and improve student satisfaction with their schools. To test whether this policy objective was achieved, I examine the causal effect of the APH school attendance on student satisfaction. In particular, I re-estimate equation 8.1 using the student satisfaction index as a new dependent variable.

Table 8.9 summarizes the OLS estimation results of equation 8.1 when the student satisfaction index is used as a dependent variable. Regardless of choice of the scope of covariates, I find that APH school students tend to report higher levels of satisfaction than their peers in regular high schools by about 0.480 to 0.550 standard deviations. To check whether this positive correlation can be attributed to the effect of APH school attendance, I instrument the APH school attendance dummy (APH_s) with the first-born indicator ($First_{is}$). The 2SLS estimation results in Table 8.10 show that the APH schools greatly improved student satisfaction levels by about 1.175 to 1.435 standard deviations.

SUMMARY AND FUTURE RESEARCH

This study evaluates the causal effect of attending the APH schools on educational outcomes of students. Comparing test scores of students who entered the APH schools in 2010 with those of students in regular high schools over the period 2010–12, I do not find any clear evidence that APH school attendance is causally related to improvement in test scores. However, I find some evidence that APH school attendance substantially increases levels of student satisfaction.

This study can be extended in the following ways. First, the effect on other educational outcomes, such as students' careers after graduation (for example, college entrance rates), can be investigated. Second, the empirical analysis in this study can be extended to different datasets from younger

Table 8.9   OLS estimation results for student satisfaction

Dependent variable: Student satisfaction index (Z score)	Specification		
	(1)	(2)	(3)
APH school attendance	0.540***	0.480***	0.550***
	(0.158)	(0.142)	(0.135)
Pregrade for all subjects = poor		−0.102**	−0.101**
		(0.042)	(0.042)
Pregrade for all subjects = fair		−0.046	−0.038
		(0.030)	(0.029)
Pregrade for all subjects = good		0.030	0.030
		(0.044)	(0.042)
Pregrade for all subjects = excellent		0.132***	0.129***
		(0.036)	(0.036)
Female		0.111*	0.113*
		(0.062)	(0.065)
Number of siblings		0.001	−0.003
		(0.030)	(0.030)
Disabled		−0.005	−0.009
		(0.059)	(0.059)
Having single parent		0.023	0.019
		(0.055)	(0.053)
Father's education < high school graduate		0.037	0.057
		(0.089)	(0.090)
Father's education = some college		−0.007	−0.013
		(0.050)	(0.049)
Father's education = college graduate		−0.005	−0.003
		(0.036)	(0.036)
Father's education > college graduate		0.038	0.034
		(0.061)	(0.060)
Mother's education < high school graduate		0.027	0.005
		(0.059)	(0.063)
Mother's education = some college		0.016	0.011
		(0.047)	(0.048)
Mother's education = college graduate		−0.009	−0.002
		(0.037)	(0.036)
Mother's education > college graduate		−0.082	−0.070
		(0.090)	(0.089)
Father's age < 50		0.009	0.000
		(0.195)	(0.197)
Father's age ≥ 60		0.029	0.037
		(0.038)	(0.037)
Mother's age < 50		0.030	0.012
		(0.077)	(0.078)

Table 8.9   (continued)

Dependent variable: Student satisfaction index (Z score)	Specification		
	(1)	(2)	(3)
Mother's age ≥ 60		−0.018	−0.021
		(0.059)	(0.057)
Free lunch recipient		0.021	0.018
		(0.049)	(0.047)
Family income (monthly, in million won)		0.003	0.004*
		(0.002)	(0.002)
Only mother employed		0.011	0.023
		(0.059)	(0.058)
Mother and father employed		0.014	0.013
		(0.024)	(0.024)
Neither employed		−0.126	−0.133
		(0.122)	(0.125)
Hours of self-study for all subjects		0.014***	0.014***
		(0.002)	(0.002)
Science-oriented track		0.053	0.055*
		(0.032)	(0.030)
Year 2011		0.019	0.008
		(0.037)	(0.036)
Year 2012		0.016	0.004
		(0.042)	(0.044)
Private school			0.138
			(0.088)
Autonomous public school			0.320**
			(0.144)
Co-educational school			−0.023
			(0.089)
Grade enrollment (in 1000 students)			−0.255
			(0.389)
Class size			−0.003
			(0.011)
Observations	10 349	8079	8079
R-squared	0.029	0.058	0.068

Note: Huber–White robust standard errors allowing for unrestricted error correlation within schools are in parentheses. *** $p < 0.01$, ** $p < 0.05$, * $p < 0.1$.

cohorts who entered the APH schools a few years after the APH schools had become well established, so that the teachers and school administrators of those schools have had enough time to adjust themselves to the new school system.

Table 8.10   2SLS estimation results for student satisfaction

Dependent variable: Student satisfaction index (Z score)	Specification		
	(1)	(2)	(3)
APH school attendance	1.710***	1.175**	1.435*
	(0.652)	(0.587)	(0.760)
Pregrade for all subjects = poor		−0.083*	−0.081*
		(0.043)	(0.044)
Pregrade for all subjects = fair		−0.019	−0.013
		(0.035)	(0.033)
Pregrade for all subjects = good		0.019	0.016
		(0.047)	(0.047)
Pregrade for all subjects = excellent		0.108**	0.116***
		(0.043)	(0.043)
Female		0.175**	0.203**
		(0.078)	(0.093)
Number of siblings		0.017	0.004
		(0.034)	(0.032)
Disabled		0.010	−0.002
		(0.063)	(0.061)
Having single parent		0.025	0.020
		(0.047)	(0.047)
Father's education < high school graduate		0.041	0.078
		(0.092)	(0.099)
Father's education = some college		0.011	−0.004
		(0.054)	(0.051)
Father's education = college graduate		−0.002	−0.018
		(0.039)	(0.036)
Father's education > college graduate		0.026	0.004
		(0.069)	(0.066)
Mother's education < high school graduate		0.058	0.035
		(0.062)	(0.068)
Mother's education = some college		−0.003	−0.014
		(0.051)	(0.054)
Mother's education = college graduate		−0.035	−0.034
		(0.043)	(0.044)
Mother's education > college graduate		−0.155	−0.157
		(0.112)	(0.119)
Father's age < 50		0.057	0.044
		(0.182)	(0.184)
Father's age ≥ 60		0.014	0.027
		(0.044)	(0.042)
Mother's age < 50		0.030	0.015
		(0.077)	(0.076)

Table 8.10   (continued)

Dependent variable: Student satisfaction index (Z score)	Specification		
	(1)	(2)	(3)
Mother's age ≥ 60		−0.025	−0.020
		(0.059)	(0.060)
Free lunch recipient		0.007	0.004
		(0.054)	(0.056)
Family income (monthly, in million won)		0.002	0.002
		(0.003)	(0.003)
Only mother employed		0.016	0.049
		(0.060)	(0.062)
Mother and father employed		0.025	0.034
		(0.028)	(0.030)
Neither employed		−0.177	−0.191
		(0.141)	(0.145)
Hours of self-study for all subjects		0.011***	0.009*
		(0.004)	(0.005)
Science-oriented track		0.034	0.028
		(0.038)	(0.038)
Year 2011		0.034	0.048
		(0.039)	(0.048)
Year 2012		0.040	0.060
		(0.051)	(0.069)
Private school			0.372*
			(0.218)
Autonomous public school			0.668**
			(0.308)
Co-educational school			0.041
			(0.136)
Grade enrollment (in 1000 students)			0.176
			(0.510)
Class size			0.010
			(0.017)
Observations	10 310	8069	8069
R-squared	−0.107	0.012	0.017
F statistics of excluded instrument	7.978	8.760	12.12

Note: Huber–White robust standard errors allowing for unrestricted error correlation within schools are in parentheses. *** $p < 0.01$, ** $p < 0.05$, * $p < 0.1$.

ACKNOWLEDGMENTS

I thank Julian Betts, Changhui Kang, Jaehoon Kim and WooRam Park (in alphabetical order) for their useful comments for this research. I was also greatly helped by Sohyun Park while writing this chapter.

NOTES

1. For this reason, students who moved from overseas are also removed from my sample.
2. For the APH schools, the dummy for private schools is set to 0 instead of 1, although the APH schools are privately owned and operated. This allows me to interpret the coefficient on *APH* in equation 8.1 as a difference in educational outcomes between regular public high schools and the APH schools rather than between the APH schools and regular private high schools. I am appreciative to Julian Betts for bringing this issue to my attention.
3. This allows for any correlation among the error components within each school. The number of schools in my sample is 73.

REFERENCES

Altonji, Joseph G., Todd E. Elder and Christopher R. Taber (2005a), "An evaluation of instrumental variable strategies for estimating the effects of Catholic schooling," *Journal of Human Resources*, **40**(4), 791–821.
Altonji, Joseph G., Todd E. Elder and Christopher R. Taber (2005b), "Selection on observed and unobserved variables: assessing the effectiveness of Catholic schools," *Journal of Political Economy*, **113**(1), 151–84.
Coleman, James, Thomas Hoffer and Sally Kilgore (1982), "Cognitive outcomes in public and private schools," *Sociology of Education*, **55**(2), 65–76.
Evans, William N. and Robert M. Schwab (1995), "Finishing high school and starting college: do Catholic schools make a difference?" *Quarterly Journal of Economics*, **110**(4), 941–74.
Kim, Yangboon, Wijung Kim, Hyunjung Lim and Jiyoung Namgoong (2012), "Analysis on school and student characteristics by school types," in *Proceedings of the Second SELS Forum for Education Policy*, Seoul: Seoul Education Research and Information Institute, pp. 35–72 (in Korean).
Neal, Derek (1997), "The effects of Catholic secondary schooling on educational achievement," *Journal of Labor Economics*, **15**(1), 98–123.
Ryu, Deockhyun and Changhui Kang (2013), "Do private tutoring expenditures raise academic performance? Evidence from middle school students in South Korea," *Asian Economic Journal*, **27**(1), 59–83.

PART IV

Human capital and the labor market

9. Building labor market skills among disadvantaged US workers: four-year college degrees and alternatives

Harry J. Holzer

INTRODUCTION

The basic economic model of investment in human capital implies that, when labor market returns to skills (or to the credentials that signal them) are very high, students will invest more heavily in attaining them. As the supply of skills thus grows, the labor market returns to them will decline over time, thus reducing earnings inequality between those who have attained these skills and those who have not (for example, Becker 1996).[1]

In the United States (US), labor market returns to higher education have been historically high for over 30 years. Enrollments in higher education, and to a lesser extent degree attainment, have risen over time, but not in sufficient quantities to reduce the returns in education and labor market inequality associated with it (Goldin and Katz 2008; Autor 2014).[2]

This is especially true for minorities or those growing up in disadvantaged families. If anything, the gaps in higher educational attainment between children from different socioeconomic strata in the United States have been rising in recent decades (Bailey and Dynarski 2011). When low-income students attend four-year colleges and universities, their completion rates lag behind those of other students by very large amounts; and when they attend two-year colleges – as they do more frequently than other students – their completion rates are also very low (Holzer and Dunlop 2013).

This chapter reviews the recent empirical evidence on skill-building among low-income youth and adults in the United States. I focus on those skills and credentials that are well rewarded in the labor market, and the different means of attaining them.

Accordingly, I begin with some discussion of the experiences of low-income students in the United States in higher education – both Bachelor of Arts (BA) degree programs at four-year colleges and universities as well as a range of sub-BA programs, mostly at two-year colleges. I also consider various alternatives to higher education in the United States, such as high-quality career and technical education (CTE), models of work-based learning and sectoral training for youth or adults. Efforts to integrate higher education and workforce policy more broadly will be discussed as well. I review both the strengths and the limitations of these models, and some of the difficulties of providing the best ones at scale. I close with some policy proposals on these issues and a discussion of their limitations as well as strengths.

HIGHER EDUCATION: BA AND SUB-BA PROGRAMS

A great deal of empirical evidence, from both survey and newer administrative data, has been generated on the higher education outcomes of Americans, including the disadvantaged. The latter data, in particular, are drawn from state-level administrative records from public colleges and universities that are being linked by Social Security numbers to the quarterly earnings records of virtually all workers in the Unemployment Insurance system. This enables us to study student experiences and achievements at all levels of school in great detail, as well as the extent to which the skills and credentials they attain are rewarded in the job market (for example, Jacobson and Mokher 2009; Jepsen et al. 2014; Kreisman et al. 2013; Backes et al. 2014).[3]

The recent evidence suggests the following:

- Disadvantaged high school graduates enroll in college at roughly the same rate as more advantaged students, but the poor are also more likely to attend lower-quality four-year colleges and universities as well as two-year ones.
- Their completion rates in two-year and especially four-year colleges and universities lag dramatically behind those of their middle- and upper-income counterparts.[4]
- Labor market returns vary hugely at any level of educational attainment, with technical degrees and those in high-demand fields (such as healthcare, business and law) paying much more than those in the social sciences and humanities.
- Because their achievement levels coming out of secondary school lag behind those of other students, the disadvantaged are less likely to enroll in more strenuous fields of study, such as those in the science, technology, engineering and math (STEM) fields and others that are more highly rewarded in the labor market.

- Average returns at the Associate of Arts (AA) degree are half or less than those of BAs, and certificate credentials generally provide even lower returns, but those in technical or high-demand fields are much stronger than average and even dominate the lower end of BA credentials.[5]
- Most AA students, particularly the disadvantaged, concentrate in humanities (or "liberal studies") that have very low completion rates and generate very low labor market earnings (Holzer and Dunlop 2013; Backes et al. 2014).

Why do completion rates lag behind for the disadvantaged? Their lower-quality academic preparation before college is certainly a major factor; as Cunha and Heckman (2007) have emphasized, "skills beget skills"; in other words, there is some "dynamic complementarity" over time in which developing early skills affects one's ability to achieve higher-level skills and educational attainment somewhat later in the life cycle. More concretely, the high rate at which disadvantaged Americans fail to complete their high school education is also a barrier to greater levels of higher education, even if the dropout rates have improved somewhat recently (Murnane 2013).

But, controlling for earlier academic achievement and high school diploma attainment, other factors reduce the attainment of higher education credentials among the poor as well. For instance, the financial costs of higher education can hurt families facing liquidity constraints, especially when capital markets are imperfect (Belley and Lochner 2007; Brown et al. 2011; Lovenheim 2011). For low-income (and often single) parents, their inability to attend college full-time (often because of family obligations) reduces their ability to accumulate academic credits in their chosen fields of study. School quality matters too: for a student of given ability, attending a better school with stronger students appears to raise average completion rates, given the superior resources and support services at higher-quality schools (Bound et al. 2009).

And access to higher-quality schools among the disadvantaged is limited not only by low academic achievement but also by limited information about better schools that are located somewhat further away from their own neighborhoods (Hoxby and Turner 2013). These choices are likely reinforced by admissions policies that put great weight on test scores with limited predictive power regarding ultimate student performance (College Board 2013). Changing admissions practices in ways that help socioeconomically disadvantaged students – particularly in an era when race-based affirmative action is being increasingly challenged by state and federal courts as well as in state legislatures or popular referenda – would help as well.[6]

The fields in which certificates are well rewarded include construction and manufacturing, health technology and other health, security, transportation, and engineering. At the AA level rewards are similar in pattern, with strong returns to health and legal programs. And at the BA level returns are strong to the STEM fields, and also medicine, business and legal studies (Holzer and Dunlop 2013; Backes et al. 2014).

Chosen fields of concentration are, no doubt, affected by student preferences as well as their early skill development, especially in math and science (for the STEM fields) or in English reading (for some humanities). But the high concentrations of students in humanities and liberal studies, especially in two-year colleges, are unlikely to be fully accounted for by earlier skills or preferences. Many AA students would likely benefit from some reallocation: either into better-compensated AA programs, or into BA programs (for higher-level performers) or certificate programs (for lower-level performers).

Instead, the currently high concentrations in AA liberal studies programs likely reflect imperfect information about the labor market among students, and very imperfect incentives to respond to that market among the public colleges. Regarding information, some recent studies (Wiswall and Zafar 2013; Long et al. 2014) suggest that new information about labor market returns have only modest impacts on student choices of major. But it is not clear that this is true among disadvantaged students, especially those in two-year colleges.

In the two-year colleges, most students get virtually no career (or even academic) counseling before or during college; most never obtain any workforce services of the type routinely provided in a jobs center (or "one-stop shop") financed by the US Department of Labor. Indeed, the student experience at most two-year colleges has been described by one prominent researcher as akin to a "shapeless river" in which students float along but receive little structure of guidance and even little assistance while navigating across programs (Scott-Clayton 2011; Jenkins and Cho 2013). This stands in sharp contrast to some traditional proprietary vocational colleges (Rosenbaum 2001), where course-taking and curricula are very structured and job placement assistance is quite strong.

But, even if student choices were better-informed and therefore more optimal, they would be constrained by limited teaching capacity in high-demand fields and other institutional features that are common at two-year colleges and the less-prestigious four-year programs where resources are very limited. Because instructors and equipment are frequently more expensive in the high-demand fields, and because subsidies from the states are for student "seat time," regardless of academic or subsequent labor market success, college administrators have little incentive to expand instructional capacity in these high-demand areas (Holzer 2014).

But many states now experiment with "performance-based subsidies" to higher education, where performance is measured by credits attained or program completion rates, especially among disadvantaged or minority students (National Conference of State Legislatures 2014); and I would also encourage states to include subsequent employment outcomes as performance measures as well. Of course, it is important to make sure that these incentives do not induce further "creaming" in college admissions or lowering of completion standards by colleges. The administrative data needed to measure both academic and employment outcomes for students of each public institution are becoming increasingly available and also usable by policymakers and practitioners.[7]

Other features of lower-quality public colleges and universities and a range of policies exacerbate these problems. For instance, the Federal Pell Grant Program, which distributes roughly $35 billion to low-income students, is simply a voucher for attending college, with few mandated supports or performance requirements built in (College Board 2013). For many older students, who simply want a credential that will directly improve their earnings potential, a lack of both academic and labor market guidance can be costly in terms of their ability to choose a sensible academic program that they can complete in a timely manner. Knowing more about fields in high demand (both locally or statewide and nationally), and about academic programs that make them qualified for employment there (and which they have the academic skills to master), would be quite helpful to many.

Regulations that limit the extent to which for-profit colleges can receive federal student financial aid, especially when their student outcomes lag behind those of public two-year colleges (Deming et al. 2013), may be important. And rising debt burdens, especially for students who do not complete their degree programs, could be limited by capping the required percent of debt repayment as a percentage of earnings on student loans.

Also, when many low-income students show up at college, large fractions of them are steered toward "developmental" (or remedial) classes in English or algebra. But the tests that steer them into these classes have little predictive power with regard to later academic performance (Scott-Clayton and Rodriguez 2015), and requirements that they pass algebra classes make little sense in many fields in which they plan to concentrate (such as health technology). In addition, most remedial programs have little positive, and even possibly have negative, effects on completion measures (Clotfelter et al. 2015; Bettinger et al. 2013).

Thus, a rethinking of both financial aid and especially remedial education would make sense (Long 2014). Providing more counseling and other supports to low-income students, and changing remediation practices along a variety of dimensions – how students are allocated to remediation, the nature of these programs (which have stronger outcomes when they are accelerated and/or integrated directly into the curriculum), and when they are allowed to take for-credit classes) – would be sensible. Stronger links of these programs to labor market information and/or vocational training seem effective as well.[8]

Overall, a policy agenda emerges from this research. Such an agenda would likely include the following:

- Changing college recruitment and admissions criteria so that more disadvantaged students with strong academic ability can attend higher-quality colleges and universities.
- The provision of adequate counseling to disadvantaged students, both younger and older, about programs of study that fit their tastes and academic backgrounds, and also about the labor market and career opportunities, both before they choose a college and/or program and during the program.
- Reforms in financial aid programs to require more supports and performance incentives, along with reforms in remedial education on a number of dimensions.
- Changing institutional incentives, by implementing higher education subsidies from the states that reward both academic and labor market performance, which would make public colleges improve their academic student outcomes as well as employment outcomes afterwards.

These policy changes and reforms would likely help disadvantaged students pick academic and vocational programs at the BA and sub-BA levels that are better suited to their abilities and interests and would help them to achieve stronger academic and employment outcomes afterwards.

OTHER PATHWAYS TO SUCCESS

For students who might not be bound for college or universities, especially right after high school, a number of other approaches to enhance their labor market skills are being developed and are under consideration in a number of states and localities. These include high-quality CTE programs in high school, work-based learning models such as apprenticeships, and innovative approaches to adult training such as sectoral models. I consider each of these approaches below.

Career and Technical Education

Traditionally, non-college-bound students, and especially those from minority or disadvantaged backgrounds, have enrolled in vocational education in the United States; or have been "tracked" there against their will. These programs prepared students mostly for low-wage jobs, and often in declining sectors. Beginning in the 1960s, resentment from minority families and communities over tracking led to declining enrollments in these programs, though they never disappeared. Even when the US School-to-Work programs of the 1990s briefly received federal funding (Neumark 2007), traditional vocational programs went largely untouched. And, though their quality has improved somewhat in recent years, CTE programs have not become a large-scale alternative to academic programs that prepare students for "college only."[9]

But a number of newer CTE models have been emerging that no longer force students to choose between college and "career" and instead try to prepare them for both (Holzer et al. 2013). The best-known of these programs are the Career Academies, which are programs within more general high schools that prepare students for careers in a particular sector, such as healthcare, information technology or finance. Students take courses within the academy as well as outside of it, and often find part-time or summer work within the sector. Evaluation evidence shows strong and lasting impacts on the earnings of enrollees, especially disadvantaged boys, whose earnings remain nearly 20 percent higher than those in the control group eight years after enrollment. There is also no evidence of lasting effects (positive or negative) on high school completion or college enrollment (Kemple 2008). More recent versions of Career Academies put more emphasis on maintaining strong college preparatory curricula while still maintaining the emphasis on specific sectors and careers.

Other models, perhaps less well-known or less rigorously evaluated, also try to prepare students for both college and careers. These include the High Schools that Work in many southern states, Linked Learning in California, and High Tech High Schools (Holzer et al. 2013). Virtually all students at these schools get some career exposure and exploration. Wherever possible, high-quality academic material is incorporated into work-based or project-based learning, to contextualize the material and make it more relevant to students. Links to employers in targeted industries, and professional development for staff, are emphasized as well. A network of "pathway states" aims to expand the best models and increase student and school participation in them.[10]

In all of these cases, as well as those listed below, it is important to remember the trade-off between developing general versus occupation- or sector-specific skills, where the former might be more highly compensated in the short run but less in the long run, as individuals change jobs or careers and as labor demand shifts across careers and sectors in often unpredictable ways (Malamud 2010; Hanushek et al. 2011). High-quality CTE, and sector-specific training models described below, must generate an appropriate balance between more general and specific skills to enhance students' labor market success in both the short and long runs.

Work-Based Learning

Work-based learning models, sometimes called "learning while earning," have enjoyed a recent surge of interest, even outside of school CTE programs. These models include internships, co-op programs at colleges, apprenticeships and "career pathways."

Many such programs provide students with paid work experience as well as a postsecondary credential of value in the labor market (Holzer and Lerman 2014). At a time when young people were experiencing low employment rates (due to the Great Recession and weak labor market recovery afterwards), combining work experience with postsecondary attainment is an appealing option. The paid work experience also motivates many students, especially those with family responsibilities and income needs, and also contextualizes the learning.

Apprenticeships, in particular, give students strong paid work experience while they gain an occupational credential. Wages might be somewhat below market levels, so that employers do not have to bear the cost of such training.[11] But this means that public sector costs are quite low. Employers thus seem to like the program. German companies, in particular, have introduced such programs in the United States, though not necessarily in identical form to the well-known apprenticeship model widely used in Germany (Schwartz 2013).

In the United States, certain states – such as South Carolina, Wisconsin and Georgia – are encouraging employers to expand apprenticeships through marketing campaigns and modest financial incentives to help offset costs (Lerman 2014). Indeed, while employers often find them appealing, few would develop them completely on their own, due to a variety of market failures.[12]

Incumbent worker training is another model of work-based learning. A range of states have provided subsidies for such training, at least before the Great Recession began (Hollenbeck 2008). The training was mostly limited to nonprofessional and nonmanagerial starting employees, and the training was usually designed to help them advance within the companies (or to prevent them from being laid off). And, to prevent the training from being too narrowly focused (or too "customized," in more modern lingo) on the needs of the specific employer, especially when public funds for the training are being provided, the states attempt to ensure that skills are at least somewhat general and "portable" to other employers and sectors. Evidence suggests positive impacts both on workers and on their performance in the workplace (Holzer et al. 1993; Ahlstrand et al. 2003).

Finally, a number of states are trying to develop "career pathways" that combine classroom work in a certificate or AA program with various amounts of work experience as they move up an occupational ladder of some type. For instance, students might first become certified nursing assistants and then licensed practical nurses, with some ultimately becoming registered nurses. A network of states are receiving technical assistance and support for developing a range of these programs (Center for Law and Social Policy 2014) within broader career pathway "systems." But little evidence exists to date on the impacts of these efforts (Fein et al. 2013).

Sectoral Training Programs

Training outside of the workplace that nonetheless targets jobs in a particular growing or high-wage sector, with the active involvement of particular employers, is known as "sectoral training." Workforce intermediaries bring together employers in that sector, training providers (either community colleges or others) and workers. The intermediaries help provide access to needed supports and services, including transportation and childcare. The intermediaries also work with providers and employers to make sure that the training fits their needs. Employers come to trust the intermediaries over time to screen workers and refer only those with strong skills and work habits.

Rigorous evaluations (Maguire et al. 2010; Roder and Elliott 2013) have shown that sectoral programs can generate large impacts on the earnings of adults and youth – of 30 percent or more – within two years of the onset of training. But the training generally works only for disadvantaged workers with quite strong basic skills and job-readiness, rather than the "hard to employ." Questions also remain about the extent to which impacts survive over time, particularly after workers leave their current jobs and maybe even that sector of employment.

Many states have begun efforts to scale up "sectoral" models, by creating partnerships between community colleges and employers or industry associations (National Governors Association 2014). Efforts in many cities and substate regions of the country have been undertaken as well (National Fund for Workforce Solutions 2014).[13] The Obama administration also embraced "demand-driven" or job-driven training as ways to meet the needs of the long-term unemployed and other disadvantaged workers (see White House 2014).

But little data exist to date measuring the outcomes achieved, in terms of numbers of workers trained or employed in these broader efforts, much less what the impacts are on worker earnings. Tensions can sometimes exist between the time it takes to build local or state "partnerships" between employers, intermediaries and service providers, on the one hand, and the often changing skill needs of employers and workers in a dynamic labor market, on the other. Making sure that these models are not just windfalls for employers who would otherwise provide the training themselves, or that the training serves at least somewhat disadvantaged workers, whom employers might be reluctant to hire, requires some vigilance on the part of intermediaries or state officials.

INTEGRATING HIGHER EDUCATION AND WORKFORCE POLICY AT THE STATE AND FEDERAL LEVELS

Virtually all of the programs and policies discussed above are designed to improve the skills that low-income workers bring to the labor market, mostly by making sure that higher education or job training efforts are consistent with the skills that employers actually seek (but do not always provide on their own). They try to ensure that our higher education institutions and training providers are responsive to the labor market, especially the forces of labor demand.

But there is also some question of how to make sure that higher education and workforce institutions are responsive to each other, and work together to generate a well-educated and well-trained workforce. Too often, our public higher education institutions and our local workforce institutions – where the latter include local Job Centers (formerly known as "One-Stop" Centers) and local Workforce Investment Boards (or WIBs) – are "siloed" from one another, with each relying on funding streams and performance measures from their respective federal agencies (the US Departments of Education and Labor) but cooperating with one another very little on the ground. Even so, joint efforts between these two agencies have certainly expanded in recent years, with a number of jointly administered grants programs, and cooperation has expanded somewhat on the ground in a number of local jurisdictions.[14] Still, it is likely that the vast majority of college students never receive labor market information or workforce services from a Job Center, or that most unemployed displaced workers never enroll on a certificate or AA program in a community college.

This situation is in many ways unfortunate. Funding levels for programs operated by the Department of Labor – primarily through its Workforce Innovation and Opportunity Act (WIOA) – have declined very dramatically over time, and at about $6 billion now constitute less than 20 percent of their peak levels in 1980 (Holzer 2009).[15] Funding from other federal agencies is limited, and spread over a wide range of other programs which sometimes overlap and conflict (US Government Accountability Office 2011).[16] Instead, Pell grant funding for vocational training now outstrips all of these other efforts combined.[17]

But, as noted earlier, a program that merely gives low-income students vouchers to attend college, with no other services provided or required, is hardly an optimal way of providing them with workforce services and training. Many ideas discussed above are efforts to provide such labor market information and career counseling to college students, and are efforts to make sure that any education or training provides strong labor market rewards.

These efforts might be encouraged in a number of ways. In Holzer (2011), I propose a set of federal grants to states or regions with the explicit goal of better integrating their higher education and workforce systems while making both more responsive to labor demand. Reauthorizations of federal workforce legislation such as the Workforce Investment Act (WIA), as well as education legislation such as the Elementary and Secondary Education Act (ESEA), the Higher Education Act (HEA) and the Perkins Act, should all encourage more such integration and responsiveness.

And states, through the building of their sectoral or career pathways systems and partnerships, should do more to encourage these efforts. But, to make them effective, it is likely not sufficient to simply build "partnerships" between employers, colleges and intermediaries; services must be provided and incentives put into place to encourage broader participation of employers and students or workers, along with high-quality education and training for disadvantaged youth and adults who otherwise would not get them.

CONCLUSION

In this chapter I have reviewed the benefits and limitations of college attendance for disadvantaged youth and adults, at both the BA and sub-BA levels. The data show strong average returns to those who complete degree programs, but also very high noncompletion rates among the disadvantaged, and tendencies to concentrate quite heavily in academic programs (such as humanities and liberal arts studies in AA programs) that are not well compensated in the labor market. I suggest a range of policies to improve these outcomes, such as recruitment and admission policies that open high-ranking colleges and universities to more disadvantaged students, better academic and career counseling, reforms in financial aid and remediation practices, and state subsidies based at least partly on the academic and employment outcomes of their students.

I also review a range of alternatives to college programs, including high-quality career and technical education, work-based learning programs and sectoral training, which have great promise but need to be carefully scaled up (and evaluated) before they will reach their potential. And I argue for policies to encourage better integration of our education and labor market programs and institutions, while making both more responsive to the job market.

None of this implies that traditional liberal arts programs are not valid or should be discouraged. These programs often teach valuable writing and critical thinking skills, while exposing students to intellectual and social perspectives that can be life-changing, especially at prestigious private colleges and universities. And even in the public institutions, preserving such options remains important. On the other hand, for low-income youth or adults who simply want to gain skills at public colleges and universities that directly raise their earnings potential, those options should be stronger than they are now. Either way, students will remain completely free to choose their paths ahead.

Other caveats need to be listed as well. For instance, there is some tension between providing students with broadly based and general skills, on the one hand, and those targeted to more specific sectors and careers, on the other. While sectoral training clearly can have large impacts on disadvantaged worker earnings within the short term (usually measured as two years), and this targeted training can make the trained workers quite attractive to their first set of employers, we do not have longer-term evidence on the extent to which these gains persist, especially after workers change firms or even sectors. Such training must contain enough general skills to maintain the higher earnings of workers, even when mobility across firms and sectors occurs. In a dynamic labor market where labor demand can shift fairly quickly, and in unanticipated ways, the appropriate balance between general and specific skills will not always be obvious.

Scaling up the most successful models can also be very challenging. While we see great success stories (such as those in Maguire et al. 2010), these are often found in agencies that have taken many years to improve their practices and to gain the confidence of the employers with which they work. There is also the usual question, regarding replication of particular models, of the extent to which the newer ones should maintain complete fidelity to the models they seek to replicate, or try to adapt to possibly different circumstances.

And there are likely to be many pitfalls in implementing the policies and practices suggested above. For instance, using performance measures to decide the magnitudes of higher education subsidies could lead to "cream-skimming" in admissions, where students with weaker observed skills would become more excluded; it can also lead to lower academic completion standards, especially in high-demand fields. It will take time to develop the appropriate incentives and performance measures that do not lead to such unanticipated consequences.

The ongoing softness of the US job market, especially for young workers, remains problematic too. Absent high aggregate labor demand, some trained workers will have difficulty finding jobs in their chosen fields, which could also lead to some backlash against these policies. On the other hand, those with strong postsecondary education or training will, on average, have better employment outcomes in a softer job market than those without it, and especially in a slack market where young workers without postsecondary education have fared worse in the downturn than those who have it.

Finally, good postsecondary education and workforce programs will mostly not make up for poor kindergarten to twelfth grade (K–12) academic preparation. Indeed, the policies described above require some relatively strong basic skills among students or workers, and will not be successful for the "hard to employ." The need for other policies to strengthen early education outcomes, or to provide incentives to and assist workers whose skills will remain very poor, remains in effect.[18]

Needless to say, there remains a great deal we do not know about how to successfully implement the higher education and workforce policies I have described above. Ongoing experimentation with and rigorous evaluation of any new federal, state or local initiatives would thus be an important part of any policy proposal.

NOTES

1. This model implies, of course, that investment decisions are made by well-informed and forward-looking young people whose discount rates for future benefits are not terribly high, and for whom liquidity constraints are not a serious problem, especially because capital markets work well for such investments. Becker himself recognized that these assumptions do not always hold. A number of economic models of these investments have also been developed that recognize imperfect student expectations of future earnings and/or lags in the investment process that might cause market earnings to oscillate, perhaps in a "cobweb" manner (for example, Freeman 1971).
2. Autor, however, notes that the rising supply of college graduates since 2000 has caused the college–high school premium to flatten since that time.

3. Of course, these data have their limitations, such as the omission of individuals who go out-of-state for college or work, or those who attend private colleges. Quarterly earnings also do not enable researchers to distinguish high wages from high numbers of hours or weeks worked. Of the studies listed that use such data, only Backes et al. (2014) include K–12 data also, which allows them to control for earlier academic achievement that is usually unobservable in most studies.

4. Backes et al. (2014) show that, in Florida, poor students have completion rates of 23 and 48 percent, respectively, in two-year and four-year colleges, while nonpoor students have rates of 34 and 62 percent.

5. Backes et al. (2014) show that, in Florida, young students with AA degrees on average earn about US$2400 more per quarter of work than high school graduates, and those with BAs earn about US$4700– US$5300 more, controlling only for work experience and tenure, demographics and high school achievement test scores. Those with certificates earn about US$1900 more. But returns to those with more technical Associate of Applied Science (AAS) degrees earn substantially more than the average for AAs, while the majority of AA students with humanities and liberal arts studies degrees earn much less. It is also noteworthy that the omission of students who attend private colleges and/ or those out-of-state likely biases downwards the returns to BA degrees but not AAs.

6. The most recent Supreme Court ruling on the use of affirmative action in admissions programs at public colleges or universities is *Fisher v. University of Texas* (2016), in which the judges upheld that affirmative action based on the race of the applicant can be used to achieve diversity. Several other states, including California, Michigan, Florida and Washington, have outlawed the use of affirmative action based on race in admissions at their public colleges and universities, and the flagship universities in these states have been developing alternative admissions procedures based on various measures of family or community disadvantage. See also Cashin (2014). But a new lawsuit challenging Harvard's use of affirmative action in admissions was filed in 2018, alleging that affirmative action generates discrimination against Asian-Americans.

7. States have been encouraged by the federal government to make these data more widely available. This has been done through grants for State Longitudinal Data Systems from the US Department of Education, as well as Workforce Data Quality grants from the Department of Labor. See Zinn and Van Kluenen (2014) for more information.

8. As Bettinger et al. (2013) note, two programs with some evidence of success include the Integrated Basic Education and Skills Training Program (I-BEST) in the state of Washington, and the General Education Development (GED) Bridge program at LaGuardia Community College in New York. I-BEST provides two teachers in every vocational training classroom: one to teach the vocational material and the other to remediate basic skills that are needed to understand the vocational material. For this reason, its costs are relatively high and perhaps hard to scale, though other states are trying to replicate the model. Evaluation evidence so far has also been positive but not very rigorous. The GED Bridge model contextualizes the GED preparatory material by linking it to information about the labor market, and specifically jobs where these skills are needed. This program has been rigorously evaluated and been shown to improve GED pass rates and college enrollments among high school dropouts, though the overall outcomes remain low in both cases.

9. Some recent changes have been driven by the latest reauthorization of the federal Perkins Act in 2007, which requires states to identify growing or high-wage "career clusters" and to generate "paths of study" to move students into these sectors. See Holzer et al. (2013).

10. Much of this work has been based on an influential report titled *Pathways to Prosperity* (Symonds et al. 2011) and also on Hoffmann (2011).

11. As Becker has pointed out, the more general the training, the less employers will be willing to pay for it, since workers could leave at any time before employers recoup the costs of their investments.

12. Economists, in particular, often wonder why certain activities that benefit both workers and employers are undertaken more frequently on their own. A range of market failures,

such as high fixed costs, limited information and wage rigidities in their firms, could impede these undertakings.

13. The National Fund is an effort funded by several philanthropic foundations to expand and scale sectoral training models at the city or regional level. It operates at over 30 sites around the country.

14. The Trade Adjustment Assistance Community College to Career Training grants, jointly administered through the US Departments of Education and Labor, are one such example. By the end of 2014 roughly US$2 billion worth of grants had been distributed through this effort. Co-locations of Job Centers on community college campuses have also grown in recent years.

15. While funding through the WIA, compared with its predecessor programs – the Comprehensive Employment and Training Act and the Job Training Partnership Act – has declined very dramatically, evaluation evidence for at least some of these programs (mostly the one for adults) has been relatively positive. See Heinrich et al. (2011) and Andersson et al. (2013).

16. There were roughly 47 federal programs to fund workforce development until 2014, though the vast majority of these are very small and targeted to specific populations. Some program consolidation that year reduced that number by about a third. Total expenditures in this area still constitute just 0.1 percent of gross domestic product in the United States, which is very low compared with other industrial nations.

17. The College Board (2013) estimates that roughly half of Pell grants are spent on programs that could be called vocational, especially for older students, which would constitute US$18 billion annually for such training.

18. Such policies might include expansions of the Earned Income Tax Credit, a tax-based subsidy for earnings in low-income families, or publicly subsidized employment for those who have difficulty getting or keeping jobs in the private sector on their own.

REFERENCES

Ahlstrand, Amanda, Laurie Bassi and Daniel McMurrer (2003), *Workplace Education for Low-Wage Workers*, Kalamazoo, MI: W.E. Upjohn Institute for Employment Research.

Andersson, Fredrik, Harry Holzer, Julia Lane, David Rosenblum and Jeffrey Smith (2013), "Does federally-funded job traning work? Non-experimental estimates of WIA training impacts using longitudinal data on firms and workers," NBER Working Paper 19446, Cambridge, MA: National Bureau of Economic Research.

Autor, David (2014), "Skills, education, and the rise of earnings inequality among the 'other 99 percent'," *Science*, **344**(6186), 843–51.

Backes, Benjamin, Harry Holzer and Erin Dunlop Velez (2014), "Is it worth it? Postsecondary education and labor market outcomes for the disadvantaged," CALDER Working Paper 117, Washington, DC: National Center for the Analysis of Longitudinal Data in Education Research, American Institutes for Research.

Bailey, Martha and Susan Dynarski (2011), "Inequality in post-secondary education," in Greg Duncan and Richard Murnane (eds), *Whither Opportunity? Rising Inequality, Schools, and Children's Life Chances*, New York: Russell Sage Foundation, pp. 117–32.

Becker, Gary (1996), *Human Capital*, second edition, Chicago, IL: University of Chicago Press.

Belley, Philippe and Lance Lochner (2007), "The changing role of family income and ability in determining educational achievement," NBER Working Paper 13527, Cambridge, MA: National Bureau of Economic Research.

Bettinger, Eric, Angela Boatman and Bridget Terry Long (2013), "Student supports: developmental education and other academic programs," *Future of Children*, **23**(1), 93–115.

Bound, John, Michael Lovenheim and Sarah Turner (2009), "Why have college completion rates declined? An analysis of changing student preparation and collegiate resources," NBER Working Paper 15566, Cambridge, MA: National Bureau of Economic Research.

Brown, Meta, J. Karl Scholz and Ananth Seshadri (2011), "A new test of borrowing constraints for education," *Review of Economic Studies*, **79**(2), 511–38.

Cashin, Sheryl (2014), *Place, Not Race: A New Vision of Opportunity in America*, Boston, MA: Beacon Press.

Center for Law and Social Policy (2014), *Shared Vision, Strong Systems: The Alliance for Quality Career Pathways Framework 1.0*, Washington, DC: Center for Postsecondary and Employment Success.

Clotfelter, Charles, Helen Ladd, Clare Muschkin and Jacob Vigdor (2015), "Developmental education in North Carolina community colleges," *Educational Evaluation and Policy Analysis*, **37**(3), 354–75.

College Board (2013), *Rethinking Pell Grants*, Washington, DC: College Board.

Cunha, Flávio and James Heckman (2007), "The technology of skill formation," *American Economic Review*, **97**(2), 31–47.

Deming, David, Claudia Goldin and Lawrence Katz (2013), "For-profit colleges," *Future of Children*, **23**(1), 137–64.

Fein, David, Howard Rolston, David Judkins and Karen N. Gardiner (2013), "Learning 'what works' in career pathways programs: the ISIS evaluations," paper presented at the Association of Public Policy and Management Annual Conference, Washington, DC, November 7–9.

Freeman, Richard (1971), *The Market for College-Trained Manpower*, Cambridge, MA: Harvard University Press.

Goldin, Claudia and Lawrence Katz (2008), *The Race between Education and Technology*, Cambridge, MA: Harvard University Press.

Hanushek, Eric, Ludger Woessmann and Lei Zhang (2011), "General education, vocational education, and labor-market outcomes over the life cycle," NBER Working Paper 17504, Cambridge, MA: National Bureau of Economic Research.

Heinrich, Carolyn, Peter R. Mueser, Kenneth R. Troske, Kyung-Seong Jeon and Daver C. Kahvecioglu (2011), "A nonexperimental evaluation of WIA programs," in Douglas J. Besharov and Phoebe H. Cottingham (eds), *The Workforce Investment Act: Implementation Experiences and Evaluation Findings*, Kalamazoo, MI: W.E. Upjohn Institute for Employment Research, pp. 371–404.

Hoffman, Nancy (2011), *Schooling in the Workplace: How Six of the World's Best Vocational Education Systems Prepare Young People for Jobs and Life*, Cambridge, MA: Harvard Education Press.

Hollenbeck, Kevin (2008), "Is there a role for public support of incumbent worker on-the-job training?" Upjohn Institute Working Paper 08-138, Kalamazoo, MI: W.E. Upjohn Institute for Employment Research.

Holzer, Harry (2009), "Workforce development as an antipoverty strategy: What do we know? What should we do?" in M. Cancian and S. Danziger (eds),

Changing Poverty, Changing Policies, New York: Russell Sage Foundation, pp. 301–29.

Holzer, Harry (2011), *Raising Job Quality and Skills for American Workers: Creating More Effective Workforce Development Systems in the States*, Washington, DC: Hamilton Project, Brookings Institution.

Holzer, Harry (2014), "Improving education and employment outcomes for disadvantaged students," in Melissa Kearney and Benjamin Harris (eds), *Policies to Address Poverty in America*, Washington, DC: Hamilton Project, Brookings Institution, pp. 87–95.

Holzer, Harry, Richard Block, Marcus Cheatham and Jack Knott (1993), "Are training subsidies for firms effective? The Michigan experience," *Industrial and Labor Relations Review*, **46**(1), 625–36.

Holzer, Harry and Erin Dunlop (2013), "Just the facts ma'am: postsecondary education and employment outcomes in the U.S.," CALDER Working Paper 86, Washington, DC: National Center for the Analysis of Longitudinal Data in Education Research, American Institutes for Research.

Holzer, Harry and Robert Lerman (2014), "Work-based learning to expand opportunities for youth," *Challenge*, **27**(4), 3–16.

Holzer, Harry, Dane Linn and Wanda Monthey (2013), *The Promise of High-Quality Career and Technical Education*, Washington, DC: College Board.

Hoxby, Caroline and Sarah Turner (2013), "Expanding college opportunity for high-achieving, low-income students," SIEPR Discussion Paper 12-014, Stanford, CA: Stanford Institute for Economic Policy Research.

Jacobson, Louis and Christine Mokher (2009), *Pathways to Boosting the Earnings of Low-Income Students by Increasing Their Educational Attainment*, New York: Hudson Institute.

Jenkins, Davis and Sung-Woo Cho (2013), *Get with the Program: Accelerating Community College Students' Entry into and Completion of Academic Programs*, New York: Community College Research Center, Columbia University.

Jepsen, Christopher, Kenneth Troske and Paul Coomes (2014), "The labor-market returns to community college degrees, certificates and diplomas," *Journal of Labor Economics*, **32**(1), 95–121.

Kemple, James (2008), *Career Academies: Long-Term Impacts on Student Earnings, Marriage and Transition to Adulthood*, New York: Manpower Demonstration Research Corporation.

Kreisman, Daniel, Brian Jacob, Susan Dynarski and Peter Bahr (2013), "The returns to course credits, certificates and degrees: evidence from Michigan's community colleges," unpublished paper, Gerald Ford School of Public Policy, University of Michigan.

Lerman, Robert (2014), "Expanding apprenticeship opportunities in the United States," in Melissa Kearney and Benjamin Harris (eds), *Policies to Address Poverty in America*, Washington, DC: Hamilton Project, Brookings Institution, pp. 79–86.

Long, Bridget (2014), "Addressing the academic barriers to higher education," in Melissa Kearney and Benjamin Harris (eds), *Policies to Address Poverty in America*, Washington, DC: Hamilton Project, Brookings Institution, pp. 67–78.

Long, Mark, Dan Goldhaber and Nick Huntington-Klein (2014), "Do student college major choices respond to changes in wages?" paper presented at CALDER Research Conference, American Institutes for Research, Washington, DC, January 23–24.

Lovenheim, Michael (2011), "The effect of liquid housing wealth on college enrollment," *Journal of Labor Economics*, **29**(4), 741–71.

Maguire, Sheila, Joshua Freely, Carol Clymer, Maureen Conway and Deena Schwartz (2010), *Tuning into Local Labor Markets: Findings from the Sectoral Employment Impace Study*, Philadelphia, PA: P/PV Public/Private Ventures.

Malamud, Ofer (2010), "Breadth v. depth: the timing of specialization in higher education," NBER Working Paper 15943, Cambridge, MA: National Bureau of Economic Research.

Murnane, Richard (2013), "U.S. higher school graduation rates: patterns and explanations," *Journal of Economic Literature*, **51**(2), pp. 370–422.

National Conference of State Legislatures (2014), "Performance-based funding for higher education," available at http://www.ncsl.org/research/education/performance-funding.aspx.

National Fund for Workforce Solutions (2014), "Regional collaboratives," web page of the National Fund for Workforce Solutions, Washington, DC, available at www.nfwsolutions.org/regional-collaboratives.

National Governors Association (2014), *State Sector Strategies Coming of Age: Implications for State Workforce Development Policy*, Washington: NGA Center for Best Practices.

Neumark, David (ed.) (2007), *Improving School-to-Work Transitions*, New York: Russell Sage Foundation.

Roder, Anne and Mark Elliott (2013), *A Promising Start: Year Up's Initial Impacts on Low-Income Young Adults Earnings and Careers*, New York: Economic Mobility Corporation.

Rosenbaum, James (2001), *Beyond College for All*, New York: Russell Sage Foundation.

Schwartz, Nelson (2013), "Where factory apprenticeship is latest model from Germany," *New York Times*, November 27, p. 1.

Scott-Clayton, Judith (2011), "Shapeless river: does a lack of structure inhibit student progress at community colleges?" Community College Research Center Working Paper, New York: Columbia University.

Scott-Clayton, Judith and Olga Rodriguez (2015), "Development, discouragement or diversion? New evidence on the effects of college remediation policy," *Education Finance and Policy*, **10**(1), 4–45.

Symonds, William, Robert Schwartz and Ronald Ferguson (2011), *Pathways to Prosperity*, Cambridge, MA: Graduate School of Education, Harvard University.

United States Government Accountability Office (2011), *Multiple Employment and Training Programs: Providing Information on Colocating Services and Consolidating Administrative Structures Could Promote Efficiencies*, Washington, DC: United States Government Accountability Office.

White House (2014), "Job-driven training for workers," Presidential Memorandum, January 30, Washington, DC: Office of the Press Secretary, White House, available at www.whitehouse.gov/the-press-office/2014/01/30/presidential-memorandum-job-driven-training-workers.

Wiswall, Matthew and Basit Zafar (2013), "How do college students respond to public information about earnings?" Staff Report 516, New York: Federal Reserve Bank of New York.

Zinn, Rachel and Andy Van Kluenen (2014), *Making Workforce Data Work: How Improved Education and Workforce Data Systems Could Help Us Compete in the 21st Century*, Washington, DC: National Skills Coalition.

10. Effects of human capital on technology intensity in the OECD manufacturing sector

WooRam Park

INTRODUCTION

The empirical magnitude of the impact of human capital on various outcomes has been a subject of interest in economic research. On the micro side, since Becker (1964) and Mincer (1974), the relation between schooling and wage at the individual level has been explored using various methods. The majority of the previous studies established a strong positive relation between years of schooling and income (Card 1999). However, unlike the well-established relation at the individual or micro level, the effect of average educational attainment at the national level is often found to be weak. In particular, Lucas's (1988) emphasis on the role of human capital on growth was followed by empirical support from Barro (1991) and Mankiw et al. (1992). However, subsequent literature has found little positive relation at the national level (Benhabib and Spiegel 1994; Pritchett 2001). Overall, as Lange and Topel (2006) argue, the evidence regarding the relation between education and economic growth is inconclusive.[1]

A paper by Ciccone and Papaioannou (2009) tries to extend the understanding on the effect of education using alternative specifications. In particular, rather than focusing on the effect of human capital on economic growth as a whole, they explore the heterogeneous effect of educational attainment across industries. Focusing on the complementarity between skill and technology, they argue that an increase in human capital will facilitate the growth of human capital-intensive industries.

The goal of the present chapter is to improve their finding by examining the heterogeneity in the effect of human capital on growth of the industries by technology intensity. In particular, I argue that if human capital facilitates a technology adoption as argued by Nelson and Phelps (1966), then the increase in human capital level will mostly affect the growth of technology-intensive industries. I test this hypothesis by examining whether human capital increases the share of high-tech industries and lowers the share of low-tech industries in terms of value-added and employment in the manufacturing sector. In other words, I test whether the human capital accumulation increases the technology intensity of the manufacturing sector.

For the empirical analysis, I use data at the industry level from Organisation for Economic Co-operation and Development (OECD) countries which have been collected based on the technological characteristics. Specifically, I try to overcome the limitations of the previous literature by using technology characteristics of industries that could be applied to most countries in my sample. Using the dataset, I find that the education attainment – regardless of the levels of educational attainment – does not increase the share of technology-intensive industries in terms of value-added and employment. This might imply that the technologies adopted by high-tech industries among developed countries are likely to be labor-replacing.

The second section of this chapter provides an overview of the main data, OECD Structural Analysis (STAN) database data and Barro and Lee (2013). The third section presents the empirical strategy, followed by the main empirical results in the fourth section and conclusions in the fifth section.

DATA

To examine the effect of human capital on the technology intensity of the manufacturing sector, I exploit data on both country-industry and country level. For the data on the employment and the value-added at the country-industry level, I use the STAN database of the OECD. In particular, I use the International Standard Industrial Classification (ISIC) revision 3 version of STAN, where industries are categorized according to the International Standard Industrial Classification of All Economic Activities, revision 3 version of STAN.[2] The data cover 32 OECD countries and information up to 2009.

More importantly, for the manufacturing sector, the dataset has also been collected based on the technology intensity of the industry. Specifically, the OECD has categorized the manufacturing sector into four groups – high-tech, medium-high-tech, medium-low-tech and low-tech industries – using the research and development (R&D) intensity of each industry of 12 OECD countries.[3] The detailed classification by technology intensity using the definition of the OECD is summarized in Table 10.1.

I believe that using OECD data has advantages compared with using

Table 10.1   Classification of manufacturing industries based on technology

Category	ISIC revision 3	Mean R&D intensity
High-technology industries	–	9.3
Aircraft and spacecraft	353	13.3
Pharmaceuticals	2423	10.5
Office, accounting and computing machinery	30	9.2
Radio, TV and communciations equipment	32	8.0
Medical, precision and optical instruments	33	7.7
Medium-high-technology industries	–	3.0
Electrical machinery and apparatus, n.e.c.	31	3.9
Motor vehicles, trailers and semi-trailers	34	3.5
Chemicals excluding pharmaceuticals	24 excl. 2423	3.1
Railroad equipment and transport equipment, n.e.c.	352 + 359	2.9
Machinery and equipment, n.e.c.	29	2.1
Medium-low-technology industries	–	0.8
Building and repairing of ships and boats	351	1.0
Rubber and plastics products	25	0.9
Coke, refined petroleum products and nuclear fuel	23	0.9
Other nonmetallic mineral products	26	0.9
Basic metals and fabricated metal products	27–28	0.6
Low-technology industries	–	0.3
Manufacturing not elsewhere classified; recycling	36–37	0.5
Wood, pulp, paper, paper products, printing and publishing	20–22	0.3
Food products, beverages and tobacco	15–16	0.3
Textiles, textile products, leather and footwear	17–19	0.3

Notes: R&D intensity is defined as direct R&D expenditures as a percentage of production (gross output), calculated after converting the country's R&D expenditures and production using GDP purchasing power parities (PPPs). "n.e.c." = not elsewhere classified.

Source: OECD (2003).

data from countries facing various degrees of development. First of all, the data are reliable and consistent since they are collected from the developed countries, which usually have well-organized national statistical offices. In addition, the homogeneity, in terms of economic development among the countries, mitigates concerns regarding biased results which could have been mainly driven from the unobserved heterogeneity across countries, which is usually correlated with economic development. Finally, I believe the R&D intensity provided by technological intensity reflects the technological characteristics better than the previously used measures, such as average years of schooling of workers in each industry.[4]

One of the main issues in documenting the effect of educational attainment on growth and various outcomes at the national level is the measurement error embedded in the aggregate educational attainment measures. In particular, measurement error will often lead to attenuation bias that will result in masking the effect of human capital. Some recent literature argues that improving the measure of educational attainment could significantly change the results of the effect of human capital growth. In particular, de la Fuente and Domenech (2006) and Cohen and Soto (2007) criticize Barro and Lee's (2001) widely used educational attainment data and create their own dataset.

Despite the criticism, I use educational attainment data from Barro and Lee (2013) for this analysis, as it has a number of advantages compared with the two other datasets. First, Barro and Lee (2013) cover all then-current 34 OECD countries, whereas the other two datasets have information for a subset of OECD countries. In particular, de la Fuente and Domenech (2006) cover only 21 OECD countries, and Cohen and Soto (2007) cover 26 of them. Second, Barro and Lee (2013) provide the most updated educational attainment data among the three. In particular, their study contains information from 1950 to 2010, whereas de la Fuente and Domenech (2006) provide information only up to 1995, and Cohen and Soto (2007) only up to 1990. Third, the Barro and Lee (2013) study has been significantly updated from Barro and Lee (2001), and many aspects of the data have addressed earlier criticisms and comments. Finally, unlike two other datasets, which provide only the overall years of educational attainment, Barro and Lee (2013) provide information about the educational attainment for three educational levels – primary, secondary and tertiary – based on the International Standard Classification of Education (ISCED) maintained by the United Nations Educational, Scientific and Cultural Organization (UNESCO). This allows us to identify the level of education that matters most for the technology adoption and productivity improvement.

Table 10.2 presents summary statistics of the data used in the analysis in two separate periods: from 1970 to 1990, and from 1995 to 2005. The table shows the education attainment increase with the time period. In particular, the majority of the increase in average years of educational attainment is driven by the increase in secondary education attainment. As a result of this increase, the percentage of individuals reporting primary education as their highest level of education attainment decreases dramatically.

Table 10.2 Summary statistics

Variable	1970–90			1995–2005		
	Obs	Mean	SD	Obs	Mean	SD
Average years of schooling attained (age 25+)	170	8.062	2.146	102	10.094	1.697
Average years of primary schooling attained (age 25+)	170	5.415	1.441	102	5.811	1.249
Average years of secondary schooling attained (age 25+)	170	2.287	1.111	102	3.609	1.135
Average years of tertiary schooling attained (age 25+)	170	0.360	0.242	102	0.674	0.315
Value-added shares of low-tech among manufacturing	113	41.960	10.500	96	37.972	10.436
Value-added shares of high-tech and med-high-tech among manufacturing	82	34.193	9.301	93	37.672	11.075
Employment shares of low-tech among manufacturing	89	47.147	9.639	87	44.168	9.853
Employment shares of high-tech and med-high-tech among manufacturing	64	30.934	7.709	83	32.594	8.608
Value-added shares of manufacturing relative to total economy	116	22.134	4.661	101	19.089	4.954
Employment shares of manufacturing in total economy	91	22.414	4.204	98	17.959	4.592
Log of number of employees in high-tech and medium-high-tech	59	12.960	1.519	83	12.776	1.526
Log of number of employees in low-tech	84	13.410	1.372	87	13.021	1.377
Log of number of employees in manufacturing	93	14.169	1.357	96	13.769	1.529
Log of per employee value-added in manufacturing	78	10.271	0.445	92	10.876	0.893
Log per capita GDP	138	9.734	0.460	102	10.062	0.449
Log of population (age 25+)	164	15.687	1.531	96	15.909	1.557

Note: The table is based on OECD STAN data and Barro and Lee (2013). Obs is the number of observations, and SD stands for standard deviation. All monetary values are expressed in constant US dollars.

The trends in the share of high-tech and medium-high-tech industries in terms of the employment and the value-added in the manufacturing sector show that the manufacturing sector became more technology-intensive. However, the change in the shares of high-tech and medium-high-tech in the manufacturing sector is not as drastic as the increase in the educational attainment. Moreover, the decrease in employment, and in the value-added of the manufacturing sector to that of the total economy, reflect the tertiarization of the economy.

EMPIRICAL STRATEGY

The longitudinal dataset at the country and industry level allows us to examine the effect of improvement in human capital on the technology intensity of the manufacturing sector. In particular, I estimate the following equation:

$$Y_{i,t} = \beta_0 + \beta_1 \, Edu_{i,t} + \mathbf{X}'_{i,t} \, \Phi + \gamma_i + \tau_t + \varepsilon_{it} \qquad (10.1)$$

where $Y_{i,t}$ denotes various outcome variables such as the employment share of high-tech industries. $Edu_{i,t}$ stands for education level of each country i at time t, which is arguably a good proxy for the human capital level in country i. The size and the significance of β_1 will thus summarize the impact of the change in human capital level on the outcome variables. $\mathbf{X}_{i,t}$ indicates the set of explanatory variables that could potentially affect the outcome variable, such as population and per capita gross domestic product (GDP). τ_t indicates the set of year dummies, which controls the time-specific shocks that are constant across countries but changes over time. The set of country fixed effects, γ_i, controls for the factors that change little over time and are specific to each OECD country, such as social and cultural norms, economic system, the area of land and the geographic location of the country.

The underlying identification assumption for the fixed-effect regression is that the major source of the endogeneity is the unobserved time-invariant characteristics. However, it does not address time-varying country-specific shocks being correlated with the educational attainment of each country. In particular, time-varying unobserved shocks of countries are likely to be positively correlated with the educational attainment, resulting in a positive bias in the estimate of β_1. Thus we use the five-year lag of educational attainment as an instrument for $Edu_{i,t}$, to mitigate the possible endogeneity in the educational attainment. The five-year lag of the educational attainment is arguably a good instrumental variable, since it is correlated with the current educational attainment but less likely to be correlated with current time-varying region-specific shocks. Another reason for using the five-year lag of educational attainment is to allow the outcome to be variable to response to the change in the educational attainment, as the change in the educational outcome might not immediately affect employment and productivity. Finally, to address possible serial correlation, I cluster the error term at the country level.

Moreover, to examine the effect of the initial level of human capital on the subsequent growth of industries by technology intensities, I estimate the following cross-country specification:

$$\Delta Y_{i,t\sim(t-v)} = \alpha_0 + \alpha_1 Edu_{i,t-v} + X'_{i,t}\Omega + \tau_t + \varepsilon_{it} \qquad (10.2)$$

where $\Delta Y_{i,t\sim(t-v)}$ denotes the change in the outcome variable Y between t and year $t-v$; that is, $\Delta Y_{i,t\sim(t-v)} = Y_{i,t} - Y_{i,(t-v)}$. $Edu_{i,t-v}$ represents the initial level of human capital for each country. Thus, the coefficient of interest, α_1, summarizes the effect of initial human capital level on the change in the outcome variable Y. As before, $X_{i,t}$ indicates the set of variables that could potentially affect the change in the outcome variable. In this specification, a country in different time periods is considered a different country. I also use Huber–White standard errors since the variance of the error term is likely to vary with the level of educational attainment.

RESULTS

In this section, I examine the impact of educational attainment on the technology intensity of manufacturing by the level of educational attainment. There is a conjecture that the increase in the level of human capital is associated with a higher rate of technology adoption (Nelson and Phelps 1966; Acemoglu 2003). If this is the case, the education attainment would matter more in terms of the growth of the technologically intensive industries. In particular, I examine whether an increase in human capital positively affects the share of technology-intensive industries and lowers the share of low-tech industries in terms of value-added and employment in the manufacturing sector. Table 10.3 reports the results from estimating equation (10.1) by using the share of high-tech and medium-high-tech industries in the manufacturing sector in terms of employment as an outcome variable. Columns (1) and (2) report the result from the unconditional estimate. The point estimate in column (2) shows that the

Table 10.3   Effect of change in educational attainment on the employment share of high-tech and mid-high-tech manufacturing (five-year lag as independent variable)

Dependent variable: employment share in manufacturing	Specification			
	(1)	(2)	(3)	(4)
Average years of schooling	0.552	–	−0.080	–
	(1.270)		(0.401)	
Average years of primary schooling	–	1.794	–	0.424
		(3.008)		(1.010)
Average years of secondary schooling	–	−0.336	–	−0.299
		(1.239)		(0.620)
Average years of tertiary schooling	–	8.762	–	−0.260
		(8.685)		(2.284)
Number of observations	147	147	137	137
Number of countries	28	28	28	28
Adjusted R-squared	0.272	0.303	0.839	0.838
Additional control	N	N	Y	Y
Year fixed effects	Y	Y	Y	Y
Country fixed effects	Y	Y	Y	Y

Notes: All specifications include year fixed effects and country fixed effects. All educational attainment indicates a five-year lagged value, which is used as an instrumental variable for current value. Specifications (3) and (4) additionally control for time-varying characteristics of countries such as population ages over 25, log of per capita GDP and value-added and employment shares of manufacturing. Standard errors in parentheses are clustered at the country level. *** $p < 0.01$, ** $p < 0.05$, * $p < 0.1$.

effect of increase in the level of tertiary education is large: a one-year increase in the tertiary educational attainment increases the employment share of technology-intensive industries in the manufacturing sector by 9 percentage points. However, the coefficient is statistically insignificant due to the large standard errors. Moreover, after controlling for the factors that could affect the technological intensity of the manufacturing sector, the estimated coefficient becomes close to zero. Specifically, all estimates in columns (3) and (4) of Table 10.3, are small and statistically insignificant.

Table 10.4 reports the effect of the increase in human capital levels on the share of low-tech industries. Column (2), reporting the unconditional effect of the educational attainment, shows that an increase in educational attainment in the primary and tertiary education levels decreases the employment share of low-tech industries among the entire manufacturing sector. However, the point estimate is not precisely estimated and is

Table 10.4   *Effect of change in educational attainment on the employment share of low-tech manufacturing (five-year lag as independent variable)*

Dependent variable: employment share in manufacturing	Specification			
	(1)	(2)	(3)	(4)
Average years of schooling	−2.607	–	−0.695	–
	(2.232)		(0.617)	
Average years of primary schooling	–	−7.819*	–	−1.460
		(4.508)		(1.371)
Average years of secondary schooling	–	−0.445	–	−0.363
		(1.303)		(0.721)
Average years of tertiary schooling	–	−8.417	–	−0.926
		(8.182)		(2.331)
Number of observations	176	176	160	160
Number of countries	29	29	29	29
Adjusted R-squared	0.348	0.42	0.916	0.916
Additional control	N	N	Y	Y
Year fixed effects	Y	Y	Y	Y
Country fixed effects	Y	Y	Y	Y

Notes: All specifications include year fixed effects and country fixed effects. All educational attainment indicates a five-year lagged value, which is used as an instrumental variable for current value. Specifications (3) and (4) additionally control for time-varying characteristics of countries such as population ages over 25, log of per capita GDP and value-added and employment shares of manufacturing. Standard errors in parentheses are clustered at the country level. *** $p < 0.01$, ** $p < 0.05$, * $p < 0.1$.

thus statistically significant only at the 10 percent level. Moreover, after controlling for the additional covariates, the size of the estimates is reduced dramatically. In particular, one can verify that the coefficients are small and statistically insignificant in column (4).

I also examine the whether the human capital accumulation induces the manufacturing sector to become more technology-intensive in terms of value-added. Tables 10.5 and 10.6 report the effect of human capital levels on the value-added shares of high-tech and low-tech industries, respectively. Overall, the pattern of the effect of human capital on the value-added share is consistent with the effect on the employment share. In particular, I find a large but statistically insignificant effect of tertiary education on the value-added share among the manufacturing sector from the unconditional estimates, and a negligible effect – regardless of statistical significance – for all levels of educational attainment after controlling for other potential determinants.

Table 10.5   Effect of change in educational attainment on the value-added share of high-tech and mid-high-tech manufacturing (five-year lag as independent variable)

Dependent variable: value-added share to manufacturing	Specification			
	(1)	(2)	(3)	(4)
Average years of schooling	0.875	–	0.104	–
	(1.073)		(0.787)	
Average years of primary schooling	–	2.628	–	1.425
		(2.105)		(1.571)
Average years of secondary schooling	–	−0.356	–	−0.078
		(1.330)		(0.709)
Average years of tertiary schooling	–	9.833	–	−0.724
		(9.250)		(3.877)
Number of observations	175	175	156	161
Number of countries	32	32	31	31
Adjusted R-squared	0.370	0.392	0.667	0.669
Additional control	N	N	Y	Y
Year fixed effects	Y	Y	Y	Y
Country fixed effects	Y	Y	Y	Y

Notes: All specifications include year fixed effects and country fixed effects. All educational attainment indicates a five-year lagged value, which is used as an instrumental variable for current value. Specifications (3) and (4) additionally control for time-varying characteristics of countries such as population ages over 25, log of per capita GDP and value-added and employment shares of manufacturing. Standard errors in parentheses are clustered at the country level. *** $p < 0.01$, ** $p < 0.05$, * $p < 0.1$.

Furthermore, I find that the effect of the initial level of education on the technology intensity of the manufacturing sector is limited. The estimation results for estimating equation (10.2) for the five-year change in the share of value-added and employment as outcome variables are summarized in Tables 10.7 to 10.10. The results are fairly consistent with the impact of the change in educational attainment level on industrial structure. Specifically, the effects of the initial educational attainment on the changes in the shares of employment and value-added are close to zero after controlling for the factors that could affect the value-added and employment shares of industries.

Robustness Check

In this section, I provide several robustness checks for the results. To begin, I use the current value (instead of the five-year lag) of educational

Table 10.6   Effect of change in educational attainment on the value-added share of low-tech manufacturing (five-year lag as independent variable)

Dependent variable: value-added share to manufacturing	Specification			
	(1)	(2)	(3)	(4)
Average years of schooling	−2.815	–	−0.742	–
	(1.892)		(0.655)	
Average years of primary schooling	–	−4.021	–	0.428
		(4.015)		(2.216)
Average years of secondary schooling	–	−2.058	–	−1.682**
		(1.499)		(0.798)
Average years of tertiary schooling	–	−9.819	–	−2.521
		(7.027)		(3.910)
Number of observations	209	209	175	180
Number of countries	33	33	32	32
Adjusted R-squared	0.325	0.339	0.747	0.718
Additional control	N	N	Y	Y
Year fixed effects	Y	Y	Y	Y
Country fixed effects	Y	Y	Y	Y

Notes: All specifications include year fixed effects and country fixed effects. All educational attainment indicates five-year lagged value which is used as an instrumental variable for current value. Specifications (3) and (4) additionally control for time-varying characteristics of countries such as population ages over 25, log of per capita GDP and value-added and employment share of manufacturing. Standard errors in parentheses are clustered at the country level. *** $p < 0.01$, ** $p < 0.05$, * $p < 0.1$.

attainment for estimating the effect of the change in human capital level on technology intensity. Tables 10.11 and 10.12 summarize the results from estimating equation (10.1) using the employment shares of high-tech and low-tech industries, respectively. The results are both qualitatively similar to the main result. In particular, the unconditional estimates show that educational attainment increases the share of high-tech industries and lowers the share of low-tech industries. Moreover, tertiary educational attainment seems to matter most in terms of the technological intensity, as its absolute magnitude is the largest among the three educational levels for the unconditional estimates. However, the coefficient is not precisely estimated and is statistically insignificant. Tables 10.13 and 10.14 document the impact of the change in human capital level on technology intensity of the manufacturing sector measured by value-added. The results are qualitatively similar to the previous result with the employment share.

Table 10.7   *Effect of initial level in educational attainment on the five-year change in employment share of high-tech and mid-high-tech manufacturing*

Dependent variable: five-year change in employment share	Specification			
	(1)	(2)	(3)	(4)
Average years of schooling	0.055	–	0.043	–
	(0.154)		(0.101)	
Average years of primary schooling	–	0.462*	–	0.066
		(0.267)		(0.278)
Average years of secondary schooling	–	0.120	–	0.065
		(0.217)		(0.192)
Average years of tertiary schooling	–	−1.723**	–	−0.135
		(0.821)		(1.167)
Number of observations	119	119	111	111
Adjusted R-squared	−0.030	0.039	0.236	0.220
Additional control	N	N	Y	Y
Year fixed effects	Y	Y	Y	Y
Country fixed effects	N	N	N	N

Notes: All specifications include year fixed effects. All educational attainment indicates initial level five-year lagged value. Specifications (3) and (4) additionally control for time-varying characteristics of countries such as population ages over 25, log of per capita GDP and value-added and employment shares of manufacturing. Huber–White standard errors are in parentheses. *** $p < 0.01$, ** $p < 0.05$, * $p < 0.1$.

Table 10.8   *Effect of initial level in educational attainment on the five-year change in employment share of low-tech manufacturing*

Dependent variable: five-year change in employment share	Specification			
	(1)	(2)	(3)	(4)
Average years of schooling	0.059	–	0.081	–
	(0.134)		(0.130)	
Average years of primary schooling	–	−0.153	–	−0.160
		(0.177)		(0.237)
Average years of secondary schooling	–	0.213	–	0.219
		(0.227)		(0.251)
Average years of tertiary schooling	–	0.229	–	0.729
		(0.957)		(1.179)
Number of observations	147	136	136	136
Adjusted R-squared	0.054	0.153	0.247	0.249

Table 10.8 (continued)

Dependent variable: five-year change in employment share	Specification			
	(1)	(2)	(3)	(4)
Additional control	N	N	Y	Y
Year fixed effects	Y	Y	Y	Y
Country fixed effects	N	N	N	N

Notes: All specifications include year fixed effects. All educational attainment indicates initial level five-year lagged value. Specifications (3) and (4) additionally control for time-varying characteristics of countries such as population ages over 25, log of per capita GDP and value-added and employment shares of manufacturing. Huber–White standard errors are in parentheses. *** $p < 0.01$, ** $p < 0.05$, * $p < 0.1$.

Table 10.9 *Effect of initial level in educational attainment on the five-year change in value-added share of high-tech and mid-high-tech manufacturing*

Dependent variable: five-year change in value-added share	Specification			
	(1)	(2)	(3)	(4)
Average years of schooling	0.171	–	0.247	–
	(0.168)		(0.154)	
Average years of primary schooling	–	0.658*	–	0.444
		(0.364)		(0.325)
Average years of secondary schooling	–	0.312	–	0.462*
		(0.288)		(0.252)
Average years of tertiary schooling	–	−2.453	–	−1.465
		(1.515)		(1.208)
Number of observations	143	143	119	119
Adjusted R-squared	0.059	0.099	0.243	0.236
Additional control	N	N	Y	Y
Year fixed effects	Y	Y	Y	Y
Country fixed effects	N	N	N	N

Notes: All specifications include year fixed effects. All educational attainment indicates initial level five-year lagged value. Specifications (3) and (4) additionally control for time-varying characteristics of countries such as population ages over 25, log of per capita GDP and value-added and employment shares of manufacturing. Huber–White standard errors are in parentheses. *** $p < 0.01$, ** $p < 0.05$, * $p < 0.1$.

Table 10.10 Effect of initial level in educational attainment on the five-year change in value-added share of low-tech manufacturing

Dependent variable: five-year change in value-added share	Specification			
	(1)	(2)	(3)	(4)
Average years of schooling	−0.077	–	−0.328*	–
	(0.139)		(0.167)	
Average years of primary schooling	–	−0.390	–	−0.291
		(0.245)		(0.310)
Average years of secondary schooling	–	−0.106	–	−0.635**
		(0.372)		(0.304)
Average years of tertiary schooling	–	0.930	–	0.525
		(1.252)		(1.199)
Number of observations	176	148	139	139
Adjusted R-squared	0.063	0.057	0.357	0.354
Additional control	N	N	Y	Y
Year fixed effects	Y	Y	Y	Y
Country fixed effects	N	N	N	N

Notes: All specifications include year fixed effects. All educational attainment indicates initial level five-year lagged value. Specifications (3) and (4) additionally control for time-varying characteristics of countries such as population ages over 25, log of per capita GDP and value-added and employment shares of manufacturing. Huber–White standard errors are in parentheses. *** $p < 0.01$, ** $p < 0.05$, * $p < 0.1$.

Table 10.11 Effect of change in educational attainment on the employment share of high-tech and mid-high-tech manufacturing (current value of educational attainment)

Dependent variable: employment share in manufacturing	Specification			
	(1)	(2)	(3)	(4)
Average years of schooling	0.160	–	0.043	–
	(0.816)		(0.273)	
Average years of primary schooling	–	−0.721	–	0.804
		(2.607)		(0.907)
Average years of secondary schooling	–	−0.188	–	−0.278
		(0.762)		(0.397)
Average years of tertiary schooling	–	7.614	–	−0.031
		(6.520)		(1.513)
Number of observations	147	147	137	137
Number of countries	28	28	28	28
Adjusted R-squared	0.266	0.300	0.839	0.839

Table 10.11   (continued)

Dependent variable: employment share in manufacturing	Specification			
	(1)	(2)	(3)	(4)
Additional control	N	N	Y	Y
Year fixed effects	Y	Y	Y	Y
Country fixed effects	Y	Y	Y	Y

Notes: All specifications include year fixed effects and country fixed effects. All educational attainment indicates current value. Specifications (3) and (4) additionally control for time-varying characteristics of countries such as population ages over 25, log of per capita GDP and value-added and employment shares of manufacturing. Standard errors in parentheses are clustered at the country level. *** $p < 0.01$, ** $p < 0.05$, * $p < 0.1$.

Table 10.12   Effect of change in educational attainment on the employment share of low-tech manufacturing (current value of educational attainment)

Dependent variable: employment share in manufacturing	Specification			
	(1)	(2)	(3)	(4)
Average years of schooling	−1.501	–	−0.686	–
	(1.702)		(0.565)	
Average years of primary schooling	–	−5.293	–	−1.599
		(5.012)		(1.113)
Average years of secondary schooling	–	−0.236	–	−0.246
		(1.037)		(0.660)
Average years of tertiary schooling	–	−7.792	–	−1.992
		(7.091)		(1.752)
Number of observations	176	176	160	160
Number of countries	29	29	29	29
Adjusted R-squared	0.310	0.354	0.917	0.918
Additional control	N	N	Y	Y
Year fixed effects	Y	Y	Y	Y
Country fixed effects	Y	Y	Y	Y

Notes: All specifications include year fixed effects and country fixed effects. All educational attainment indicates current value. Specifications (3) and (4) additionally control for time-varying characteristics of countries such as population ages over 25, log of per capita GDP and value-added and employment shares of manufacturing. Standard errors in parentheses are clustered at the country level. *** $p < 0.01$, ** $p < 0.05$, * $p < 0.1$.

Table 10.13 *Effect of change in educational attainment on the value-added share of high-tech and mid-high-tech manufacturing (current value of educational attainment)*

Dependent variable: value-added share to manufacturing	Specification			
	(1)	(2)	(3)	(4)
Average years of schooling	0.076	–	−0.208	–
	(0.712)		(0.509)	
Average years of primary schooling	–	0.272	–	0.911
		(2.161)		(1.483)
Average years of secondary schooling	–	−0.291	–	0.447
		(0.783)		(0.590)
Average years of tertiary schooling	–	4.723	–	−2.846
		(8.476)		(4.346)
Number of observations	175	175	156	161
Number of countries	32	32	31	31
Adjusted R-squared	0.361	0.362	0.639	0.632
Additional control	N	N	Y	Y
Year fixed effects	Y	Y	Y	Y
Country fixed effects	Y	Y	Y	Y

Notes: All specifications include year fixed effects and country fixed effects. All educational attainment indicates current value. Specifications (3) and (4) additionally control for time-varying characteristics of countries such as population ages over 25, log of per capita GDP and value-added and employment shares of manufacturing. Standard errors in parentheses are clustered at the country level. *** $p < 0.01$, ** $p < 0.05$, * $p < 0.1$.

Furthermore, I examine the long-term effect of the initial level of human capital in technology intensity of the manufacturing sector. Tables 10.15 and 10.16 report, respectively, the results from estimating equation (10.2) using a ten-year difference in employment shares in high-tech and low-tech industries (that is, v equal to 10) as an outcome variable. Overall, the results do not provide supportive evidence on the effect of human capital accumulation on the technology intensity of the manufacturing sector. Moreover, Tables 10.17 and 10.18 report the effect of the initial level of human capital on the value-added share by technology intensity. Similar to the result using the employment share, I do not find strong evidence that human capital either increases the value-added share of high-tech or lowers the value-added share of low-tech industries.

Table 10.14   *Effect of change in educational attainment on the value-added share of low-tech manufacturing (current value of educational attainment)*

Dependent variable: value-added share to manufacturing	Specification			
	(1)	(2)	(3)	(4)
Average years of schooling	−1.685	–	−0.378	–
	(1.477)		(0.804)	
Average years of primary schooling	–	−2.447	–	−1.147
		(3.266)		(2.189)
Average years of secondary schooling	–	−1.053	–	−1.318*
		(1.184)		(0.768)
Average years of tertiary schooling	–	−9.347	–	−1.252
		(7.560)		(3.699)
Number of observations	209	209	175	180
Number of countries	33	33	32	32
Adjusted R-squared	0.284	0.302	0.716	0.636
Additional control	N	N	Y	Y
Year fixed effects	Y	Y	Y	Y
Country fixed effects	Y	Y	Y	Y

Notes: All specifications include year fixed effects and country fixed effects. All educational attainment indicates current value. Specifications (3) and (4) additionally control for time-varying characteristics of countries such as population ages over 25, log of per capita GDP and value-added and employment shares of manufacturing. Standard errors in parentheses are clustered at the country level. *** $p < 0.01$, ** $p < 0.05$, * $p < 0.1$.

Table 10.15   *Effect of initial level in educational attainment on the ten-year change in employment share of high-tech and mid-high-tech manufacturing*

Dependent variable: ten-year change in employment share	Specification			
	(1)	(2)	(3)	(4)
Average years of schooling	0.121	–	0.084	–
	(0.329)		(0.185)	
Average years of primary schooling	–	1.119*	–	−0.237
		(0.613)		(0.492)
Average years of secondary schooling	–	0.134	–	−0.123
		(0.482)		(0.375)
Average years of tertiary schooling	–	−3.798*	–	2.332
		(1.963)		(2.252)
Number of observations	91	91	87	87

Table 10.15 (continued)

Dependent variable: ten-year change in employment share	Specification			
	(1)	(2)	(3)	(4)
Adjusted R-squared	−0.050	0.071	0.523	0.520
Additional control	N	N	Y	Y
Year fixed effects	Y	Y	Y	Y
Country fixed effects	N	N	N	N

Notes: All specifications include year fixed effects. All educational attainment indicates initial level ten-year lagged value. Specifications (3) and (4) additionally control for time-varying characteristics of countries such as population ages over 25, log of per capita GDP and value-added and employment shares of manufacturing. Huber–White standard errors are in parentheses. *** $p < 0.01$, ** $p < 0.05$, * $p < 0.1$.

Table 10.16 *Effect of initial level in educational attainment on the ten-year change in employment share of low-tech manufacturing*

Dependent variable: ten-year change in employment share	Specification			
	(1)	(2)	(3)	(4)
Average years of schooling	0.192	–	0.197	–
	(0.291)		(0.262)	
Average years of primary schooling	–	−0.286	–	−0.231
		(0.343)		(0.425)
Average years of secondary schooling	–	0.736	–	0.604
		(0.572)		(0.464)
Average years of tertiary schooling	–	0.276	–	0.777
		(2.133)		(2.294)
Number of observations	118	107	111	111
Adjusted R-squared	0.003	0.139	0.467	0.475
Additional control	N	N	Y	Y
Year fixed effects	Y	Y	Y	Y
Country fixed effects	N	N	N	N

Notes: All specifications include year fixed effects. All educational attainment indicates initial level ten-year lagged value. Specifications (3) and (4) additionally control for time-varying characteristics of countries such as population ages over 25, log of per capita GDP and value-added and employment shares of manufacturing. Huber–White standard errors are in parentheses. *** $p < 0.01$, ** $p < 0.05$, * $p < 0.1$.

Table 10.17   *Effect of initial level in educational attainment on the ten-year change in value-added share of high-tech and mid-high-tech manufacturing*

Dependent variable: ten-year change in value-added share	Specification			
	(1)	(2)	(3)	(4)
Average years of schooling	0.178	–	0.348	–
	(0.347)		(0.290)	
Average years of primary schooling	–	1.116	–	0.700
		(0.785)		(0.570)
Average years of secondary schooling	–	−0.098	–	0.301
		(0.692)		(0.457)
Average years of tertiary schooling	–	−2.883	–	−1.186
		(3.632)		(2.439)
Number of observations	112	112	96	96
Adjusted R-squared	−0.030	0.031	0.463	0.457
Additional control	N	N	Y	Y
Year fixed effects	Y	Y	Y	Y
Country fixed effects	N	N	N	N

Notes: All specifications include year fixed effects. All educational attainment indicates initial level ten-year lagged value. Specifications (3) and (4) additionally control for time-varying characteristics of countries such as population ages over 25, log of per capita GDP and value-added and employment shares of manufacturing. Huber–White standard errors are in parentheses. *** $p < 0.01$, ** $p < 0.05$, * $p < 0.1$.

CONCLUSION

This chapter examines the effect of the human capital level on the technology intensity in the manufacturing sector. In particular, the goal is to shed light on the possible mechanism by which educational attainment could have a positive impact on the economy. It also explores whether the social returns from education depend on the level of education, as a number of studies in the recent literature show that the returns from education could vary across educational levels. For the empirical analysis, I use data from the OECD that contains information at the country-industry level, where industries in the manufacturing sector are categorized based on technological intensity. By examining the effect of both changes and the initial level of educational attainment, I do not find strong support for the argument that an increase in human capital affects the share of high-tech industries in terms of employment or value-added among the manufacturing sector.

I plan to extend this work by using alternative measures of educational

Table 10.18 Effect of initial level in educational attainment on the ten-year change in value-added share of low-tech manufacturing

Dependent variable: ten-year change in value-added share	Specification			
	(1)	(2)	(3)	(4)
Average years of schooling	2.095	–	1.275	–
	(1.487)		(0.880)	
Average years of primary schooling	–	0.287	–	1.759
		(2.096)		(1.499)
Average years of secondary schooling	–	4.129	–	0.671
		(2.519)		(1.560)
Average years of tertiary schooling	–	5.374	–	1.156
		(7.327)		(7.667)
Number of observations	139	114	115	115
Adjusted R-squared	0.028	0.386	0.721	0.718
Additional control	N	N	Y	Y
Year fixed effects	Y	Y	Y	Y
Country fixed effects	N	N	N	N

Notes: All specifications include year fixed effects. All educational attainment indicates initial level ten-year lagged value. Specifications (3) and (4) additionally control for time-varying characteristics of countries such as population ages over 25, log of per capita GDP and value-added and employment shares of manufacturing. Huber–White standard errors are in parentheses. *** $p < 0.01$, ** $p < 0.05$, *$p < 0.1$.

attainment, such as the proportion of individuals who attain at least secondary schooling. I will also provide several robustness checks using alternative periods and additional controls, such as the physical capital intensity of a country.

NOTES

1. Several factors could lead to finding rather disappointing results. In particular, many papers suspect that measurement errors in the education attainment will generally lead to attenuation bias (Krueger and Lindahl 2001; de la Fuente and Domenech 2006; Cohen and Soto 2007). Also, several papers argue that educational attainment measured by year is not comparable across countries, as it does not reflect differences in educational quality (Hanushek and Kimko 2000; Schoellman 2012).
2. The OECD's STAN database is based on ISIC revision 4 which, at the time of the analysis, provided data for only 15 countries.
3. OECD (2003) provides detailed information on how the intensities are measured. Although the classification is based on the four levels, I merge the high- and mid-high-technology categories for the empirical estimation, since STAN does not have separate information for both categories for many years and countries. Also, I omit the low-medium-tech industries, as the information is often missing in the dataset.

4. Furthermore, the OECD categorizes the manufacturing sector using the average of R&D intensity from 12 countries, whereas Ciccone and Papaioannou (2009) calculate the schooling intensities of each industry using only one country (the United States) as a benchmark.

REFERENCES

Acemoglu, D. (2003), "Patterns of skill premia," *Review of Economic Studies*, **70**(2), 1199–230.

Barro, R.J. (1991), "Economic growth in a cross section of countries," *Quarterly Journal of Economics*, **106**(2), 407–43.

Barro, R.J. and J.W. Lee (2001), "International data on educational attainment: updates and implications," *Oxford Economic Papers*, **53**(3), 541–63.

Barro, R.J. and J.W. Lee (2013), "A new data set of educational attainment in the world, 1950–2010," *Journal of Development Economics*, **104**, 184–98.

Becker, G.S. (1964), *Human Capital: A Theoretical and Empirical Analysis, with Special Reference to Education*, New York: National Bureau of Economic Research, distributed by Columbia University Press.

Benhabib, J. and M.M. Spiegel (1994), "The role of human capital in economic development: evidence from aggregate cross-country data," *Journal of Monetary Economics*, **34**(2), 143–73.

Card, D.E. (1999), "The causal effect of education on earnings," in O. Ashenfelter and D. Card (eds), *Handbook of Labor Economics, Volume 3, Part A*, Amsterdam: Elsevier (North-Holland Publishing Company), pp. 1801–63.

Ciccone, A. and E. Papaioannou (2009), "Human capital, the structure of production, and growth," *Review of Economics and Statistics*, **91**(1), 66–82.

Cohen, D. and M. Soto (2007), "Growth and human capital: good data, good results," *Journal of Economic Growth*, **12**(1), 51–76.

de la Fuente, A. and R. Domenech (2006), "Human capital in growth regressions: how much difference does data quality make?" *Journal of the European Economic Association*, **4**(1), 1–36.

Hanushek, E.A. and D.D. Kimko (2000), "Schooling, labor-force quality, and the growth of nations," *American Economic Review*, **90**(5), 1184–208.

Krueger, A.B. and M. Lindahl (2001), "Education for growth: why and for whom?" *Journal of Economic Literature*, **39**(4), 1101–36, available at http://ideas.repec.org.

Lange, F. and R. Topel (2006), "The social value of education and human capital," in E. Hanushek and F. Welch (eds), *Handbook of the Economics of Education, Volume 1*, Amsterdam: Elsevier (North-Holland Publishing Company), pp. 459–509.

Lucas, R.E. (1988), "On the mechanics of economic development," *Journal of Monetary Economics*, **22**(1), 3–42.

Mankiw, N.G., D. Romer and D.N. Weil (1992), "A contribution to the empirics of economic growth," *Quarterly Journal of Economics*, **107**(2), 407–37.

Mincer, J.A. (1974), *Schooling, Experience, and Earnings*, New York: National Bureau of Economic Research, distributed by Columbia University Press.

Nelson, R.R. and E.S. Phelps (1966), "Investment in humans, technological diffusion, and economic growth," *American Economic Review*, **56**(1–2), 69–75.

Organisation for Economic Co-operation and Development (OECD) (2003), *OECD Science, Technology and Industry Scoreboard 2003*, Paris: Organisation for Economic Co-operation and Development.

Pritchett, L. (2001), "Where has all the education gone?" *World Bank Economic Review*, **15**(3), 367–91.

Schoellman, T. (2012), "Education quality and development accounting," *Review of Economic Studies*, **79**(1), 388–417.

11. Intragenerational income mobility in Korea since 2000

Yong-seong Kim

INTRODUCTION

What makes an individual's income different from that of others? How freely can an individual move up and down the socioeconomic ladder? These are topics of various debates and of interest to both policymakers and economists in all countries.

Numerous studies on these topics have been conducted for the United States (US) and other developed countries.[1] Surprisingly, studies for developing countries are limited. Despite a growing concern about the imbalance between income growth and its distribution, little attempt has been made to address this issue. One of the major obstacles in the majority of developing countries is the limited availability of panel datasets, upon which these studies heavily rely. From this perspective, Korea is extremely fortunate to possess a micropanel dataset that provides researchers a unique opportunity and tools to understand income inequality and mobility for Korea.

A study of the Korean case is particularly interesting. As is well known, Korea has experienced dramatic economic development. From one of the poorest countries in the 1960s, it became a member of the Organisation for Economic Co-operation and Development (OECD) in 1996. The period under consideration in this chapter, 2001–13, is particularly interesting, because of salient economic growth. Per capita gross domestic product (GDP) increased from US\$19330 in 2001 to US\$27990 in 2012 (in 2005 constant dollars), according to OECD National Account Statistics. This growth, and extraordinary incidents (immediately after the financial crisis of 1997 and the global crisis beginning in 2008), provide a rare opportunity to examine the dynamic impacts on income distribution and mobility.

The well-being of societal members is determined by various aspects of living, including income. The primary purpose of this chapter is to observe how an individual's income evolves over a lifetime, with a focus on intragenerational mobility, particularly changes in income. For clarity, intragenerational mobility deals mainly with within-generation issues, while intergenerational mobility is concerned mainly with those between generations (Burkhauser and Couch 2009). However, this is not equivalent to saying that these two mobilities are separate and independent, but rather that they are closely linked through complex channels in a society.

The importance of intragenerational mobility was succinctly put by Sorensen (1975: 456) in stating that intragenerational mobility "is generated by persons' attempts to maximize their status and income." In spite of its significant implication on one's lifetime well-being, intragenerational mobility has received little attention compared with intergenerational mobility. From an individual point of view, intragenerational mobility is a strong stimulus in motivating oneself for a pursuit of better life in the future. With intragenerational mobility secured, one could be willing to commit to education and to invest in human capital, in the hopes that one's children will have better chances to surpass their parents. In a society with persistent inequality, however, differences in the earning gap due to the parental backgrounds leads to unequal opportunities for children, which is then transmitted to socioeconomic disparity in the subsequent generations. Compounding this problem is the fact that such a process could itself be accelerated in a vicious cycle. For this reason, intragenerational mobility has a profound influence on shaping the intergenerational mobility of a society.

In short, the result of this chapter indicates that income mobility began declining in Korea from 2000. An examination of the transition process based on relative income positions over time reveals that the direction of mobility has become downward rather than upward, with income becoming less mobile. When an income is decomposed into its components, income variations due to the permanent part become dominant over time, and this is particularly true for the "less educated" group. Such income mobility trends raise serious concerns about the future of Korean society.

The next section surveys previous studies, both cross-country and on Korea, and briefly reports their main findings. The third section presents the trends of income inequality and analyzes mobility in Korea since 2000, and is followed by conclusions.

LITERATURE REVIEW

There have been voluminous studies on intragenerational income mobility. Recent observations of rising income inequality raise serious concerns about income mobility within generations as well as between generations.

The first category of research on income mobility focuses on the transition process of income between two points of time. The mobility based on the relative positions is particularly suitable to identify the degree and direction of mobility for specific income groups, such as households at the top and the bottom of the income distribution. The empirical studies on US income mobility based on relative positions suggest that the results are somewhat mixed. Auten and Gee (2009), using data on US income tax returns for 1987–96 and 1996–2005, report a salient US income mobility by showing that more than half of the taxpayers in the bottom quintile at the beginning advanced to higher income groups by the end of each period, while those at the top were likely to move down to lower income groups. Based on the Panel Study for Income Dynamics (PSID) for 1984–2004, Acs and Zimmerman (2008) conclude that recent US income mobility has been lower than the past; and Bradbury (2011: 12), using PSID data for 1969–2006, shows that "the number of deciles the average person moved declined from 1.9 [during the 1970s] to 1.7 [during 1995–2005]." Kopczuk et al. (2007) analyze Social Security Administration data since 1937 and find that there has been little change in the rank-based measure of mobility over time.

Another set of papers focus on the relationship between income inequality at a point of time and income mobility over time. The most common approach in these studies is to relate cross-sectional income inequality to multi-period measures for income inequality (Gottschalk and Moffitt 1994; Baker and Solon 1999; Burkhauser and Couch 2009; Bayaz-Ozturk et al. 2014). The underlying hypothesis is that income becomes less mobile if rising income inequality is driven by the volatility of a persistent (not transitory) income component. Studies on income volatility trends of the United States have generally agreed that income volatility increased from the 1970s until the early 1990s. There is less consensus on the direction of income volatility since the 1990s. Moffitt and Gottschalk (2008) and Dahl et al. (2011) find that income volatility has remained quite stable; whereas Shin and Solon (2009) find that income volatility has continued to rise. The majority of the studies report that there is no apparent positive or negative relationship between the two measures of income inequality and mobility. Burkhauser and Couch (2009) conclude that the relationship between income inequality and mobility is ambiguous, even though a sizable portion (60–90 percent) of total income is a permanent component.

While many studies explore income mobility for the United States and other countries that are mostly developed nations, research on income mobility in developing countries is rare. For instance, Bayaz-Ozturk et al. (2014) examine the overall trends of income mobility in the United States and Germany. Gottschalk (1993) carries out a comparative study on income inequality in seven industrialized countries, and Baker and

Solon (1999) do so for Canada. Blanden et al. (2005a, 2005b) find that rapid educational upgrading and increased returns to human capital over time results in falling social mobility in the United Kingdom. Among the few studies on income mobility for developing countries, Fields et al. (2007a, 2007b) analyze intragenerational income mobility in Latin America.

Studies on income mobility in Korea are at an early stage, as a panel dataset has been available only since 1998. The results of the previous studies on Korean income mobility are mixed. Nam (2007), which is based on the Markov transition process of each income group using 1998–2004 data from the Korean Labor and Income Panel Study (KLIPS), finds that income became less mobile (with the probability of staying in the middle class equal to 0.5 over 1998–2004) and that those in the middle class were more likely to move downward (29 percent) rather than upward (21 percent). Kang (2011) shows that the probability of changing income deciles decreased from 64.3 percent (1990–97) and 62.9 percent (1998–2002) to 57.7 percent during 2003–08. A similar result is reported by Oh and Choi (2014).

On the other hand, Kim (2007) calculates the correlation coefficient and the Shorrocks mobility index using Household Panel Survey data for 1999–2002 and 2003–06. She concludes that income mobility increased in terms of the correlation coefficient, but decreased when measured by the Shorrocks index. According to her research, the trends of income mobility appear sensitive to the choice of mobility measures. Yoon and Hong (2012) analyze income mobility using KLIPS data for 1998–2008. They argue that income mobility increased over the period because the impact of income during the initial years declined in the subsequent years.

INEQUALITY AND MOBILITY IN KOREA

Data and Income Variable

This chapter utilizes two datasets for the analysis: the Household Income and Expenditure Survey (HIES) from the Korean National Statistical Office and the Korea Labor and Income Panel Study (KLIPS) from the Korea Labor Institute.

The purpose of HIES is to collect repeated cross-sectional information on household income and expenditures. It started in 1963 with 1700 households residing in urban areas, and currently boasts a sample size of about 5000 to 10 000. Until 2002, it restricted its samples to wage and salaried urban households. From 2003, it covered households residing in

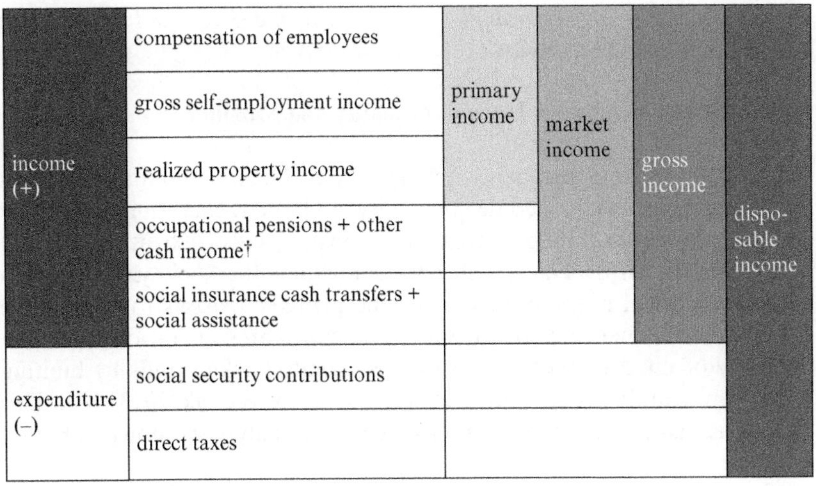

income (+)	compensation of employees	primary income	market income	gross income	dispo- sable income
	gross self-employment income				
	realized property income				
	occupational pensions + other cash income†				
	social insurance cash transfers + social assistance				
expenditure (−)	social security contributions				
	direct taxes				

Note: †"Other cash income" includes private income transfers, childcare subsidies, support for parents and other cash transfers on a regular basis.

Source: Adapted from Yoo and Kim (2003: 15, Table 2.2).

Figure 11.1   Various definitions of income

urban areas in addition to households in rural regions. In spite of HIES's long history, it is difficult to look at the trends of income distribution, due to changes in sample selection. In order to see the long-term trends of income distribution, this chapter inevitably follows only households in urban areas.

An important source of information on income mobility is KLIPS, a longitudinal household survey launched in 1998. KLIPS annually interviews members of 5000 households from seven metropolitan cities and urban areas in eight provinces. It contains rich information on labor market activities as well as household income and individuals, which allows researchers to conduct analysis on the dynamic aspects of economic activities.

There are various definitions of income (see Figure 11.1), and studies yield different results depending on the choice of income variable. Studies commonly use market income or disposable income, or both. The difference between these two income variables is that market income does not include public transfers (such as social assistance). Hence, one could assess the effectiveness of government redistributive policies by comparing distributions between market and disposable incomes. The income measure used in this chapter is based on market income,[2] which is defined as:

*market income = labor earnings + business income + realized income from
properties + private transfers*

The Relationship between Income Inequality and Mobility

What does income inequality tell us about income mobility? Thanks
to numerous studies, income inequality and intergenerational mobility
are understood to have an inverse relationship with each other (OECD
2010; Corak 2013). That is, the more unequal the society, the less its
intergenerational mobility is. One of the primary reasons for a negative
correlation is that income inequality lowers intergenerational income
mobility of children with disadvantaged family backgrounds by limiting
their opportunity to advance socioeconomically (Corak 2013: 85). This
linkage is easily verified from the cross-country analysis as shown in Figure
11.2.

Can one find a pattern in the relationship between the income inequality and intragenerational mobility? Unfortunately, the answer is unclear.
Although certain connections between income inequality and mobility are
bound to be present, there is no one-to-one match. What is unambiguous
is that income inequality could be mitigated if people could easily move

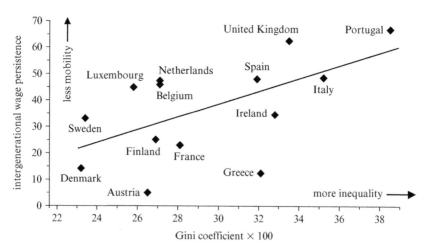

Note: Data are for men aged 35 to 44. The straight line represents the relationship between
mobility and inequality.

Source: OECD data.

Figure 11.2   *Income inequality and intergenerational mobility in selected
OECD countries, 2010*

up and down in their relative positions over the income distribution. One might be tempted to say that high income inequality reduces mobility by widening the distances between the rungs within the ladder. If such is the case, rising income inequality of today should be a precursor to deteriorating income mobility in the forthcoming days.

Consider another case where the distances between rungs within the ladder are close, but not sufficiently close for one to climb, and the bottom and the top of the income ladder are quite far apart. What can be inferred about income mobility in such a case? Thus, income inequality at a certain point of time gives us little information on the nature and the direction of intragenerational income mobility.

Figure 11.3 is an example of an obscure relationship between income inequality and mobility. According to a study of German and US cases during 1984–2006,[3] both countries experienced rising income inequality (measured by the Theil index) since the mid-1980s. In contrast, the income

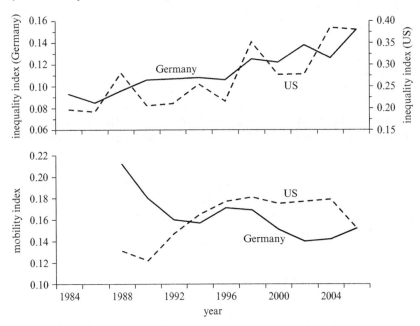

Note: Only western states of Germany were included in the study. Disposable income was used for calculation.

Source: Bayaz-Ozturk et al. (2014); income inequality indexes are from Table 1 (p. 436), and income mobility values are recalculated by converting income rigidity reported on Table A1 (p. 442).

Figure 11.3   German and US income inequality and mobility, 1984–2006

mobilities of the two countries (measured by M_{SR}, which is defined below) took different paths: the income mobility of Germany declined (that is, a lower value for M_{SR}), whereas the United States saw a slight increase (a higher value for M_{SR}).

The existence of a trade-off relationship between income inequality and mobility heavily relies on the causes of changes in the income distribution. If rising income inequality is a consequence of persistent factors, decline in income mobility may follow suit. Otherwise, income inequality might not be as serious to income mobility as it appears. What is more important are income prospects over a lifetime, rather than income differences at a specific point in that lifetime.

Trends of Income Inequality in Korea

Until the mid-1990s, Korean income inequality was considered relatively stable and low. Income inequality measured by the Gini coefficient from repeated cross-sectional data was around 0.27, and the income of the top 20 percent was only 2.2 times higher than that of the bottom 20 percent (see Figure 11.4).[4]

The financial crisis of the late 1990s dramatically changed income distribution in Korea. Income inequality soared from a Gini coefficient of 0.27 in 1997 to 0.32 in 1999, and the 80:20 income ratio rose from 2.2 to 2.6 during the same period. In the course of recovery from the aftermath of the financial crisis during 1999–2002, Korea's income inequality seemed to be

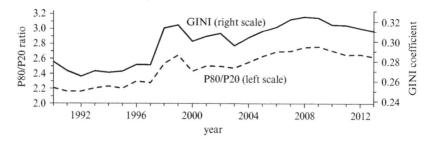

Note: Samples are restricted to households with more than two members residing in urban areas (the nonagricultural sector). Numbers are based on household market income adjusted by household size.

Source: Korean National Statistical Office, Household Income and Expenditure Survey data.

Figure 11.4   *The 80:20 ratio and income inequality (Gini coefficient) in Korea, 1990–2013*

declining, although income inequality appeared to remain higher than the pre-crisis level. The income inequality index presented here is interpreted in a cautious manner, as the index is calculated only from households in urban areas. Thus, when all types of households are included, income inequality is likely to be higher.[5]

Income inequality began to rise again in 2003, culminating in 2008. Simultaneously, the 80:20 ratio showed a similar pattern (Figure 11.4). In the early 1990s, income at 80 percent in the distribution was 2.2 times higher than that of income at 20 percent. The ratio rose to 2.7 in 2008. Deteriorating income distribution from 2003 raised grave concerns that this may be a reflection of a structural tendency rather than temporal variations. Issues on income distribution are taken particularly seriously, because this one occurred simultaneously with the rapid expansion of the social protection systems.

Figure 11.5 shows the possibility of polarization in Korea's income distribution. In the early 1990s, the richest top 20 percent of the households earned 37 percent of the total household income, and this share rose to approximately 40 percent in 2008. Meanwhile, the share of the poorest 20 percent of households stood at 8 percent in the early 1990s, and continuously declined to 5 percent during the same period. Over time, the income gap between the rich and the poor became wider.

Who are in the bottom and the top quintile? Is there a notable difference between them? To answer these questions, the characteristics of rich and poor households are compared and presented in Table 11.1. Several points merit particular attention. First, the proportion of male-headed households is generally higher among the rich than among the poor. Second, the average age of heads of poor households substantially increased from 41

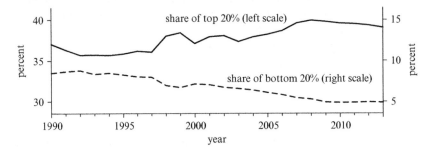

Source: Korean National Statistical Office, Household Income and Expenditure Survey data.

Figure 11.5   Income shares of top 20 percent and bottom 20 percent (market income) of Korean households, 1990–2013

Table 11.1 *Household characteristics of upper and lower income quintiles in Korea, 1993 and 2013*

Characteristics	Poorest 20%		Richest 20%	
	1993	2013	1993	2013
Households with male head (%)	73.49	66.29	94.30	91.78
Average age of household head (years)	40.76	59.46	43.28	47.48
Educational level of household head (%)				
Less than high school	42.04	45.06	17.77	4.77
High school	42.43	35.09	35.10	25.30
College and more	15.54	19.33	47.13	67.50
Household size (persons)	3.28	2.44	4.30	3.65

Source: Korean National Statistical Office, Household Income and Expenditure Survey (various years).

in 1993 to 59 in 2013. The disproportional share of low-income households among the elderly is attributed to both rapid population aging and the limited accessibility of income sources for the elderly. Third, there are clear differences in the educational distribution between the rich and the poor. As expected, heads of rich households are more likely to have more education than heads of poor households.

One can decompose total income inequality by educational groups. Figure 11.6 shows the result of the decomposition. Two points merit special attention. First, compared with within-group inequalities, between-group inequality has a tendency to increase despite the relatively small magnitude. Second, within-group inequalities show different shapes over time by educational group. For the less educated, within-group inequality rises substantially. In contrast, within-group inequality among the educated remains quite stable for identical periods. This implies that the increase in overall inequality is mostly due to rising income inequality among the less educated.

Income Mobility

Income mobility can be measured in various ways. A straightforward method is to compare intertemporal changes in the amount of income or in the relative positions on income distributions. That is, one could assess intertemporal changes in one's relative position (say, ranking) in such a way that improved or worsened positions over time can be thought of, respectively, as upward or downward mobility.

Figure 11.7 shows upward mobility based on movements between

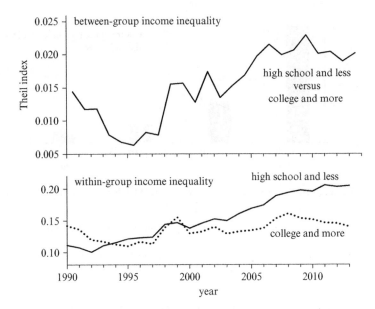

Note: The Theil index is used to measure income inequality.

Source: Korean National Statistical Office, Household Income and Expenditure Survey data.

Figure 11.6 Income inequality by educational groups in Korea, 1990–2013

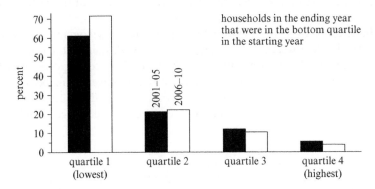

Source: Korean Labor and Income Panel Study data for the years 2001, 2005, 2006 and 2010.

Figure 11.7 Relative upward mobility out of the bottom income quartile in Korea, 2001–05 and 2006–10

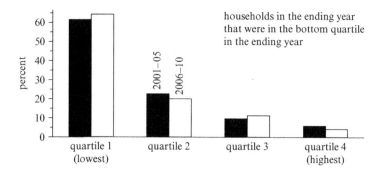

Note: Starting-year quartile of households who were at the bottom quartile in the ending year.

Source: Korean Labor and Income Panel Study for the years 2001, 2005, 2006 and 2010.

Figure 11.8   *Relative downward mobility: mobility into the bottom income quartile in Korea, 2001–05 and 2006–10*

quartiles of household income during two sample periods, 2001–05 and 2006–10. Among the households in the bottom quartile in 2001, 61.2 percent remained in the bottom quartile in 2005, and 71.6 percent remained there during the period 2006–10. At the same time, upward mobility into a higher quartile was declining exponentially. For example, 21.3 percent of bottom-quartile households in 2001 succeeded in moving to the next quartile after five years, whereas the share moving from the bottom into the highest quartile was a mere 5.5 percent.

In order to observe downward mobility, the households in the bottom quartile in 2005 were selected and compared with their initial quartiles in 2001. Among the bottom quartile in 2005, 61.7 percent had belonged to the bottom quartile in 2001, whereas only 5.8 percent had belonged to the top income quartile the same year (Figure 11.8). Thus, the percentage that fell into the bottom quartile in the ending year decreased with income quartiles in the starting year.

Relative mobilities into or out of a certain quintile over time can be ascertained from Tables 11.2 and 11.3. In the tables, the households in the shaded diagonal cells did not experience any changes in their income quintiles, while those in off-diagonal cells did experience changes (either upward or downward) between the starting and the ending year. A comparison of the two tables shows that the shares of each diagonal cell are higher during 2006–10 than during 2001–05. In addition, by comparing the upper-triangular off-diagonal cells corresponding in the two tables, one finds that the cells in Table 11.2 generally have higher shares than those in

Table 11.2   *Transition matrix by quintile income groups in Korea: number of households in 2001 versus 2005*

2001	2005					2001 total
	Q1	Q2	Q3	Q4	Q5	
Q1	363	130	65	32	28	618
	(0.59)	(0.21)	(0.11)	(0.05)	(0.05)	(1.00)
Q2	147	218	175	95	43	678
	(0.22)	(0.32)	(0.26)	(0.14)	(0.06)	(1.00)
Q3	66	145	196	183	67	657
	(0.10)	(0.22)	(0.30)	(0.28)	(0.10)	(1.00)
Q4	26	92	169	281	188	756
	(0.03)	(0.12)	(0.22)	(0.37)	(0.25)	(1.00)
Q5	18	51	56	110	375	610
	(0.03)	(0.08)	(0.09)	(0.18)	(0.61)	(1.00)
2005 total	620	636	661	701	701	3319

Note: Q1 = richest and Q5 = poorest 20 percent. Numbers in parentheses are row-shares in the table (% of 2001 total households).

Source: Korean Labor and Income Panel Study for the years 2001 and 2005.

Table 11.3   *Transition matrix by quintile income groups in Korea: number of households in 2006 versus 2010*

2006	2010					2006 total
	Q1	Q2	Q3	Q4	Q5	
Q1	472	138	64	37	15	726
	(0.65)	(0.19)	(0.09)	(0.05)	(0.02)	(1.00)
Q2	162	287	177	96	38	760
	(0.21)	(0.38)	(0.23)	(0.13)	(0.05)	(1.00)
Q3	73	170	269	202	77	791
	(0.09)	(0.22)	(0.34)	(0.26)	(0.10)	(1.00)
Q4	40	93	187	307	181	808
	(0.05)	(0.12)	(0.23)	(0.38)	(0.22)	(1.00)
Q5	31	34	81	167	501	814
	(0.04)	(0.04)	(0.10)	(0.20)	(0.62)	(1.00)
2010 total	778	722	778	809	812	3899

Note: Q1 = richest and Q5 = poorest 20 percent. Numbers in parentheses are row-shares in the table (% of 2006 total households).

Source: Korean Labor and Income Panel Study for the years 2006 and 2010.

Table 11.3, and that the opposite is true for lower-triangular off-diagonal cells. These transitional tables, which hint that there has been a decline in income mobility since the 2000s, suggest that downward mobility is more likely than upward mobility over time.

One way to summarize the mobility in a transition table is to calculate the Shorrocks M index proposed by Shorrocks (1978a), which is defined as:

$$M_{sm}(P) = \frac{n - trace(P)}{n - 1} \tag{11.1}$$

where P is a transition matrix (table) and n is the number of income categories (such as quintiles). By its construction, $M_{sm}(P) = 0$ for a perfectly immobile transition table (that is, $P = I$). A perfectly mobile case is a transition matrix with identical rows, yielding $M_{sm}(P) = 1$ since trace (P) = 1.

Table 11.4 presents Shorrocks M income mobility overall and by educational level of household heads. As shown, the Shorrocks M index based on both income quintiles and deciles decreased over the periods, indicating that Korea has become a less income-mobile society since 2001. Mobility indexes by educational groups also show that income mobility declined for both educational groups.

The shortcomings of the Shorrocks M index based on relative positions (as a transition matrix) are twofold. First, it does not reflect the mobility due to economic growth. That is, an individual's income may increase in absolute amounts without changing their relative position in the income distribution. Shorrocks M is unable to capture income mobility as long

Table 11.4   *Income mobility overall and by educational group in Korea, 2001–11*

Period	Quintile transition matrix			Decile transition matrix		
	Overall	High school education	College education	Overall	High school education	College education
2001–05	0.702	0.735	0.712	0.827	0.842	0.862
2003–07	0.678	0.713	0.688	0.798	0.816	0.821
2005–09	0.681	0.722	0.695	0.801	0.832	0.804
2007–11	0.664	0.684	0.719	0.799	0.810	0.848

Note: Shorrocks M is not decomposable in the sense that the sum of income mobilities by educational groups is not equal to overall mobility.

Source: Korean Labor and Income Panel Study, various waves.

as a relative position remains unchanged. Second, the equal treatment of upward and downward mobility results in failure to deliver any information concerning the direction of mobility, which has important policy implications. One needs to complement these shortcomings by using different measures for income mobility.

Alternatively, income mobility can be perceived as income equality over a lifetime. By arguing that "mobility is measured by the extent to which the income distribution is equalized as the accounting period is extended," Shorrocks (1978b: 378) proposed an alternative measure for income mobility called Shorrocks R, given as:

$$m_{SR} = 1 - \frac{I(E_t[y_{it}])}{\sum_t \dot{w}_t I(y_{it})} \qquad (11.2)$$

where $I(\bullet)$ is an inequality index and $E_t[y_{it}] = \sum_t y_{it}/T_i$, $w_t = \mu_t/\mu$ is the ratio of average income at t to overall average income. Shorrocks R is one minus the ratio of inequality over multi-year averaged income to a weighted average of inequalities over single year incomes. The ratio, m_{SR}, takes the value of 1 in the case of perfect mobility (that is, $m_{SR} = 1$) and 0 if perfect immobility (that is, $m_{SR} = 0$).

Like m_{SM}, m_{SR} tells us little about the direction of income mobility. To address this disadvantage, Fields and Ok (1999) propose a directional measure of mobility such as:

$$m_{F0} = \frac{1}{n} \sum_i (\ln y_{is} - \ln y_{it}) y_{it} \qquad (11.3)$$

where y_{is} and y_{it} are an individual i's income at the ending and starting points, respectively. A positive value of m_{F0} implies that people's income has improved on average, and implies the opposite for a negative value.

Table 11.5 presents the results of m_{SR} and m_{F0}. First, as indicated by m_{SR}, the mobility declined not only for the overall group but also for both educational groups over time. The result is consistent with the findings of m_{SM}. Second, for the period of 2001–05, the income mobility of the "less educated" ($m_{SR} = 0.197$) was higher than that of the "more educated" ($m_{SR} = 0.156$). During 2007–11, the income mobility of the less educated declined sharply ($m_{SR} = 0.111$), while that of the more educated group showed a moderate decrease ($m_{SR} = 0.1244$). Third, an intertemporal comparison of m_{F0} provides a surprising result. For the period 2007–11, m_{F0} becomes negative for the overall group ($m_{F0} = -0.026$), meaning that the direction of mobility is not income-improving but rather income-deteriorating. This results seem to be driven by the less educated group ($m_{F0} = -0.049$).

Table 11.5   Income mobility (m_{SR} and m_{FO}) overall and by educational group in Korea, 2001–11

Period	m_{SR}			m_{FO}		
	Overall	High school education	College education	Overall	High school education	College education
2001–05	0.166	0.197	0.156	0.227	0.202	0.293
2003–07	0.166	0.188	0.163	0.118	0.081	0.217
2005–09	0.113	0.124	0.127	−0.005	−0.051	0.089
2007–11	0.111	0.111	0.138	−0.026	−0.049	0.020

Note: Incomes are converted into constant values in order not to capture price effect over time.

Source: Korean Labor and Income Panel Study, various waves.

Income Mobility by Decomposition

Conceptually, an income can be thought of as the sum of two parts: the transitory and the permanent components. Transitory income reflects year-to-year income volatility, primarily due to contemporaneous shocks. Income inequality due to the transitory component is less fundamental because its impact on income distribution should fade away as the shocks disappear. For example, one may have windfalls or downfalls over a lifetime, but overall ups and downs could be averaged out without having a long-lasting impact. To make this point clear, consider the following log earning ($\ln y_{it}$) equation for an individual i at time t:

$$\ln y_{it} = \chi_{it}\beta + u_{it}, \text{ where } u_{it} = \delta_i + v_{it} \qquad (11.4)$$

where the independent variable χ_{it} is a vector of observable attributes of an individual (such as age, experience, education, and so on) that affect earnings. Note that the error term (u_{it}) consists of two components: (1) a time-invariant part specific to an individual (δ_i) with mean zero and the variance equal to σ_δ^2; and (2) a time-varying transitory shock (v_{it}) having mean zero and the variance equal to σ_v^2. Thus, δ_i represents unmeasurable individual characteristics affecting the income persistently over time. Examples of such variables are motivation, intelligence, interpersonal skills and appearance (if it matters), among many others. The v_{it} can be interpreted as a transitory or temporal deviation from an individual's life-cycle earning trajectory.

For the purpose of tractability, assume that δ_i and v_{it} are mutually independent and for all i, $\text{cov}(v_{it}, v_{is}) = 0$ if $t \neq s$. Thus, the variance of the log earnings:

$$\text{var}(\ln y_{it} | x_{it}) = \sigma_u^2 = \sigma_\delta^2 + \sigma_U^2. \qquad (11.5)$$

What matters in income mobility is the income inequality caused by the persistent and permanent component. A transitory component (v_{it}) results in income volatility without long-lasting consequences on lifetime earnings inequality (Solon 2001: 156). The proportion of the variance of the component to overall variance:

$$\rho = \sigma_\delta^2 / (\sigma_\delta^2 + \sigma_v^2)$$

is similar to the income rigidity part in the Shorrocks R, in the sense that two measures are based on the comparison of income inequality of lifelong (multi-year) earnings to cross-sectional income inequality (Burkhauser and Couch 2009).

Let $r_{it} = \ln y_{it} - \ln \hat{y}_{it}$ and $\bar{r} = [\sum_i (\sum_t r_{it} / T_i)] / N$. Following Gottschalk (1993), Gottschalk and Moffitt (1994) and Solon (2001), the permanent (r_i^P) and transitory (r_{it}^T) components can be approximated by $r_i^P = [\sum_t r_{it}] / T_i$ and $r_{it}^T = r_{it} - r_i^P$, respectively. The variances of each component can be easily obtained by (Bayaz-Ozturk et al. 2014: 434–35):

$$\sigma_v^2 = (1/N) \times \sum_i [1/(T_i - 1)] \sum_t (r_{it} - r_i^P)^2 \qquad (11.6)$$

where $\bar{T} = \sum_i T_i / N$.

Table 11.6 presents the results of the decomposition of residual earnings by educational groups. It is worth interpreting the table cross-sectionally and intertemporally. From the cross-sectional point of view, the following are worth noting. First, overall income variation ($\sigma_\delta^2 + \sigma_v^2$) is higher for the less educated group than the more educated group. In 2001–05, overall income variance for the less educated group was 0.576, whereas for the more educated group it was 0.471. A similar pattern is observed for 2007–11.

Second, once decomposed, the permanent component is a dominant cause of income variance. During 2001–05, the variance of the permanent component was larger than the variance of the transitory component for both educational groups. The pattern is similar during 2001–11. As a result, the variance of the permanent income component (ρ) explains 66.3 percent of overall income variance during 2001–05. During 2007–11, the proportion of the variance of the permanent component to overall variance rose to 73.0 percent.

Table 11.6   Decomposition of income variances in Korea, 2001–11

Period	Overall			High school education			College education		
	σ_δ^2	σ_v^2	ρ	σ_δ^2	σ_v^2	ρ	σ_δ^2	σ_v^2	ρ
2001–05	0.373	0.190	0.663	0.376	0.201	0.652	0.301	0.170	0.639
2003–07	0.373	0.166	0.692	0.382	0.161	0.704	0.303	0.178	0.630
2005–09	0.393	0.163	0.706	0.403	0.163	0.712	0.310	0.163	0.655
2007–11	0.422	0.157	0.730	0.455	0.168	0.730	0.298	0.136	0.686

Notes: For 2001–05, observations total 21 792 from 5205 distinctive households. For 2003–07, observations total 23 275 from 5384 distinctive households. For 2005–09, observations total 24 129 from 5503 distinctive households. For 2007–11, observations total 28 667 from 7084 distinctive households.

Source: Korean Labor and Income Panel Study, various waves.

From the intertemporal point of view, there are a couple of points to mention. First, overall variance of income slightly increased to 0.579 during 2007–11, from 0.563 during 2001–05. While overall income variances remained relatively stable during the two sample periods, the variances of permanent and transitory components moved in different directions. Over the two sample periods, the variance of the transitory income component declined from 0.190 to 0.157, while the permanent income component increased from 0.373 to 0.422. A similar intertemporal pattern appears for both educational groups. As a result, the overall income rigidity measure (ρ) increased from 0.663 during 2001–05, to 0.730 during 2007–11, hinting at a move toward a less income-mobile society for Korea.

Second, for the two educational groups, the fractions of permanent income variance to overall variance, ρ, were around 0.64–0.65 during 2001–05. During 2007–11, however, income rigidity for the less educated group was 0.73, considerably higher than the more educated group's income rigidity of 0.69. This implies that income for the less educated group became less mobile during the two sample periods.

In short, income inequality measured by variance of log income slightly increased over the two periods 2001–05 and 2006–11. As the results of the decomposition indicate, this is because the permanent income component raised income inequality, whereas the transitory component lowered it over the two sample periods. Even though overall income inequality changed little, the rising variance of permanent-component income had profound negative impacts on the income mobility of Korean society. What happened during these periods is a substantial deterioration of income mobility with a minor impact on income inequality. This phenomenon is particularly noticeable for the less educated group.

CONCLUSION

An important element of a sound society is the presence of socioeconomic mobility in which higher status can be attained through efforts and accomplishments throughout one's lifetime, and not be confined or determined by where and how one started. Such intragenerational mobility is an engine in moving a society forward, as it profoundly affects the children's well-being in the next generations.

Until the financial crisis of the late 1990s, Korea was known to have achieved a relatively equal society, with significant improvement in living standards from generation to generation in the course of its rapid economic growth, which lasted several decades. However, the financial crisis dramatically altered the course of the Korean economy in an unprecedented manner. Income inequality suddenly soared and continued to rise, and the gap between the haves and the have-nots widened. All these negative aspects of Korea's income distribution portend a serious potential problem in income mobility.

This study, motivated by curiosity to discover the state of the income distribution since the financial crisis, looks at the trends of Korea's intragenerational income mobility and measures income mobility by various indexes for cross-checking. The findings of the chapter are as follows.

First, rising income inequality observed since 2000 seems to be driven by an increase in within-group inequality, particularly for the less educated, whereas the more educated remain relatively stable over time. The size of the between-group inequality is deemed too small to explain the overall trends of income inequality, despite the fact that it is rising.

Second, income mobility measures based on transitional tables indicate that income became less mobile over the period 2001–11. In particular, income mobility, which used to be higher for the less educated than the more educated in the early 2000s, has sharply declined. The direction in recent years is problematic, as income moves downward rather than upward.

Third, a decomposition approach shows that income inequality is primarily due to the permanent component of income, with its share of total income variation increasing over time. This implies that a substantial part of income inequality has a persistent element, making it harder for income to be mobile. This trend is apparent for the less educated group.

To summarize, Korea's rising income inequality during the first decade of the new century was accompanied by a decline in income mobility. Deteriorating income mobility may cause serious challenges to social cohesion and intergenerational mobility for future generations. Hence, Korean society needs to be actively involved in correcting this problem.

NOTES

1. For comparative studies on this subject, see Gottschalk (1993) on income inequality in seven industrialized countries, and Baker and Solon (1999) for Canada. Burkhauser and Couch (2009) give a nice summary on this topic.
2. $AdjI = I/S^E$, where $AdjI$ is household size adjusted income, I is household market income, S is the size of household and E is an equivalent scale set to 0.5.
3. For details, see Bayaz-Ozturk et al. (2014).
4. Long-run historical data for income distribution are available only for nonagricultural households with more than two members. This implies that income inequality is likely to be higher than reported if the sample coverage scope (say, single households, or households in the rural areas) is expanded. For a detailed discussion on this issue, see Kim and Kim (2013).
5. Kim and Kim (2013) point out that income inequality using HIES is likely to be underestimated due to serious sampling errors, such as the attrition of top-earners. In this case, the income inequality index would be even higher than reported.

REFERENCES

Acs, Gregory and Seth Zimmerman (2008), "U.S. intragenerational economic mobility from 1984 to 2004: trends and implications," a report of the Economic Mobility Project (an initiative of the Pew Charitable Trusts), available at www.urban.org.

Auten, Gerald E. and Geoffrey Gee (2009), "Income mobility in the United States: new evidence from income tax data," *National Tax Journal*, **62**(2), 301–28.

Baker, Michael and Gary Solon (1999), "Earnings dynamics and inequality among Canadian men, 1976–1992: evidence from longitudinal income tax records," NBER Working Paper 7370, Cambridge, MA: National Bureau of Economic Research.

Bayaz-Ozturk, G., R. Burkhauser and A. Couch (2014), "Consolidating the evidence of income mobility in the western states of Germany and the United States from 1984 to 2006," *Economic Inquiry*, **52**(1), 431–43.

Blanden, J., P. Gregg and S. Machin (2005a), "Educational inequality and intergenerational mobility," in S. Machin and A. Vignoles (eds), *What's the Good of Education? The Economics of Education in the United Kingdom*, Princeton, NJ: Princeton University Press, pp. 99–114.

Blanden, J., P. Gregg and S. Machin (2005b), "Intergenerational mobility in Europe and North America," a report supported by the Sutton Trust, available at www.suttontrust.com.

Bradbury, Katharine (2011), "Trends in U.S. family income mobility, 1996–2006," Working Paper 11-10, Boston, MA: Federal Reserve Bank of Boston.

Burkhauser, Richard V. and Kenneth A. Couch (2009), "Intragenerational inequality and intertemporal mobility," in Wiemer Salverda, Brian Nolan and Timothy M. Smeeding (eds), *The Oxford Handbook of Income Inequality*, Oxford: Oxford University Press, pp. 522–46.

Corak, Miles (2013), "Income inequality, equality of opportunity, and intergenerational mobility," *Journal of Economic Perspectives*, **27**(3), 79–102.

Dahl, Molly, Thomas DeLeire and Jonathan A. Schwabish (2011), "Estimate of year-to-year volatility in earnings and in household income from administrative, survey, and matched data," *Journal of Human Resources*, **46**(4), 750–74.

Fields, G., R. Duval-Hernandez, S. Freije and M. Puerta (2007a), "Earnings mobility in Argentina, Mexico, and Venezuela: testing the divergence of earnings and the symmetry of mobility hypothesis," IZA Discussion Paper 3184, Bonn: Institute of Labor Economics.

Fields, G., R. Duval-Hernandez, S. Freije, M. Puerta, O. Arias, O. Assuncao and J. Assuncao (2007b), "Intragenerational income mobility in Latin America," *Economia*, **7**(2), 101–54.

Fields, Gary S. and Efe A. Ok (1999), "Measuring movement of incomes," *Economica*, **66**(264), 455–71.

Gottschalk, P. (1993), "Changes in inequality of family income in seven industrialized countries," *American Economic Review: Papers and Proceedings*, **83**(2), 136–42.

Gottschalk, P. and R. Moffitt (1994), "The growth of earnings instability in the U.S. labor market," *Brookings Papers on Economic Activity*, **2**, 217–72.

Kang, Shinwook (2011), "Trends in income mobility," *Health and Welfare Issue and Focus*, **93**(25), Seoul: Korea Institute for Health and Social Affairs.

Kim, Hae Ryun (2007), "Analysis on income mobility and poverty dynamics," SRI Issue Paper 2007-01, Seoul: Statistical Research Institute.

Kim, Nak Nyeon and Jong-il Kim (2013), "Revisit on index on Korean income distribution," *Korean Economic Analysis*, **19**(2), 1–64.

Kopczuk, Wojciech, Emmanuel Saez and Jae Song (2007), "Uncovering the American dream: inequality and mobility in social security earnings data since 1937," NBER Working Paper 13345, Cambridge, MA: National Bureau of Economic Research.

Moffitt, Robert and Peter Gottschalk (2008), "Trends in the transitory variance of male earnings in the U.S. 1970–2004," Boston College Working Paper 697, Boston, MA: Boston College.

Nam, Jun-Woo (2007), "The size of middle class and changing income distribution after economic crisis," *Quarterly Journal of Labor Policy*, **7**(4), 1–24.

Oh, Hyngna and Yun Jeong Choi (2014), "Limited income mobility in Korea," Research Working Paper 2014-rwp-64, Seoul: Yonsei Economics Research Institute, Yonsei University, available at https://ideas.repec.org.

Organisation for Economic Co-operation and Development (OECD) (2010), "A family affair: intergenerational social mobility across OECD countries," in OECD (ed.), *Economic Policy Reforms: Going for Growth, Part II*, Paris: Organisation for Economic Co-operation and Development, pp. 181–98, available at www.oecd.org.

Shin, Donggyun and Gary Solon (2009), "Trends in men's earnings volatility: what does the Panel Study of Income Dynamics show?" *Journal of Public Economics*, **95**(7–8), 973–82.

Shorrocks, A. (1978a), "The measurement of mobility," *Econometrica*, **46**(5), 1013–24.

Shorrocks, A. (1978b), "Income inequality and income mobility," *Journal of Econometric Theory*, **19**, 376–93.

Solon, Gary (2001), "Mobility within and between generations," in Finis Welch (ed.), *The Causes and Consequences of Increasing Inequality*, Chicago, IL: University of Chicago Press, pp. 153–68.

Sorensen, Aage B. (1975), "The structure of intragenerational mobility," *American Sociological Review*, **40**, 456–71.

Yoo, Gyeongjoon and Daeil Kim (2003), *Cross-country Comparison of Income Distribution and Poverty Study*, Seoul: Korea Development Institute (in Korean).

Yoon, Jungyoll and Kiseok Hong (2012), "An empirical analysis of intragenerational income mobility in Korea," *Korean Journal of Labor Economics*, **35**(2), 43–77.

Index